GMAT®
Math Foundations

Third Edition

The Staff of Kaplan Test Prep

PUBLISHING

New York

This publication is designed to provide accurate and authoritative information in regard to the subject matter covered. It is sold with the understanding that the publisher is not engaged in rendering legal, accounting, or other professional service. If legal advice or other expert assistance is required, the services of a competent professional should be sought.

© 2013 Kaplan, Inc.

Published by Kaplan Publishing, a division of Kaplan, Inc.
395 Hudson Street, 4th Floor
New York, NY 10014

Printed in the United States of America

10 9 8 7 6 5 4 3 2 1

ISBN: 978-1-60978-678-6

Kaplan Publishing books are available at special quantity discounts to use for sales promotions, employee premiums, or educational purposes. For more information or to purchase books, please call the Simon & Schuster special sales department at 866-506-1949.

CONTENTS

INTRODUCTION

Do positive and negative numbers make your head swim? Do you use ten steps to solve a problem when you could have used three? Are you confused about the difference between a trapezoid and a rectangle? And when was the last time you had to add a bunch of fractions without a calculator? Being able to apply math skills and concepts is the most basic foundation for doing well on the GMAT. The problem is you may not have seen all the topics tested lately. Plus, improving your skills is often a boring, tedious process. But it doesn't have to be! Allow us to introduce the Foundations Method.

Devised by the experts at Kaplan, it makes learning mathematics as painless as possible. Unlike other books on math skills review, this book covers only the principles and concepts you need to master for the GMAT—nothing more, nothing less—using a systematic routine for memorization that uses your own real-life situations as practice exercises. It's the most convenient way to learn math while going about your everyday life.

HOW TO USE THIS BOOK

All the math you need for the GMAT you probably learned by your sophomore year in high school. Yes, *high school*! In fact, the math that appears on the GMAT is almost identical to the math tested on the SAT or ACT. You don't need to know trigonometry or calculus!

No matter how much your memories of high school algebra classes have dimmed, don't panic. The GMAT tests a limited number of core math concepts in predictable ways. Certain topics come up in every test, and chances are these topics will be expressed in much the same way; even some of the words and phrases appearing in the questions are predictable. Since the test is so formulaic, we can show you the math you're bound to encounter.

The 12 chapters in this book are divided into three sections—arithmetic, geometry, and algebra—the only math topics you need for the GMAT. Each chapter contains four key components.

1. Detailed Lessons

Each chapter focuses on a specific math topic. We'll explain the concepts involved in detail, provide lots of relevant examples, and offer strategies to help you remember what you need to know. In the process, we'll help you review the fundamentals from previous chapters.

2. Plentiful Practice

Here's a phrase you'll hear over and over throughout this book: *repetition is the key to mastery*. So be prepared to practice, practice, practice! You'll find everything from simple matching exercises to exercises that ask you to apply the skills you're learning to practical, real-life situations. By "learning from all sides," so to speak, you're much more likely to retain the information. And remember, don't start a new chapter if you haven't mastered the earlier material—you'll be building on a weak foundation.

3. Summary

Each chapter concludes with a summary for quick review of important key facts you should take from the lesson.

4. Chapter Test

At the end of each chapter, you'll take a test to practice what you've learned and assess how well you've learned it. The tests cover material in that chapter, sometimes combined with key concepts from previous chapters. The chapter test will help you make sure you have mastered the material in that chapter before you move on to the next lesson.

Cumulative Test

The last section of this book is a test that covers all the concepts you've learned and reviewed throughout the whole book. It's more great review and focused practice.

A strong building needs a strong foundation. To improve your skills in math and get a high GMAT score, you need to begin with a strong foundation too—a solid understanding of basic math concepts. The chapters in this book are arranged from basic skills to more advanced topics, beginning with the properties of numbers, so every skill builds upon a firm base. With a system as focused and structured as this, good math skills are well within your reach. All you have to do is take the first step. Good luck!

SECTION I

Arithmetic

Properties of Numbers

In this first chapter, you will review the basic facts of working with numbers, including the different classifications of numbers, the order of operations when simplifying numerical expressions, and the three basic properties of numbers.

WORKING WITH NUMBERS

All the numbers that you'll see on the GMAT are **real numbers**. The real numbers, all of the numbers that you encounter each day, are classified into various sets and subsets. All real numbers are either rational numbers or irrational numbers.

You don't really have to be concerned about numbers that aren't real, but if you're wondering, numbers that aren't real are called imaginary. For example, the square root of −1 is imaginary. If that sounds complicated, don't worry; there aren't any imaginary numbers on the test.

Rational Numbers

The **rational numbers** are the numbers that can be expressed as a fraction in the form $\frac{a}{b}$, where a and b are integers and b does not equal 0. A rational number can take various forms:

- 5 can also be written as $\frac{5}{1}$.

- 1.2 can be written as $\frac{12}{10}$ or $\frac{6}{5}$.

- −7 can be written as $\frac{-7}{1}$.

- $0.\overline{3}$ can be written as $\frac{1}{3}$.

When written as a decimal, a rational number is either terminating or repeating.

TERMINATING DECIMALS

Terminating decimals are numbers such as 0.25 or 3.2897; in other words, they are decimals that end. They may extend to just one or two decimal places or for dozens, hundreds, or more.

REPEATING DECIMALS

Repeating decimals are decimals that form a pattern of digits, such as 1.282828... or 3.29712971... To indicate that the number continues into infinity, you may see an ellipses used (...), or sometimes you'll see a bar over the repeating digit or digits. For example, 1.282828...could also be written as $1.\overline{28}$.

Fractions and decimals will be covered in depth in chapter 3.

Irrational Numbers

Irrational numbers are called "irrational" because they cannot be written as the ratio of two integers and cannot be expressed as fractions. It's easier to think of irrational numbers as nonrepeating, nonterminating decimals. Irrational numbers are decimals that extend into infinity without ever forming a pattern. Some examples are $\sqrt{2}, \sqrt{3}, \sqrt{5}$, and π.

The decimal equivalent of π, as you may know, stretches on and on: 3.141592653... etc. Even when mathematicians look at millions and millions of its digits, no pattern forms. The number π is by far not the only irrational number; many square roots (such as the square root of 2) and some other kinds of numbers are also irrational.

REMEMBER THIS!

The **rational numbers** can be classified into subsets:

The **natural numbers**, also known as the counting numbers:
  {1, 2, 3, 4, 5, 6, 7...}

The **whole numbers** are the natural numbers, plus 0:
  {0, 1, 2, 3, 4, 5, 6, 7...}

The **integers** are the whole numbers and their opposites:
  {...−3, −2, −1, 0, 1, 2, 3...}

Here are some things you should know about integers:

- All numbers greater than 0 are positive numbers.

- All numbers less than 0 are negative numbers.

- Zero is neither positive nor negative.

- The even integers are divisible by 2 and include the number 0.

- The odd integers are not divisible by 2.

The integers will be covered in more depth in the next chapter.

PRACTICE 1

For each set of numbers in the first column, find the letter that corresponds with the correct set classification name. Choose the most descriptive name for the set. Answers and explanations are located at the end of the chapter.

1. $\{\sqrt{7}, \sqrt{11}, \pi, 5.1101001000...\}$ A. Rational numbers

2. $\{...-3, -1, 1, 3...\}$ B. Whole numbers

3. $\{0, 1, 2, 3, 4...\}$ C. Natural numbers

4. $\{-3, 0.4, -1.5, 0, 6.3\}$ D. Irrational numbers

5. $\{1, 2, 3...\}$ E. Odd integers

The Order of Operations

You encounter formulas in everyday life. When traveling abroad, you may need to convert a temperature from degrees Celsius to degrees Fahrenheit to know whether to wear a coat or not. You many need to calculate the perimeter or area of your back-yard to build a fence. Formulas exist for all kinds of situations.

When simplifying a mathematical expression after you have plugged values into your formula, you do not simply work from left to right, as you do when you read a book. Just as there are rules for driving an automobile, there are rules for order when performing arithmetic operations.

For example, here's a fairly straightforward math problem: $4 + 3 \times 2$.

If someone simply performed the steps from left to right, the result would be

$$4 + 3 \times 2$$
$$= 7 \times 2$$
$$= 14$$

But someone else who chose to do the multiplication first would get a different result:

$$4 + 3 \times 2$$
$$= 4 + 6$$
$$= 10$$

PEMDAS

Clearly, the order in which we perform math steps can make a difference. That order is a predetermined **order of operations** used to evaluate expressions. Perhaps you remember the mnemonic for remembering the order of operations: PEMDAS. Or some of you may have used the memory tool "Please Excuse My Dear Aunt Sally" to recall the correct order.

REMEMBER THIS!

The order of operations is:

P   **P**arentheses (grouping symbols)

E   **E**xponents

MD   **M**ultiply and **D**ivide from left to right

AS   **A**dd and **S**ubtract from left to right

- First perform any operations within **P**arentheses. (If the expression has parentheses within parentheses, work from the inside out.)
- Next, work out any **E**xponents.
- Then do all **M**ultiplication and **D**ivision in order from left to right.
- Lastly, do all **A**ddition and **S**ubtraction in order from left to right.

Example: Evaluate $10 \div 2 - 4 + 3 + 4 \times 7 - 18 \div 9 - 7$.

There aren't any parentheses or exponents, so go straight to multiplication and division.

$$(10 \div 2) - 4 + 3 + (4 \times 7) - (18 \div 9) - 7$$
$$= 5 - 4 + 3 + 28 - 2 - 7$$

Then do the addition and subtraction:

$$= 5 - 4 + 3 + 28 - 2 - 7$$
$$= 1 + 3 + 28 - 2 - 7$$
$$= 4 + 28 - 2 - 7$$
$$= 32 - 2 - 7$$
$$= 30 - 7$$
$$= 23$$

Example: Evaluate $[4 + (3 \times 2 + 7)] - (5 - 2)^2 + 6 \times 4$.

With nested parentheses or brackets, begin on the inside and work your way outwards.

$$[4 + (3 \times 2 + 7)] - (5 - 2)^2 + 6 \times 4$$
$$= [4 + (6 + 7)] - (5 - 2)^2 + 6 \times 4$$
$$= [4 + 13] - (3)^2 + 6 \times 4$$
$$= 17 - 3^2 + 6 \times 4$$

Now evaluate the exponent: $\qquad$ $17 - 9 + 6 \times 4$

Multiply (there is no division here): $\qquad$ $17 - 9 + 24$

Then add and subtract as needed: $\qquad$ $8 + 24 = 32$

PRACTICE 2

For questions 6–9, answer TRUE or FALSE for each statement. Answers and explanations are located at the end of the chapter.

6. **T   F**   In a numeric expression, addition is always performed before subtraction.

7. **T   F**   Parentheses are evaluated before exponents.

8. **T   F**   In the expression $57 - 32 + 8$, subtraction is the last operation performed.

9. **T** **F**   In the expression $700 \div 14 \times 2$, you would first multiply 14 by 2.

10. Simplify: $4^2 - (20 \div 4 \times 2)$

11. Simplify: $(15 - 12)^3 \div 9 \times 3$

12. Simplify: $94 - 2(4)^2 + 14$

13. Simplify: $1,200 \div 10^2 - 5 \times 2$

Other Grouping Symbols

The P in PEMDAS stands for parentheses, or grouping symbols. Grouping symbols include parentheses, brackets, the absolute value symbol, and a fraction bar. So to simplify $\dfrac{(18 + 10^2 - 4 \times 2)}{(20 - 27 \div 3)}$, treat the fraction bar as a grouping symbol and first evaluate the top (the numerator) then the bottom (the denominator). Then divide as the final step.

To simplify the numerator, first simplify your exponent: $10^2 = 100$. Second, multiply 4 times 2 to get 8. The top is now $18 + 100 - 8$. Evaluate from left to right: $118 - 8 = 110$. To simplify the denominator, first divide 27 by 3 to get 9. Then subtract: $20 - 9 = 11$. Finally, divide 110 by 11 to get 10.

In the order of operations, a radical sign is evaluated on the same level of priority as an exponent. To simplify $550 - \sqrt{9 \times 4} \times 3$, you would evaluate the radical first. Under the radical sign, multiply 9 times 4 to get 36. The square root of 36 is 6. Now the problem reads $550 - 6 \times 3$. Multiply 6 by 3 next to get $550 - 18$ for a final value of 532.

When plugging numbers into formulas, a working knowledge of the order of operations is essential. For example, to convert a temperature from degrees Fahrenheit to degrees Celsius, you use the formula $C = \dfrac{5}{9}(F - 32)$, where F is the degrees in Fahrenheit and C is the degrees in Celsius. If you have a temperature of 77 degrees Fahrenheit and you want to know the equivalent degrees in Celsius, substitute 77 for F in the formula: $C = \dfrac{5}{9}(77 - 32)$. First, subtract 32 from 77 because parentheses are evaluated first: $C = \dfrac{5}{9}(45)$. Now, multiply $\dfrac{5}{9}$ by 45 to get 25 degrees Celsius.

NUMBER PROPERTIES

Certain common properties of numbers are frequently used to make adding and multiplying easier. You most likely use these properties without even realizing it when you do mental arithmetic or when you add a column of numbers. These properties give you the license to change the order of operations in certain situations. In addition to making addition and multiplication of number terms easier to calculate, these three properties are frequently used in solving algebraic equations, as explained in chapter 12.

The Commutative Property of Addition

The **commutative property of addition** states that changing the order of the addends in a sum does not change the sum.

$$a + b = b + a, \text{ where } a \text{ and } b \text{ are any real numbers}$$

For example: $12.3 + 6.9 + 7.7 = 12.3 + 7.7 + 6.9$

The order of operations dictates that 12.3 first be added to 6.9. But the addition is easier if you first add 12.3 to 7.7 because the sum will equal a whole number. The commutative property of addition gives you this freedom.

The Commutative Property of Multiplication

The **commutative property of multiplication** states that changing the order of the factors in a product does not change the product.

$$a \times b = b \times a, \text{ where } a \text{ and } b \text{ are any real numbers}$$

For example: $2 \times 8 \times 5 \times 7 = 2 \times 5 \times 8 \times 7$

If you scan a group of factors to find subproducts that equal 10, 100, or 1,000, it is easiest to multiply these factors first. The commutative property allows you to make these changes to the order of operations.

When you are combining addition and subtraction, or combining multiplication and division, the key issue is the sign $(+, -, \times, \text{ or } \div)$ that precedes the number. For example, if a number is preceded by a subtraction sign, you must make sure that the number is subtracted. However, you can do the subtraction in any convenient order. Understanding this may help you do your arithmetic work.

It might be a bit frustrating or annoying to work through something like this:

$$10 - 2 + 3 - 8 + 4 - 6$$

But we can rewrite it in a more convenient order, taking care to maintain each number's sign, and this will make the arithmetic easier.

$$10 - 2 + 3 - 8 + 4 - 6$$
$$= 10 + 3 + 4 - 2 - 8 - 6$$
$$= 17 - 16$$
$$= 1$$

Simplify $120 - 2 \times 14 \times 5 + 9 \times 3 - 8 + 10 - 9 \div 3$.

$$120 - 2 \times 5 \times 14 + 9 \times 3 - 8 + 10 - 9 \div 3$$
$$= 120 - 10 \times 14 + 9 \times 3 - 8 + 10 - 9 \div 3$$
$$= 120 - 140 + 27 - 8 + 10 - 3$$
$$= 120 + 27 + 10 - 140 - 8 - 3$$
$$= 157 - 140 - 8 - 3$$
$$= 17 - 8 - 3$$
$$= 9 - 3$$
$$= 6$$

Notice that in the second step, we multiplied the 2 by the 5 before we multiplied by the 14. That made the math easier because it's easier to multiply by 10 than by just about any other number.

You'll have to be careful at first as you practice manipulating arithmetic like this, but since having a strong command of the material will greatly improve both your speed and accuracy, it is well worth the effort! Success on the GMAT often demands a creative problem-solving approach.

The Associative Property

Like the commutative property, the associative property pertains to either the addends in a sum or the factors in a product. The **associative property of addition** or **multiplication** states that changing the grouping (parentheses or brackets) of addends in a sum or the grouping of factors in a product does not change the resulting sum or product.

$a + (b + c) = (a + b) + c$, where a, b, and c are any real numbers

$a \times (b \times c) = (a \times b) \times c$, where a, b, and c are any real numbers

Sometimes, you can use the associative law (together with the commutative law) creatively to make your life easier. For example, you may want to look for numbers that are easier to add first, then add the rest. In the following problem, we can move the numbers into groups that add up to 10 to make our arithmetic easier.

$$3 + 9 + 1 + 2 + 7 + 8$$
$$= 3 + (9 + 1) + 2 + 7 + 8$$
$$= 3 + (9 + 1) + 7 + (2 + 8)$$
$$= (3 + 7) + (9 + 1) + (2 + 8)$$
$$= 10 + 10 + 10$$
$$= 30$$

We would have gotten 30 if we had added the numbers in the original order as well, but it would have been a bit more challenging. The difference is even more notable when the numbers are larger! Try to find pairs of numbers that add up to 100 in the following: $48 + 36 + 81 + 70 + 64 + 30 + 52 + 19$.

Answer:

$$48 + 36 + 81 + 70 + 64 + 30 + 52 + 19$$
$$= (48 + 52) + (36 + 64) + (81 + 19) + (70 + 30)$$
$$= 100 + 100 + 100 + 100$$
$$= 400$$

Again, simply adding the numbers in the original order would also have yielded 400. By combining them in this order, however, we make the problem much easier. Of course, not all problems will provide such perfect pairings, but it is worth your time to look for ways to make the problems easier. The payoff in speed and accuracy will be enormous down the line.

To explore the associative property of multiplication, consider the expression $7 \times 20 \times 5 \times 8$. Notice that $20 \times 5 = 100$, so change the grouping to make the multiplication easier: $7 \times (20 \times 5) \times 8$. Now evaluate from left to right: $7 \times 100 = 700$. Finally, $700 \times 8 = 5,600$.

You can also use a combination of the properties. For example, to simplify the expression $2.1 + 8.07 + 7.9 + 24.93$, scan the addends and recognize that $(2.1 + 7.9)$ and $(8.07 + 24.93)$ will produce whole numbers. Use the commutative property to get $2.1 + 7.9 + 8.07 + 24.93$. Then use the associative property to get $(2.1 + 7.9) + (8.07 + 24.93)$. Now the addition is easy to finish: $10 + 33 = 43$.

PRACTICE 3

Practice your knowledge of these properties. For each example below, answer *commutative*, *associative*, or *both*. Answers are located at the end of the chapter.

14. $7 + 11 + 3 = 7 + 3 + 11$

15. $12 \times 25 \times 4 = 12 \times (25 \times 4)$

16. $16.4 + 7.9 + (0.1 + 3) = 16.4 + (7.9 + 0.1) + 3$

17. $17.3 + 15 + 12.7 + 30 = (17.3 + 12.7) + (15 + 30)$

The Distributive Property

The distributive property involves two operations: addition and multiplication or subtraction and multiplication. The **distributive property of multiplication over addition** or **subtraction** states that multiplication distributes over addition and subtraction. In other words, this property allows us to multiply a number on the outside of parentheses with everything inside the parentheses. If we write that in algebraic terms, it would look like this:

$$a \times (b + c) = (a \times b) + (a \times c), \text{ where } a, b, \text{ and } c \text{ are real numbers}$$

$$a \times (b - c) = (a \times b) - (a \times c), \text{ where } a, b, \text{ and } c \text{ are real numbers}$$

Example: Simplify $2(3 + 6)$.

$2(3 + 6)$

$= 2 \times 3 + 2 \times 6$

$= 6 + 12$

$= 18$

We would have gotten the same result if we had added the material in the parentheses first and then multiplied:

$$2(3 + 6)$$
$$= 2(9)$$
$$= 18$$

You can also use the distributive property in reverse. For example, if you were instructed to simplify $(12 \times 6.4) + (12 \times 3.6)$, the order of operations would have you evaluate inside parentheses first, which would involve decimal multiplication. If you notice that both terms are multiplied by 12, however, you can use the distributive property to "factor out" the 12: $(12 \times 6.4) + (12 \times 3.6) = 12 \times (6.4 + 3.6) = 12 \times 10 = 120$.

Usually, if there are numbers (as opposed to variables such as x or y) inside the parentheses, it is easier to do the addition or subtraction inside the parentheses and then multiply, rather than distribute. For algebra, however, distribution will be a lot more useful to you—necessary, in fact.

DISTRIBUTIVE LAW WITH DIVISION

Division is distributive as well, though the way it works is a bit different. It's best illustrated with a few examples.

$$\frac{12 + 6}{2}$$
$$= \frac{12}{2} + \frac{6}{2}$$
$$= 6 + 3$$
$$= 9$$

This is the same result that we would have seen if we had added first and then divided, like this:

$$\frac{12 + 6}{2} = \frac{18}{2} = 9$$

You'll have to be careful, however, since this procedure doesn't work when the addition or subtraction is in the denominator (bottom) of the fraction.

$\dfrac{60}{4 + 6}$ is *not* equal to $\dfrac{60}{4} + \dfrac{60}{6}$.

$\dfrac{60}{4 + 6}$ equals $\dfrac{60}{10}$, which equals 6.

$\dfrac{60}{4} + \dfrac{60}{6}$ equals $15 + 10$, which equals 25.

So when something is being added or subtracted in the denominator of a fraction, be careful! This is a common source of error for many students, especially when this material is tested in an algebraic environment.

PRACTICE 4

To practice using the distributive property, fill in the blanks below.

18. $9(50 + 6) = (\underline{\hspace{1cm}} \times 50) + (9 \times 6)$

19. $(18 \times 24) + (18 \times 76) = \underline{\hspace{1cm}} \times (24 + 76)$

20. $(15 \times 6.6) + (15 \times 3.4) = 15(6.6 + \underline{\hspace{1cm}})$

21. $12(30 + 14) = (\underline{\hspace{1cm}} \times 30) + (12 \times 14)$

SUMMARY

Here are five main points about number properties that you should take from this chapter:

1. The correct order of operations is parentheses, then exponents, then multiplication and division, and then addition and subtraction (PEMDAS).

2. For order of operations, multiplication and division are performed from left to right; addition and subtraction are also evaluated from left to right.

3. The commutative property states that changing the order of addends or factors does not change the sum or product.

4. The associative property states that changing the grouping of addends or factors does not change the sum or product.

5. The distributive property states that multiplication distributes over addition or subtraction.

Practice Answers and Explanations

1. D

The irrational numbers cannot be expressed as fractions.

2. E

The integers are the whole numbers and their opposites. Odd numbers cannot be divided evenly by 2.

3. B

The whole numbers are the natural numbers plus 0.

4. A

The rational numbers are those that can be expressed as fractions.

5. C

The natural numbers are also known as the counting numbers.

6. False

Addition and subtraction are evaluated from left to right, as they are encountered in a problem.

7. True

Terms in parentheses are always evaluated before exponents.

8. False

Addition will be evaluated last.

9. False

Division will be evaluated first.

10. 6

Parentheses are evaluated first. Inside the parentheses, evaluate division and then multiplication: $20 \div 4 = 5$; $5 \times 2 = 10$. Next, evaluate the exponent: $4^2 = 16$. Finally, evaluate subtraction: $16 - 10 = 6$.

11. 9

Evaluate inside the parentheses first: $15 - 12 = 3$. Next, evaluate the exponent: $3^3 = 27$. Division is performed next: $27 \div 9 = 3$. Finally, $3 \times 3 = 9$.

12. 76

The term in the parentheses is already in its simplest possible form, so evaluate the exponent to get $4^2 = 16$. Next, perform multiplication: $2 \times 16 = 32$. Finally, perform addition and subtraction from left to right: $(94 - 32) + 14 = 62 + 14 = 76$.

13. 2

The exponent is evaluated first: $10^2 = 100$. Next, perform division: $1,200 \div 100 = 12$. Next, multiply: $5 \times 2 = 10$. Finally, $12 - 10 = 2$.

14. Commutative

15. Associative

16. Associative

17. Both

18. 9

19. 18

20. 3.4

21. 12

CHAPTER 1 TEST

1. Which set below features the even integers?

    (A) {2.4, 3.6, 4.8, 5.0, 6.2}

    (B) {..., −6, −4, −2, 0, 2, 4, 6...}

    (C) {0, 1, 2, 3, 4...}

    (D) {..., −7, −5, −3, −1, 1, 3, 5, 7...}

    (E) Both A and B

2. All of the elements in the set $\left\{\frac{1}{4}, \frac{1}{3}, \frac{2}{3}, \frac{3}{4}, \frac{5}{6}\right\}$ are

    (A) irrational numbers.

    (B) integers.

    (C) natural numbers.

    (D) rational numbers.

    (E) whole numbers.

3. Simplify: 56 − 24 + 12

    (A) 68

    (B) 20

    (C) 44

    (D) 92

    (E) 42

4. Simplify: 36 + 8 ÷ 2

    (A) 40

    (B) 22

    (C) 52

    (D) 25

    (E) 88

5. Simplify: $32 - 4^2 \times 2$

    (A) 32

    (B) 0

    (C) 48

    (D) 16

    (E) 80

6. Simplify $(40 + 20) \div 10$

    (A) 3

    (B) 42

    (C) 5

    (D) 1

    (E) 6

7. Simplify: $48 \div 2 + 4 \times 4 - 2$

    (A) 110

    (B) 3

    (C) 38

    (D) 30

    (E) 56

8. The number sentence $5 \times 7 \times 20 = 5 \times 20 \times 7$ is an example of which property?

    (A) Distributive

    (B) Commutative

    (C) Associative

    (D) Order of operations

    (E) None of the above

9. Which sentence below demonstrates the distributive property?

   (A) $8(40 + 7) = (8 + 40) \times (8 + 7)$
   (B) $8 + (40 \times 7) = (8 \times 40) + (8 \times 7)$
   (C) $8(40 + 7) = (8 + 40) + 7$
   (D) $8(40 + 7) = (8 \times 40) + (8 \times 7)$
   (E) $8(40 + 7) = (40 + 7)8$

10. Choose from below to fill in the blank:

   $9(50 + 6) = (9 \times 50) + (9 \times \underline{\hspace{1cm}})$

   (A) 56
   (B) 6
   (C) 9
   (D) 15
   (E) 54

11. Which example below demonstrates the associative property?

   (A) $(6.27 + 3.7) + 16.3 = 6.27 + (3.7 + 16.3)$
   (B) $6.27 + 3.7 + 16.3 = 16.3 + 6.27 + 3.7$
   (C) $7 \times (30 + 8) = (7 \times 30) + (7 \times 8)$
   (D) $(18 \times 3.7) + (18 \times 16.3) = 18(3.7 + 16.3)$
   (E) $18 \times (3.7 + 16.3) = (18 \times 3.7) + 16.3$

12. Choose the correct classification for the following numbers, in order:
   $-8, \dfrac{3}{4}, 0, \sqrt{2}, 9$

   (A) Integer, irrational, whole number, irrational, integer
   (B) Irrational, irrational, rational, irrational, rational
   (C) Integer, rational, whole number, irrational, whole number
   (D) Integer, irrational, whole number, irrational, rational
   (E) Integer, rational, natural number, irrational, natural number

13. Which of the following is an irrational number?

    (A) $3.77\overline{7}$

    (B) $\sqrt{5}$

    (C) $\dfrac{2}{3}$

    (D) Both A and B

    (E) All of the above

14. The most specific name for the set of numbers {0, 1, 2, 3, 4...} is the

    (A) irrational numbers.

    (B) natural numbers.

    (C) whole numbers.

    (D) rational numbers.

    (E) real numbers.

15. Simplify: $(15 - 12)^3 \div 9 \times 3$

    (A) 9

    (B) 3

    (C) $\dfrac{1}{3}$

    (D) 1

    (E) 27

16. Simplify: $10^2 \div (80 \div 4 \times 2)$

    (A) $\dfrac{2}{3}$

    (B) 10

    (C) $\dfrac{5}{2}$

    (D) $\dfrac{1}{2}$

    (E) 25

17. Simplify: $\dfrac{8(5 + 2) + 4}{5 + 5 \times 2}$

   (A) $\dfrac{19}{20}$

   (B) 4

   (C) 3

   (D) $\dfrac{12}{5}$

   (E) 5

18. Which choice shows the correct order of operations for the expression $12 - 2 \times 4 + 1$?

   (A) $12 - ((2 \times 4) + 1)$

   (B) $(12 - 2) \times (4 + 1)$

   (C) $((12 - 2) \times 4) + 1$

   (D) $12 - (2 \times (4 + 1))$

   (E) $(12 - (2 \times 4)) + 1$

19. Which choice shows the correct evaluation of the expression $8^2 - 4^2 \times 2$?

   (A) $(8 \times 2) - ((4 \times 2) \times 2)$

   (B) $((8 \times 2) - (4 \times 2)) \times 2$

   (C) $(8^2) - ((4^2) \times 2)$

   (D) $(64 - 16) \times 2$

   (E) $(8 \times 2) - 4 \times 2 \times 2$

20. Which statement illustrates the commutative property?

   (A) $19(70 + 7) = (19 \times 70) + (19 \times 7)$

   (B) $19 \times 70 \times 7 = 19 \times (70 \times 7)$

   (C) $19 + 3 + 21 = 19 + 21 + 3$

   (D) $19 \times 3 + 21 = 19 \times (3 + 21)$

   (E) $(19 \times 70) + (9 \times 70) = 70(19 + 9)$

Answers and Explanations

1. B

Choice (A) is not a set of even integers. Even though the numbers in this set have a last digit that is divisible by 2, they are not integers—they are decimals. Choice (C) is the set of whole numbers, both even and odd. Choice (D) is the set of odd integers.

2. D

A rational number is any number that can be expressed as a fraction. Choice (A) is incorrect; irrational numbers are real numbers that are *not* rational. Choice (B) does not describe the set; integers are not fractions. Choice (C) is not correct; natural numbers are numbers in the set $\{1, 2, 3, 4...\}$. Choice (E) is also incorrect; whole numbers are numbers in the set $\{0, 1, 2, 3, 4...\}$.

3. C

First subtract 24 from 56; $56 - 24 = 32$. Now add this result to 12: $32 + 12 = 44$.

4. A

Evaluate division first: $8 \div 2 = 4$. Then add: $36 + 4 = 40$.

5. B

The order of operations is exponents, then multiplication, and finally subtraction. $4^2 = 16$, then $16 \times 2 = 32$. Finally, $32 - 32 = 0$.

6. E

Evaluate terms in parentheses first, then divide: $40 + 20 = 60$, and $60 \div 10 = 6$.

7. C

Work from left to right, evaluating all division and multiplication first. Thus, $48 \div 2 = 24$. Next, $4 \times 4 = 16$. Then, $24 + 16 = 40$. Finally, $40 - 2 = 38$.

8. B

This example shows that changing the order of the factors does not change the resulting product, which is by definition the commutative property. Choice (A), the distributive property, states that multiplication distributes over addition. Choice (C), the associative property, deals with the grouping of factors, not the order. Choice (D), order of operations, is a ruling on the precedence of operations.

9. D

Choice (D) shows that multiplication distributes over addition. Choices (A), (B), and (C) are all false statements; they are not examples of any property of numbers. If you simplify the equation in choice (A) by using the order of operations, you get $8 \times 47 = 48 \times 15$, or $376 = 720$, which is false. If you simplify the equation in choice (B) by using the order of operations, you get $8 + 280 = 320 + 56$, or $288 = 376$, which is false. If you simplify the equation in choice (C) by using the order of operations, you get $8 \times 47 = 48 + 7$, or $376 = 55$, which is false. Choice (E) shows an example of the commutative property, which states that you can change the order of factors without changing the product.

10. B

This example of the distributive property is missing the 6, which is the second part of the sum over which 9 distributes.

11. A

Choice (A) indicates that changing the grouping of addends does not affect the resultant sum. This is, by definition, the associative property. Choice (B) is a demonstration of the commutative property. Choices (C) and (D) are examples of the distributive property. If you simplify the equation in choice (E) by using the order of operations, you get $18 \times 20 = 66.6 + 16.3$, or $360 = 82.9$, which is false.

12. C

Choice (C) is the correct classification for each of the numbers listed. Negative 8 is an integer and a rational number. Three-fourths is a rational number. Zero is an integer, a whole number, and a rational number. The square root of 2 is irrational. Nine is an integer, a whole number, a natural number, and a rational number.

13. B

Choice (B) is the only irrational number. A rational number is a number that can be expressed as a fraction. For choice (A), $3.7\overline{77} = 3\dfrac{7}{9} = \dfrac{34}{9}$ and thus is a rational number. Choice (C), a fraction, is by definition a rational number. Choice (B) is the only choice that cannot be expressed as a fraction. When converted to a decimal equivalent, $\sqrt{5}$ neither terminates nor repeats.

14. C

The most specific name for this set is the whole numbers, choice (C). This set of numbers is a set of rational numbers; all can be expressed as fractions. Therefore, choice (A) is false. Choice (D) is a true classification for the set, but it is not the most *specific* name for the set. Choice (B) is not a correct classification; the natural numbers do not include the number 0. Choice (E) is true—the numbers in this set are all real numbers—but it is not the most *specific* classification.

15. A

Evaluate terms in parentheses first: $15 - 12 = 3$. Next, evaluate the exponent: $3^3 = 3 \times 3 \times 3 = 27$. Next, divide: $27 \div 9 = 3$. Finally, multiply: $3 \times 3 = 9$.

16. C

First simplify within the parentheses. Division is located to the left of multiplication, so divide first: $80 \div 4 = 20$. Now multiply 20 by 2 to get 40. Next, evaluate the exponent: $10^2 = 100$. The final step is to divide 100 by 40: $\dfrac{100}{40} = \dfrac{5}{2}$.

17. B

This is a fractional expression. The fraction bar acts as a grouping symbol, so evaluate the numerator, evaluate the denominator, and then divide. In the numerator, add $5 + 2 = 7$ because this is contained within parentheses. Next, multiply by 8: $7 \times 8 = 56$. Add 4: $56 + 4 = 60$. In the denominator, multiplication is evaluated before addition, so $5 \times 2 = 10$, and then $5 + 10 = 15$. Finally, $60 \div 15 = 4$.

18. E

Parentheses have been added to the answer choices to show the order of preference for the operations. Multiplication is performed first, followed by subtraction (it is to the left of the addition operation), then addition.

19. C

Evaluate the exponents first. Choice (C) shows this, because these exponents are enclosed in parentheses. The outer parentheses surrounding $4^2 \times 2$ indicate that multiplication is evaluated before subtraction.

20. C

Choice (C) is the only example that demonstrates the commutative property, which states that changing the order of addends does not change the resultant sum. Choices (A) and (E) are examples of the distributive property. Choice (B) is a demonstration of the associative property. Choice (D) is not an example of any property of numbers; it is false. If you simplify the equation in choice (D) by using the order of operations, you get $57 + 21 = 19 \times 24$, or $78 = 456$.

Integers

This chapter will focus on the set of numbers known as **integers**. You encounter integers in many places each day. They are used to express temperatures above and below 0, a loss or gain of yards when playing certain sports, and the highs and lows of the stock market, to name a few. Integers provide a foundation for the real number system.

WORKING WITH INTEGERS

Integers are the set of whole numbers and their opposites. As a set, the integers are written as $\{\ldots, -3, -2, -1, 0, 1, 2, 3\ldots\}$.

Each integer has a location on a real number line, where the sign of the number determines to which side of 0 the number is located. For example, positive 5, which can also be written as +5 or simply 5, is located 5 units to the right of 0, as shown in the diagram below.

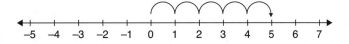

Negative 8, which can also be written as −8, is located 8 units to the left of 0, as shown in the diagram below.

It is important to remember that the number 0 is neither positive nor negative.

Absolute Value

On the GMAT, you will encounter the concept of absolute value from time to time. The **absolute value** of a number is the number stripped of its sign. For example, the absolute value of −2 is 2, and the absolute value of 9 is 9.

You can also think of absolute value as the number of units a number is away from 0 on a number line. Since absolute value is a measure of distance, it is always a positive value. The symbol for absolute value is two bars on either side of a numerical value or expression. For example, the absolute value of −7 is written as $|-7|$, and since −7 is 7 units away from 0 on a number line, $|-7| = 7$. The absolute value of 4 is written as $|4|$, and since it is 4 units away from 0 on a number line, $|4| = 4$.

Absolute value as a concept is necessary in math because sometimes we are interested in the difference between two values without worrying about which one is larger.

PRACTICE 1

Fill in the blank with the best possible word. Answers and explanations are located at the end of the chapter.

1. Negative numbers are located on the _____ side of 0 on a number line.

2. The integer −2 is located _____ spaces to the left of 0 on a number line.

3. The absolute value of 5 is equal to _____.

4. The value of $|101|$ = _____.

5. The value of $|-442|$ = _____.

6. The integer _____ is neither positive nor negative.

Ordering Integers

The value of an integer is determined by its location on the real number line, where negative numbers appear to the left of 0 and positive numbers are located to the right of 0. When comparing integers, first determine their locations on the number line. A number farther to the right is larger in value than a number farther to the left. For example, when comparing −8 and −9, −9 is farther to the left on a number line;

therefore, −9 is less than −8. This concept can also be written using the symbol for *less than* and would appear as −9 < −8.

PRACTICE 2

Now try the following TRUE/FALSE questions to test your ordering skills. Answers and explanations are located at the end of the chapter.

7. **T   F**   The integer −5 is larger than the integer −6.

8. **T   F**   The set {−65, −60, −59} is listed in ascending order.

9. **T   F**   −11 < −12.

PROPERTIES OF −1, 0, 1, AND NUMBERS IN BETWEEN

Here's a helpful refresher on some basic number properties.

Properties of Zero

Adding or subtracting zero from a number does not change the number.

- $8 + 0 = 8$
- $6 - 0 = 6$
- $\frac{1}{2} + 0 = \frac{1}{2}$
- $\frac{1}{2} - 0 = \frac{1}{2}$
- $-3 + 0 = -3$

Multiplying any number by zero always results in zero.

- $8 \times 0 = 0$
- $6 \times 0 = 0$
- $\frac{1}{2} \times 0 = 0$
- $-3 \times 0 = 0$

In math, dividing by zero is not allowed. This is because it simply doesn't make sense to say that we are dividing something into zero pieces. Thus, anything divided by zero is undefined, and you may never divide by zero or a variable that may be equal to zero.

However, it is permissible to divide zero by other numbers. The result is always zero. This is consistent with logic. After all, if we have nothing, we can divide that nothing into as many pieces as we wish and still have nothing!

- $0 \div 4 = 0$
- $\dfrac{0}{7} = 0$

Properties of 1 and −1

Multiplying or dividing a number by 1 does not change the number.

- $8 \times 1 = 8$
- $6 \div 1 = 6$
- $\dfrac{1}{2} \times 1 = \dfrac{1}{2}$
- $\dfrac{1}{2} \div 1 = \dfrac{1}{2}$
- $-3 \times 1 = -3$

Multiplying or dividing a nonzero number by −1 "flips the sign"; that is, it changes the number from positive to negative, or negative to positive, without changing the rest of the number (its absolute value).

- $8 \times -1 = -8$
- $6 \div -1 = -6$
- $\dfrac{1}{2} \times -1 = -\dfrac{1}{2}$
- $\dfrac{1}{2} \div -1 = -\dfrac{1}{2}$
- $-3 \times -1 = 3$

Accordingly, the value of 0×1 is 0. This is true because multiplying any number by 0 yields 0 and because any number multiplied by 1 is itself.

The **reciprocal** of a number is 1 divided by that number. For example, the reciprocal of 15 is $\frac{1}{15}$. It is also helpful to know that the product of a number and its reciprocal is 1. For the record, 0 has no reciprocal. It would be considered undefined. And, of course, we'll see reciprocals again in chapter 3: Fractions and Decimals.

Properties of Numbers between –1 and 1

The reciprocal of a number between 0 and 1 is greater than the number.

- The reciprocal of $\frac{1}{2}$ is 2.

- The reciprocal of $\frac{2}{7}$ is $\frac{7}{2}$.

- The reciprocal of $\frac{3}{17}$ is $\frac{17}{3}$.

The reciprocal of a number between –1 and 0 is less than the number.

- The reciprocal of $-\frac{1}{4}$ is –4; –4 is smaller than $-\frac{1}{4}$ because $-\frac{1}{4}$ is farther to the right on a number line.

- The reciprocal of $-\frac{2}{9}$ is $-\frac{9}{2}$; $-\frac{9}{2}$ is smaller than $-\frac{2}{9}$ because $-\frac{2}{9}$ is farther to the right on a number line.

If we square a number between 0 and 1, the result will be smaller than the original number.

- $\left(\frac{1}{2}\right)^2 = \frac{1}{4}$

- $\left(\frac{2}{3}\right)^2 = \frac{4}{9}$

If we multiply any positive number by a fraction between 0 and 1, the result will be smaller than the original number.

- $6 \times \frac{1}{2} = 3$

- $10 \times \frac{3}{5} = 6$

- $14 \times \frac{2}{7} = 4$

Multiplying any negative number by a fraction between 0 and 1 gives a product greater than the original number.

- $-6 \times \dfrac{1}{2} = -3$ (Note that -3 is larger than -6 because -3 is farther to the right on the number line.)

- $-10 \times \dfrac{3}{5} = -6$

- $-14 \times \dfrac{2}{7} = -4$

PRACTICE 3

If you are feeling overwhelmed by all these facts, keep in mind that they are best learned by understanding rather than by memorization. Increase your understanding now by practicing these examples! Answers and explanations are located at the end of the chapter.

10. **T F**   The reciprocal of 11 is -11.

11. **T F**   Squaring any number between 0 and 1 will increase its value.

12. **T F**   Squaring any number between 0 and -1 will increase its value.

13. **T F**   Squaring any positive number will increase its value.

14. **T F**   Multiplying a negative number less than -1 by any number greater than -1 will reduce its value.

PROPERTIES OF ODD AND EVEN NUMBERS

The terms *odd* and *even* apply only to integers. Nonintegers are neither odd nor even. Even numbers are integers that are divisible by 2, and odd numbers are integers that are not. Put more simply, if an integer's last digit is either 0, 2, 4, 6, or 8, it is even; if its last digit is 1, 3, 5, 7, or 9, it is odd. Odd and even numbers may be negative or positive, and for the record, zero is even.

Odds and evens behave in definitive patterns that can (and should!) be learned and relied upon on test day. There are no exceptions to these rules.

Addition and Subtraction Rules

$$ODD +/- ODD = EVEN$$
$$EVEN +/- EVEN = EVEN$$
$$ODD +/- EVEN = ODD$$

Multiplication Rules

A number needs just a single factor of 2 to be even, so the product of an even number and any integer will always be even. If you multiply only with odd numbers, the result will always be odd.

$$ODD \times ODD = ODD$$
$$EVEN \times EVEN = EVEN$$
$$ODD \times EVEN = EVEN$$

There are no rules for division with evens and odds.

If you ever forget the rules of odds and evens, you can prove them to yourself again by picking sample numbers. You can use 0 as your token even number and 1 as your token odd number. Zero is even and, as far as even/odd rules go, behaves like every other even number; 1 is odd and behaves just like every other odd number.

For example, on test day, if you can't remember the result of adding an odd and an even number, you can check to see what happens when you add 1 and 0. The sum of 1 and 0 is 1, which is odd. Therefore, the sum of an odd and even is odd.

PRACTICE 4

Practice is the key to learning. Demonstrate your mastery of odd and even number properties with these examples. Answers and explanations are located at the end of the chapter.

15. **T F**   An even number divided by an even number will always produce an even number.

16. **T F**   If x is an integer, then $75,392x$ will always be an even integer, regardless of the value of x.

17. **T F**   If x is an integer, then $x + 1,978$ will be an odd integer if and only if x is odd.

INTEGER OPERATIONS

The ability to add and subtract signed numbers is best learned by practice. Also, keep your common sense close at hand. In everyday life, you deal with assets and debts, so you can bring this experience to bear as you work through math problems.

Adding Integers

When adding integers, the sign of the numbers involved is very important. To help you visualize adding integers, think of any positive integer as a group of that many positives and any negative integer as a group of that many negatives. Thus, +5 would be represented as five positives.

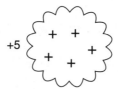

In the same way, −7 would be represented as seven negatives.

Another way to conceptualize it is to think of the positive numbers as assets and the negative numbers as debts. Combine all your assets (positive numbers), then combine all your debts (negative numbers). If the assets outweigh the debts, we have a positive mark on the ledger. And if the debts outweigh the assets, then we'll end up with a negative result.

Keep in mind that any time one positive and one negative are grouped together, this makes a neutral. They cancel each other out. You can consider this as $+1 + -1 = 0$.

When adding integers that have the same sign, just add the absolute values of the numbers and keep the sign.

Here are two examples:

$6 + 7 = 13$

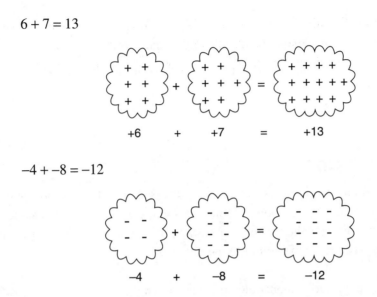

$$+6 \quad + \quad +7 \quad = \quad +13$$

$-4 + -8 = -12$

$$-4 \quad + \quad -8 \quad = \quad -12$$

When adding integers that have different signs, recall that each negative sign can pair with a positive sign to form a neutral. Each member of the pair cancels the other out. Therefore, the solution to an addition problem with integers of different signs will be the remaining positives or negatives that do not form a pair.

For example, in the problem $-3 + 5$, three negatives pair with three of the five positives to form three neutral pairs.

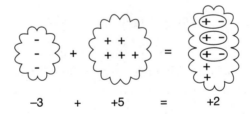

$$-3 \quad + \quad +5 \quad = \quad +2$$

You now have two positives left over that did not form a pair. Therefore, the solution to the problem $-3 + 5$ is 2.

A general rule for adding integers with different signs is to subtract their absolute values and keep the sign of the number with the larger absolute value as your answer. In the example $18 + (-25)$, subtract the absolute values to get $25 - 18 = 7$. Since -25 has a larger absolute value, take the negative sign for your answer. The final answer is -7.

REMEMBER THIS!

When adding integers:

- If the signs are the same…add and keep the sign.

- If the signs are different…subtract and take the sign of the number with the larger absolute value.

Subtracting Integers

The subtraction of any two integers can also be expressed as adding the opposite of the number being subtracted. In other words, subtracting a negative is the same as adding a positive. This way, the concept can be simplified into an addition problem, and you have only two rules to commit to memory.

Here are a few examples to demonstrate how this works.

Find the value of $19 - (-2)$.

Since this problem involves subtracting integers, change the problem so that it is adding the opposite of the number subtracted. So the subtraction sign changes to an addition sign, and the -2 changes to a $+2$. The problem now becomes $19 + (+2)$. Follow the rules for addition. Since the signs are both positive, add 19 and 2 to get 21 and keep the solution positive: $19 - (-2) = 21$.

Find the value of $-45 - 9$.

Remember that $-45 - 9$ means $-45 - (+9)$. As in the previous example, change the subtraction sign to an addition sign and change the $+9$ to a -9. The problem now becomes $-45 + (-9)$. Since the signs are both negative, add the absolute values to get $45 + 9 = 54$ and keep the solution negative: $-45 - 9 = -54$.

The temperature on a certain day dropped from $-4°F$ to $-17°F$.

What is the difference in temperature for that day?

This example illustrates how negative integers can be used to show temperature. Since you are looking for the difference between the two temperatures, subtract the two values. Then $-4 - (-17)$ becomes $-4 + 17$. The subtraction sign is changed to addition and the sign of -17 is changed to a positive. Since the signs are now different, subtract the absolute values and take the sign of the larger absolute value: $17 - 4 = 13$. The difference in temperature is 13 degrees.

FLASHBACK!

Use the number properties studied in chapter 1 to help simplify expressions with integers.

Take the expression $-4 + 5 + -6$. You can use the commutative property of addition to change the order of the expression to $-4 + (-6) + 5$. Now the negative numbers are together and can easily be combined. Since $-4 + (-6) = -10$, now add -10 to 5 to get a final answer: $-10 + 5 = -5$.

PRACTICE 5

Try the following set of questions to practice adding and subtracting integers. For each numbered problem in the first column, find the letter that corresponds with the correct sum or difference. Answers and explanations are located at the end of the chapter.

18. $-12 + 4$ A. -32

19. $14 - (-5)$ B. -1

20. $-201 - (-200)$ C. 18

21. $-18 + (-14)$ D. 19

22. $23 + (-5)$ E. -8

Multiplying and Dividing Integers

Multiplication and division of integers is a bit more straightforward than adding and subtracting. Regardless of the numbers' signs, you multiply or divide the absolute values of the numbers just as when you first learned how to multiply and divide. The only question is whether the solution is positive or negative. Since multiplication is repeated addition, use the principles of addition to make sense of the rules. In the example $6 \times (-2)$, this is the same as adding six groups of -2. Therefore, the answer would be -12.

For the problem $(-5) \times (-3)$, this is the same as the opposite of adding five groups of -3. This would have a result of 15. There are two negatives in the problem, so they cancel each other out.

Since division follows the same principle, a problem such as $-12 \div 4$ would result in an answer of -3. There is only one negative in the problem, so the answer is also negative. The negative has nothing to cancel out with.

In the example $-4 \times -9 \times -2$, the result will be the opposite of the product of 4, 9, and 2, which is -72. The solution here is negative because two negatives pair up to cancel out with one negative sign left over.

REMEMBER THIS!

When multiplying and dividing integers, if there is an even number of negatives in the problem, the solution will be positive. If there is an odd number of negatives, the solution will be negative.

PRACTICE 6

Remember, repetition is the key to mastery! Use the following bank of integers to answer the questions below on multiplying and dividing integers. Answers and explanations are located at the end of the chapter.

9	−30	−12	−9	40	−20
21	30	−35	−40	−1	−3

23. $-5 \times -6 =$

24. $-5 \times 6 =$

25. $-36 \div -4 =$

26. $21 \div -7 =$

27. $-4 \times -2 \times -5$

WORKING WITH OPERATIONS AND ABSOLUTE VALUE

When working with absolute value, expressions are simplified much in the same way as expressions that contain parentheses. Any operations contained within the absolute value bars are evaluated first, using the correct order of operations. Take, for example, the expression $|-16 + 7|$. The first step in simplifying is to combine -16 and 7, which is equal to -9. Remember that the -9 is still inside the absolute value bars. Now evaluate the absolute value of -9: $|-9| = 9$.

In a contrasting example, such as $|-16| + |7|$, only single values are contained within the absolute value bars. Evaluate within the absolute values first. Since $|-16| = 16$ and $|7| = 7$, the problem then becomes $16 + 7 = 23$. The key for both of these examples is to simplify any absolute value problem down to a single value within the absolute value bars first, and then calculate the absolute value of the number. Refer to chapter 1 of this book for any questions on the order of operations.

PRACTICE 7

Try this practice set to help you assess your understanding of operations and absolute value.

28. Find the value of the expression $|24 - (-4)|$.

29. Find the value of the expression $|-8| + |-6|$.

30. Find the value of the expression $-|-16| - |5|$.

31. Is there a difference in the solutions of the two expressions $|-15 + 9|$ and $|-15| + |9|$? Explain your answer.

SUMMARY

Here are the six main points about integers and absolute value that you should take from this chapter:

1. The absolute value of an integer is the distance the number is from 0 on a number line. This value is always positive.

2. When comparing integers, the number farther to the left on a number line is the smaller integer.

3. When adding integers with like signs, add the absolute values and keep the sign. If the signs are different, subtract the absolute values and take the sign of the number with the larger absolute value.

4. Any subtraction problem can be rewritten as an addition problem by changing the subtraction sign to an addition sign and switching the sign of the number being subtracted. Then follow the rules for addition.

5. When multiplying and dividing integers, an even number of negatives results in a positive answer. An odd number of negatives results in a negative answer.

6. Evaluate terms within any absolute value bars first in a question. When the terms within the bars are reduced to a single value, then proceed to work with that value.

Practice Answers and Explanations

1. Left

On any horizontal number line, negative numbers appear to the left of 0. The value of the numbers decreases the farther to the left you move.

2. 2

The integer −2 is located 2 places away from 0 on a number line. Since distance is always a positive value, the answer is positive 2, even though you moved to the left to get to −2.

3. 5

The absolute value of a number is the distance the number is from 0 on a number line. The number 5 is five units from 0.

4. 101

The expression $|101|$ means the absolute value of positive 101, which is equal to 101. The integer 101 is 101 units away from 0 on a number line.

5. 442

The expression $|-442|$ means the absolute value of negative 442, which is equal to 442. The integer −442 is 442 units away from 0 on a number line.

6. 0

The integer 0 is considered neutral; it is neither positive nor negative.

7. True

Negative 5 is to the right of −6 on a number line.

8. True

These numbers are in order from smallest to largest.

9. False

Negative 11 is greater than −12 because it is farther to the right on a number line.

10. False

The reciprocal of a number is its inverse, not its negative. The reciprocal of 11 is $\frac{1}{11}$.

11. False

Squaring a number between 0 and 1 will actually make it smaller. For example, $\left(\frac{1}{2}\right)^2 = \frac{1}{4}$, which is smaller than $\frac{1}{2}$.

12. True

Numbers between 0 and −1 are negative, and squaring a negative number will make it positive, which increases its value.

13. False

Although this statement is true for positive numbers greater than 1, don't forget that squaring a number between 0 and 1 makes it smaller!

14. False

A negative number less than −1 will actually increase in value if it's multiplied by a number between −1 and 1. For example, take −10:

$$-10 \times \left(-\frac{1}{2}\right) = 5$$
$$-10 \times \left(\frac{1}{2}\right) = -5$$

Both 5 and −5 are greater than −10.

15. False

There are no odd/even rules for division. This is because dividing one integer by another will not always produce an integer. For example, $6 \div 4 = 1.5$; the result is not an integer and is therefore neither odd nor even.

16. True

Multiplying an even number by any integer always produces an even integer. Because 75,392 is even, $75,392x$ is guaranteed to be even as long as x is an integer.

17. True

Because odd + even = odd and 1,978 is an even number, $1,978 + x$ will be odd if x is odd and even if x is even.

18. E

19. D

20. B

21. A

22. C

23. 30

24. −30

25. 9

26. −3

27. −40

28. 28

$$|28| = 28$$

29. 14

$$8 + 6 = 14$$

30. −21

$$-|-16| - |5| = -16 - 5 = -21$$

31. Yes

When evaluating the first expression, combine −15 and 9 first to get $|-6| = 6$. In the second expression, evaluate the absolute values first to get $15 + 9$, which is equal to 24. The order of operations for the two expressions is different, resulting in two different solutions.

CHAPTER 2 TEST

Try the following questions to test your knowledge of integers. Use the lessons and practice from the chapter to answer any questions you may have. The answer explanations following this section will also provide help and guidance.

1. The number −12 is how many units away from 0 on a number line?

    (A) −13
    (B) −12
    (C) −1
    (D) 1
    (E) 12

2. The absolute value of an integer is *ALWAYS*

    (A) equal to zero.
    (B) negative.
    (C) either zero or positive.
    (D) either positive or negative.
    (E) equal to the opposite of the number.

3. The value of $|-98| =$ _____?

    (A) −99
    (B) −98
    (C) −97
    (D) 98
    (E) 99

4. The value of $|23| =$ _____?

    (A) −24
    (B) −23
    (C) 23
    (D) 24
    (E) 46

5. Which of the following answer choices are *NOT* in ascending order?

    (A) 0, 2, 4

    (B) −5, −7, −8

    (C) −21, −20, −19

    (D) −90, −80, −70

    (E) None of these

6. For the inequality −35 < _____ < −24, which of the following could be placed in the blank to make the inequality TRUE?

    (A) −46

    (B) −36

    (C) −34

    (D) −23

    (E) −20

7. Evaluate: −13 + (−6)

    (A) −19

    (B) −7

    (C) 7

    (D) 18

    (E) 19

8. Evaluate: 20 + (−5)

    (A) −25

    (B) −15

    (C) −4

    (D) 15

    (E) 25

9. Evaluate: −19 + 4 + (−2)

    (A) −25

    (B) −21

    (C) −17

    (D) −13

    (E) 13

10. Evaluate: −27 − 11

    (A) −38

    (B) −37

    (C) −16

    (D) 37

    (E) 38

11. Evaluate: −56 − (−9)

    (A) 65

    (B) 47

    (C) −47

    (D) −65

    (E) 504

12. Evaluate: −18 ÷ (−2)

    (A) 9

    (B) 6

    (C) −9

    (D) −20

    (E) −36

13. Evaluate: -77×2

    (A) -154
    (B) 154
    (C) -75
    (D) -79
    (E) 79

14. Evaluate: $-4 \times -1 \times -9$

    (A) -14
    (B) 14
    (C) -36
    (D) 36
    (E) -32

15. Evaluate: $-6 + (14 - (-2)) - 3^2$

    (A) 1
    (B) 4
    (C) 13
    (D) -3
    (E) 0

16. Find the value of the expression $|4| - |5|$.

    (A) -20
    (B) -9
    (C) -1
    (D) 1
    (E) 9

KAPLAN

17. Find the value of the expression $|-7 + -78|$.

    (A) −85

    (B) −71

    (C) 85

    (D) −86

    (E) 71

18. Find the value of the expression $-|-10 \times 5 + (-12)|$.

    (A) −38

    (B) −62

    (C) −70

    (D) 62

    (E) 38

19. While performing an experiment, a science student measured a substance as having a temperature of −14°F. She then raised the temperature of the substance 15 degrees, before lowering the temperature 18 degrees. What was the final temperature of the substance after the experiment?

    (A) 19°F

    (B) 15°F

    (C) −13°F

    (D) −17°F

    (E) −18°F

20. Marty checks his bank account and finds that he has a balance of $231.28. He then writes checks in the amounts of $64.75, $122.20, and $49.08 to pay some of his bills. What is the balance in his account after paying the bills?

    (A) −$236.03

    (B) −$4.75

    (C) $4.75

    (D) $236.03

    (E) $467.31

Answers and Explanations

1. E

The number −12 is 12 units to the left of 0 on a number line. Choices (A), (B), and (C) cannot be correct because distance cannot be a negative value. Choice (D) is not the answer because only the numbers −1 and 1 are one unit from 0 on a number line.

2. C

The absolute value of a number is the distance the number is from 0 on a number line. Since it is a measure of distance, it is always positive or equal to zero. Choice (A) is not the correct answer because only the number 0 has an absolute value of 0. Choices (B) and (D) are not correct because the absolute value of a number is never negative. Choice (E) is not always correct; for example, the absolute value of 3 is 3, not −3.

3. D

The expression $|-98|$ represents the absolute value of −98. Since −98 is 98 units to the left of 0 on a number line, the absolute value of −98 is equal to 98.

4. C

The expression $|23|$ means the absolute value of positive 23, which is equal to 23. The integer 23 is 23 units away from 0 on a number line.

5. B

Each of the answer choices is listed in order from smallest to largest except for the numbers in choice (B). Since −5 is greater than −7 and −7 is greater than −8, these numbers are listed in descending, or decreasing, order.

6. C

To solve this problem, you need to find a number that is between −35 and −24 on a number line. Since −34 is larger than −35 and smaller than −24, it is between the two values.

7. A

Since you are adding and the signs of the numbers are the same, add the absolute values and keep the sign: $-13 + (-6) = -19$.

8. D

Since you are adding and the signs are different, subtract the absolute values of the numbers and keep the sign of the larger absolute value for your answer: $20 - 5 = 15$. The sign of the larger is positive, so the final answer is $+15$.

9. C

Since you are adding and the signs of the first two numbers are different, subtract the absolute values and keep the sign of the number with the larger absolute value: $-19 + 4 = -15$. Now add $-15 + (-2)$ by adding the absolute values and keeping the negative sign: $-15 + -2 = -17$.

10. A

Since you are subtracting, change the subtraction to addition and the sign of the number being subtracted to its opposite. Thus, $-27 - 11$ becomes $-27 + (-11)$. The operation is now addition and the signs are the same, so add the absolute values and keep the sign: $-27 + -11 = -38$.

11. C

Since you are subtracting, change the subtraction to addition and the sign of the number being subtracted to its opposite. Thus, $-56 - (-9)$ becomes $-56 + 9$. The operation is now addition and the signs are different, so subtract the absolute values and take the sign of the number with the larger absolute value for the answer: $56 - 9 = 47$. The sign of the larger number is negative; thus, the answer is -47.

12. A

Divide 18 by 2 to get 9. Since there is an even number of negatives in the problem, the answer is $+9$.

13. A

Multiply 77 by 2 to get 154. Since there is an odd number of negatives in the problem, the final answer is -154.

14. C

Multiply $4 \times 1 \times 9$ to get 36. Since there is an odd number of negatives in the problem, the final answer is -36.

15. A

Evaluate this expression by using the order of operations. The first step is to evaluate within the parentheses. In the expression $14 - (-2)$, change the subtraction sign to addition and the sign of -2 to $+2$. It then becomes $14 + 2 = 16$. Then evaluate the exponent of 2 on the base of 3: $3^2 = 9$. The entire expression is now $-6 + 16 - 9$. Combine -6 and 16 to get 10 by subtracting the absolute values and making the result positive. To complete the problem, subtract: $10 - 9 = 1$.

16. C

Since each of the terms inside the absolute value bars is a single value, evaluate the absolute values first. Thus, $|4| - |5|$ becomes $4 - 5$, which is equal to -1.

17. C

Evaluate within the absolute value bars first. Because the signs of the values are the same and you are adding, $|-7 + -78|$ becomes $|-85|$. Since the absolute value of -85 is 85, the final answer is 85.

18. B

Start by evaluating within the absolute value bars by multiplying -10 by 5. The expression then becomes $-|-50 + (-12)|$. Continue to simplify within the bars by adding -50 and -12 to get -62. Now the expression is $-|-62|$. Evaluate the absolute value of -62 to get 62. The solution includes the negative in front of the absolute value bars in the original question, so the final answer is -62.

19. D

This problem can be solved by using the expression $-14 + 15 + (-18)$, since the substance started out at $-14°$, was raised $15°$, and then was lowered $18°$. Since $-14 + 15 = 1$ and $1 + (-18) = -17$, the final answer is $-17°F$.

20. B

Since Marty has a starting balance of \$231.28, take that amount and subtract the amount of each check: $231.28 - (64.75 + 122.20 + 49.08) = 231.28 - 236.03 = 231.28 + -236.03 = -4.75$. Marty has a negative balance: $-\$4.75$.

CHAPTER 3

Fractions and Decimals

Fractions and decimals are two ways to express numbers. It is important to be comfortable with these notations and to be adept at performing mathematical operations with both types of numbers. This chapter will cover how to convert from one form of the number to the other; how to order numbers in the two forms; and how to perform the operations of addition, subtraction, multiplication, and division with both types.

FRACTION AND DECIMAL BASICS

To understand how to perform operations with fractions, you must be comfortable with the concepts of multiples, remainders, and factors.

Multiples

An integer that is divisible by another integer is a **multiple** of that integer. For example, 12 is multiple of 3, since 12 is divisible by 3 ($12 \div 3 = 4$). Also, we can find multiples of a number, for example 4, by multiplying 4 by other numbers.

- $4 \times 1 = 4$
- $4 \times 2 = 8$
- $4 \times 3 = 12$

Remainders

When we perform division, sometimes one term doesn't divide evenly into another.

A **remainder** is a whole number that represents the parts that are left over after we divide. A remainder is always smaller than the number by which we are dividing.

For example, if you divide 13 by 2, the answer is 6 with a remainder of 1.

$$\begin{array}{r} 6 \quad \text{R } 1 \\ 2\overline{)13} \\ \underline{12} \\ 1 \end{array}$$

Factors

A **factor** of a number is a whole number that divides into that number evenly without a remainder.

Another word for factor is **divisor**, because a number is always evenly divisible by its factors. A **factor pair** of a given term is a pair of factors that multiply to produce the term. For example, a factor pair of 12 is 2 and 6.

Now, find all the factors of 36. Let's begin by listing the factor pairs of 36:

$$
\begin{array}{ccc}
1 & \times & 36 \\
2 & \times & 18 \\
3 & \times & 12 \\
4 & \times & 9 \\
6 & \times & 6
\end{array}
$$

Thus, the factors of 36 are 1, 2, 3, 4, 6, 9, 12, 18, and 36.

▓ REMEMBER THIS! ▓

If you ever get the terms *factor* and *multiple* confused, you can use this mnemonic: there are **F**ew **F**actors, but **M**illions of **M**ultiples.

PRACTICE 1

Finding a number's factors is an important foundational skill. Build your expertise right here with these practice problems! Answers and explanations are located at the end of the chapter.

1. What are the factors of 48?

2. What are the factors of 77?

Prime Numbers

A **prime number** is an integer greater than 1 that has no factors other than 1 and itself. (The number 1 is not considered a prime.) The number 2 is the first prime number and the *only* even prime number. (Do you see why? All other even numbers have 2 as a factor and, therefore, are not primes.) The first ten prime numbers are 2, 3, 5, 7, 11, 13, 17, 19, 23, and 29.

PRIME FACTORIZATION

In a variety of problems on the GMAT, particularly when you are dealing with a very large number, it will be helpful for you to break a number down into its prime factors. To do this, you can create a factor tree.

Every number has a unique set of prime factors. The prime factorization of a number is the expression of the number as the product of its prime factors. You can make a factor tree to find these prime factors. Below are examples of factor trees for the numbers 28 and 80.

$$28 = 2 \cdot 2 \cdot 7 \qquad\qquad 80 = 2 \cdot 2 \cdot 2 \cdot 2 \cdot 5$$

As you can see from the example above, there may be more than one way to make a factor tree. No matter how you approach your factor tree, in the end, a whole number will break down into the same set of prime factors.

Begin by finding a pair of factors of the number you are factorizing. For example, if you are finding the prime factors of 60, you might use 5 and 12.

Since 5 is prime, we'll leave it alone and focus on breaking down 12.

Since 3 is prime, we can leave it alone and break down 4.

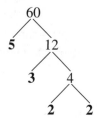

Now that all we have left are prime numbers, we are done with the factor tree and have found that the complete prime factorization of 60 is $\{2 \times 2 \times 3 \times 5\}$.

As another example, the complete prime factorization of 36 is $\{2 \times 2 \times 3 \times 3\}$.

PRACTICE 2

Check your understanding of prime factorization by answering the following questions. Answers and explanations are located at the end of the chapter.

3. What is the prime factorization of 120?

4. What is the prime factorization of 40?

The Greatest Common Factor

The **greatest common factor** (GCF) is the largest common factor of two or more numbers. The GCF is often used to simplify a fraction. Prime factorization is a convenient way to find the GCF of two or more numbers.

After finding the prime factors of the numbers you are working with, place them in a Venn diagram by pairing up all common primes. The Venn diagram that follows illustrates this process by placing all common prime factors of 28 and 80 in the intersection of the circles. The factors without a match are in the outer circles of the Venn diagram.

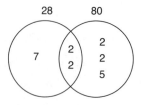

Find the greatest common factor by multiplying only the common factors in the intersection: $2 \times 2 = 4$.

With smaller numbers, it is often easier to find the greatest common factor by simply listing the factors of each number and finding the largest number they have in common.

For example, what is the greatest common factor of 20 and 30?

The factors of 20 are 1, 2, 4, 5, 10, and 20.

The factors of 30 are 1, 2, 3, 5, 6, 10, 15, and 30.

The largest number that is common to both lists is 10, so the greatest common factor is 10.

With larger numbers, it can be difficult and time-consuming to list all the factors of the numbers. In this case, it's best to use the prime factors of the numbers to help you find the greatest common factor. The greatest common factor is the product of the prime factors that the two numbers have in common.

For example, what is the greatest common factor of 150 and 84?

The prime factorization of 150 is $2 \times 3 \times 5 \times 5$.

The prime factorization of 84 is $2 \times 2 \times 3 \times 7$.

The prime factors that they have in common are one 2 and one 3, so the greatest common factor is the product of 2 and 3, which is 6.

PRACTICE 3

Use the bank of numbers to answer the following questions. Answers and explanations are located at the end of the chapter.

6   24   30   16   12   8   4

5. What is the greatest common factor of 24 and 96?
6. What is the greatest common factor of 48 and 100?

The Least Common Multiple

The **least common multiple** (LCM) is the smallest number that two or more numbers will divide into evenly. For example, the least common multiple of 3 and 10 is 30. It's important to know how to find the least common multiple because it will help you to work with fractions: the LCM of two or more numbers is used when adding or subtracting fractions.

For relatively small numbers, it's easier to find the LCM by simply listing several multiples of one of the numbers, usually the larger one, until you come to one that is divisible by the other.

For example, what is the least common multiple of 6 and 20? We'll list multiples of 20: 20, 40, 60... Since 60 is divisible by 6, we have found our LCM. The LCM of 6 and 20 is 60.

For larger numbers, prime factorization again comes in handy. For example, what is the least common multiple of 84 and 66?

$$84 = 2 \times 2 \times 3 \times 7$$

$$66 = 2 \times 3 \times 11$$

The LCM must contain the entire list of each number's prime factors, but there shouldn't be any more prime factors than needed. For example, we need only one 3, since each number has one 3 as a prime factor. There is no need to put in both 3s. The LCM is equal to $2 \times 2 \times 3 \times 7 \times 11$, which is 924.

Notice that the LCM can be evenly divided by each of the original terms:

$$\frac{924}{84} = \frac{2 \times 2 \times 3 \times 7 \times 11}{2 \times 2 \times 3 \times 7} = \frac{\cancel{2} \times \cancel{2} \times \cancel{3} \times \cancel{7} \times 11}{\cancel{2} \times \cancel{2} \times \cancel{3} \times \cancel{7}} = 11$$

$$\frac{924}{66} = \frac{2 \times 2 \times 3 \times 7 \times 11}{2 \times 3 \times 11} = \frac{\cancel{2} \times 2 \times \cancel{3} \times 7 \times \cancel{11}}{\cancel{2} \times \cancel{3} \times \cancel{11}} = 14$$

PRACTICE 4

In the following problems, match the pair of numbers on the left with the least common multiple on the right. Answers are located at the end of the chapter.

7.	48, 100	A.	60
8.	24, 96	B.	96
9.	12, 60	C.	1,200
10.	27, 90	D.	270

Divisibility Rules

In the upcoming lessons on fractions, you will be asked to find factors of a whole number. It is helpful to be familiar with divisibility rules for whole numbers. Plus, on many occasions during the GMAT, it will be worthwhile for you to determine if one number is divisible by another number without actually performing the calculation. Long division is time-consuming and often rather unpleasant, so if we can get around it, we should! This is why it is so essential for you to learn divisibility rules. It is well worth the effort to do so.

Note that the phrases "divisible by" and "multiple of" are roughly synonymous in their effect. That is to say, if a number is divisible by x, then it is a multiple of x and vice versa.

Divisibility by 2:

A number is divisible by 2 if the number is an even number.

For example, which of the following numbers are divisible by 2?

$$5, 2, 18, 43, 34, 37, 1, 99, 0, 44, 13{,}790$$

The even numbers in the list are the multiples of 2; they are 2, 18, 34, 0, 44, and 13,790.

Divisibility by 3:

A number is divisible by 3 if the sum of the individual digits in the number is divisible by 3.

For example, is 345 divisible by 3?

$$3 + 4 + 5 = 12$$

Since 12 is divisible by 3, we know that 345 is divisible by 3.

Divisibility by 4:

A number is divisible by 4 if the last two digits, taken as a two-digit number, are divisible by 4.

For example, is 1,347,936 divisible by 4?

The number formed by its last two digits, 36, is divisible by 4, so 1,347,936 is divisible by 4.

Divisibility by 5:

A number is divisible by 5 if the last digit of the number is a 5 or a 0.

For example, the numbers 10, 25, 30, and 75 are all divisible by 5 because the last digit of each is a 5 or a 0.

Divisibility by 6:

Numbers divisible by both 2 and 3 are divisible by 6.

For example, 534 is divisible by 6 because it's divisible by 2 (it's an even number) and divisible by 3 (5 + 3 + 4 = 12, which is divisible by 3).

Divisibility by 7:

Double the last digit and subtract the result from the remaining digits of the number. If the result is divisible by 7, so is the original number. If you don't know whether the result is divisible by 7, apply this rule again.

For example, 623 is divisible by 7 because its last digit can be multiplied by two $(3 \times 2 = 6)$, then subtracted from the remaining digits $(62 - 6 = 56)$ to yield a number that is divisible by 7.

Divisibility by 8:

A number is divisible by 8 if the last three digits, taken as a three-digit number, are divisible by 8.

For example, the number 3,024 is divisible by 8 because 024, or just 24, is divisible by 8. Likewise, the number 79,128 is divisible by 8 because 128 is divisible by 8: $128 \div 8 = 16$.

Divisibility by 9:

A number is divisible by 9 if the sum of the individual digits in the number is divisible by 9.

For example, the number 9,135 is divisible by 9 because $9 + 1 + 3 + 5 = 18$, which is divisible by 9. The number 414,972 is divisible by 9 because $4 + 1 + 4 + 9 + 7 + 2 = 27$, which is divisible by 9.

Divisibility by 11:

Sum every other digit and subtract remaining digits. If the result is divisible by 11, so is the number.

For example, 1,023 is divisible by 11 because $1 + 2 - 0 - 3 = 0$, which is divisible by 11: $0 \div 11 = 0$. However, 3,062 is not divisible by 11 because $3 + 6 - 0 - 2 = 7$, which is not divisible by 11.

Divisibility by 12:

Numbers divisible by both 3 and 4 are divisible by 12.

For example, 13,524 is divisible by 12 because it is divisible by 3 ($1 + 3 + 5 + 2 + 4 = 15$, which is divisible by 3) and divisible by 4 (the last two digits put together are 24, which is divisible by 4).

PRACTICE 5

Answer TRUE or FALSE for the following statements about divisibility. Answers and explanations are located at the end of the chapter.

11. **T** **F**   5,940 is divisible by 3.

12. **T** **F**   719 is divisible by 9.

13. **T** **F**   2,528 is divisible by 4.

14. **T** **F**   1,550 is divisible by 2 and 5.

FRACTIONS

A **fraction** is a rational number in the form $\frac{a}{b}$. The variable a is called the **numerator**, and the variable b is called the **denominator**. There is one restriction on b: the denominator cannot have the value of 0.

The fractional form of any rational number is the most precise way to represent the number, unless the number is an integer. There are many reasons that numbers are represented as fractions. Some fractions, or ratios, show a comparison of two numbers. This concept will be covered in chapter 4 on ratios. Fractions can also represent a part-whole relationship, as discussed in chapter 5 on percentages. And fractions are usually used to display probabilities as well; see chapter 6 on probabilities.

Equivalent Fractions

A single number can have several equivalent fractional forms. To find an equivalent fraction, just multiply or divide the fraction by 1 in the special form of $\frac{a}{a}$.

For example, $\frac{5}{35}$ is equivalent to $\frac{1}{7}$ because $\frac{5}{35} \div \frac{5}{5} = \frac{1}{7}$. To find a fraction equivalent to $\frac{3}{4}$, multiply by some fractional form of 1: $\frac{3}{4} \times \frac{6}{6} = \frac{18}{24}$.

Often, when performing operations on fractions, you will be instructed to simplify a fraction. To simplify a fraction, divide by the greatest common factor of the numerator and the denominator. For example, to simplify $\frac{28}{80}$, divide by $\frac{4}{4}$ because 4 is the GCF: $\frac{28}{80} \div \frac{4}{4} = \frac{7}{20}$.

REDUCING

One reason to change the format of a fraction is if we need to put the fraction in **lowest terms**. This will often be the last step of a problem on the GMAT—you may work through a problem and then have to put your answer in lowest terms before you can find the correct answer among the choices.

A fraction is in lowest terms if the numerator and the denominator are not divisible by any common integer greater than 1. For example, the fraction $\frac{4}{7}$ is in lowest terms, but the fraction $\frac{3}{6}$ is not, since 3 and 6 are both divisible by 3.

The method we use to put a fraction in lowest terms is called **reducing**. To reduce a fraction, we look for factors that are common to both the numerator and the denominator.

For example, reduce $\dfrac{15}{35}$ to lowest terms. First determine the largest common factor of the numerator and denominator. In this case, the largest common factor of 15 and 35 is 5. So if you write the numerator and denominator both as the product of a number and 5, the 5s cancel out and the fraction reduces to $\dfrac{3}{7}$.

$$\frac{15}{35} = \frac{3 \times 5}{7 \times 5} = \frac{3 \times \cancel{5}}{7 \times \cancel{5}} = \frac{3}{7}$$

PRACTICE 6

Use the bank of fractions to choose an equivalent value for each of the fractions given:

$$\frac{7}{5} \quad \frac{4}{5} \quad \frac{4}{7} \quad \frac{20}{30} \quad \frac{45}{60} \quad \frac{60}{90} \quad \frac{14}{25} \quad \frac{18}{25} \quad \frac{8}{25} \quad \frac{15}{63} \quad \frac{15}{42}$$

15. $\dfrac{56}{100}$

16. $\dfrac{3}{4}$

17. $\dfrac{28}{35}$

18. $\dfrac{5}{21}$

Fraction Operations

MULTIPLICATION

Multiplying with fractions is a lot easier than adding and subtracting with them. There is no need for a common denominator when you multiply—in fact, finding one will needlessly complicate things and waste time. Instead, you should simply multiply the numbers in the numerator, then multiply the numbers in the denominator.

Example: $\dfrac{7}{9} \times \dfrac{3}{16}$. Cancel out any common factors found in any of the numerators and denominators to make the multiplication easier:

$$\frac{7}{{}_3\cancel{9}} \times \frac{\cancel{3}^1}{16} = \frac{7 \times 1}{3 \times 16} = \frac{7}{48}$$

Likewise, to find $\frac{1}{9}$ of $\frac{4}{5}$, just multiply:

$$\frac{1}{9} \times \frac{4}{5} = \frac{1 \times 4}{9 \times 5} = \frac{4}{45}$$

REMEMBER THIS!

In mathematics, the word *of* most often means to multiply.

PRACTICE 7

Try the following fractional multiplication problems. Answers and explanations are located at the end of the chapter.

19. What is $\frac{1}{3}$ of $\frac{4}{7}$?

20. $\frac{5}{8} \times \frac{5}{7} = ?$

21. $\frac{3}{7} \times \frac{7}{11} = ?$

DIVISION

To divide fractions, recall that division is the inverse operation of multiplication. The multiplicative inverse of a fraction is the **reciprocal**, or "flip" of the fraction.

REMEMBER THIS!

The easiest and most common way to divide fractions is to take the first fraction and multiply it by the **reciprocal** of the second fraction.

Dividing fractions by multiplying by the reciprocal works because you are essentially doing two inverse operations (multiplying and taking the reciprocal) to result in division. For example, $\frac{5}{8} \div \frac{3}{2}$ is equivalent to $\frac{5}{8} \times \frac{2}{3} = \frac{5 \times 2}{8 \times 3} = \frac{10}{24}$.

PRACTICE 8

Repetition is the key to mastery, so try these fractional division problems. Answers and explanations are located at the end of the chapter.

22. $7 \div \dfrac{2}{3} = ?$

23. $\dfrac{12}{7} \div \dfrac{12}{2} = ?$

24. $\dfrac{8}{9} \div \dfrac{5}{3} = ?$

ADDITION AND SUBTRACTION

To add and subtract fractions, you may need to change the fractions so they have common denominators. The best common denominator to use is the least common multiple of the denominators involved. This is called the **least common denominator** (LCD).

REMEMBER THIS!

To add or subtract fractions:

1. If necessary, convert the fractions so they have an equivalent least common denominator.

2. Add or subtract the numerators and keep the denominator.

3. Simplify the resultant fraction if necessary.

For example, to add $\dfrac{13}{15}$ and $\dfrac{3}{5}$, find the LCM of the denominators. This is 15. Rewrite the problem with denominators of 15: $\dfrac{13}{15} + \dfrac{9}{15} = \dfrac{13 + 9}{15} = \dfrac{22}{15}$.

You may also be faced with positive and negative arithmetic. Take $\dfrac{1}{3} - \dfrac{19}{20}$ for instance. The common denominator in this case is 60. Rewrite the fractions. Then subtract the numerators and keep the denominator: $\dfrac{1}{3} - \dfrac{19}{20} = \dfrac{20}{60} - \dfrac{57}{60} = \dfrac{20 - 57}{60}$.

Now you can change the subtraction in the numerator to addition of the opposite. The problem becomes $\dfrac{20 + (-57)}{60}$. Finally, you subtract and keep the sign of the larger absolute value to get $-\dfrac{37}{60}$.

PRACTICE 9

Constant practice and repetition are the keys to learning math! Try these two problems for more practice adding and subtracting fractions. Answers and explanations are located at the end of the chapter.

25. $\dfrac{1}{12} + \dfrac{5}{8} = ?$

26. $-\dfrac{6}{7} + \dfrac{3}{21} = ?$

USING A COMMON DENOMINATOR

Consider this: Which is larger, $\dfrac{3}{8}$ or $\dfrac{5}{16}$? Let's use the common denominator of 16. Thus, $\dfrac{3}{8} = \dfrac{6}{16}$, but we can leave $\dfrac{5}{16}$ the same. The question now becomes, which is larger, $\dfrac{6}{16}$ or $\dfrac{5}{16}$? Since the denominators are the same, we can tell that $\dfrac{6}{16}$ is larger.

The following example involves more fractions. Arrange these in order from smallest to largest: $\dfrac{5}{9}, \dfrac{1}{3}, \dfrac{2}{3}, \dfrac{1}{2}, \dfrac{13}{18}$. We'll use the common denominator of 18:

$$\dfrac{5}{9} = \dfrac{10}{18}$$

$$\dfrac{1}{3} = \dfrac{6}{18}$$

$$\dfrac{2}{3} = \dfrac{12}{18}$$

$$\dfrac{1}{2} = \dfrac{9}{18}$$

Arranged in order, the fractions now read $\dfrac{6}{18}, \dfrac{9}{18}, \dfrac{10}{18}, \dfrac{12}{18}, \dfrac{13}{18}$. So the original fractions, arranged in order, are $\dfrac{1}{3}, \dfrac{1}{2}, \dfrac{5}{9}, \dfrac{2}{3}, \dfrac{13}{18}$.

CROSS MULTIPLYING

Another way to compare fractions that do not have the same numerator or denominator is to cross multiply. To cross multiply, multiply the denominator of the right fraction by the numerator of the left fraction and vice versa. (Make sure to move from bottom right to top left, and from bottom left to top right.) Then compare the products obtained. If the product on the left is greater, the fraction on the left is greater than the fraction on the right.

Example: Which is larger, $\frac{1}{2}$ or $\frac{3}{4}$? Cross multiply, bottom right by top left $(4 \times 1 = 4)$, then bottom left by top right $(2 \times 3 = 6)$. Since 6 is larger, $\frac{3}{4}$ is larger.

USING A COMMON NUMERATOR

Sometimes when comparing fractions, it is easier to find a common numerator. The fraction with the smaller denominator will be the larger fraction.

For example, which is larger, $\frac{3}{15}$ or $\frac{6}{27}$? We'll use the common numerator of 6, so $\frac{3}{15}$ becomes $\frac{6}{30}$. Comparing $\frac{6}{30}$ to $\frac{6}{27}$, we find that $\frac{6}{27}$ is larger since it has the smaller denominator.

PRACTICE 10

Repetition is the key to mastery. Try these exercises for comparing fractions! Answers and explanations are located at the end of the chapter.

27. Which fraction is greater: $\frac{8}{11}$ or $\frac{31}{44}$?

28. Which fraction is greater: $\frac{8}{13}$ or $\frac{3}{5}$?

29. Which fraction is greater: $\frac{15}{23}$ or $\frac{5}{8}$?

Mixed Numbers and Improper Fractions

Mixed numbers are numbers consisting of an integer and a fraction, or $A\frac{b}{c}$. For example, $1\frac{1}{2}$, $15\frac{2}{3}$, $12\frac{4}{5}$, and $2\frac{19}{20}$ are all mixed numbers. **Improper fractions** are fractions in which the numerator is greater than the denominator. For example, $\frac{18}{5}$, $\frac{20}{3}$, $\frac{4}{3}$, and $\frac{9}{8}$ are improper fractions.

You can turn mixed numbers into improper fractions and vice versa. To change a mixed number to an improper fraction, you multiply $c \times A$ and add it to b. Then put this new number over c: $\dfrac{(A \times c) + b}{c}$.

For example, turn $3\dfrac{4}{9}$ into an improper fraction. First we multiply the denominator of the fraction, 9, by the whole number, 3. This gives us 27. Next we add the numerator of the fraction, 4, to the result of the previous step. This gives us $27 + 4 = 31$. Finally, write that number over the original denominator, which is 9. The final answer is $\dfrac{31}{9}$.

Here's an example of the reverse process: turn $\dfrac{7}{3}$ into a mixed number. Find the multiple of 3 that's closest to, but smaller than, 7. That number is 6, which is 3×2. This means we have two complete 3s in $\dfrac{7}{3}$. So we have 2 with some left over. The next step is to subtract 6 from 7 to see how many thirds are left over. Since 7 minus 6 is 1, we have one-third left over. Putting it all together, the mixed number is $2\dfrac{1}{3}$.

OPERATIONS WITH MIXED NUMBERS AND IMPROPER FRACTIONS

When performing operations using mixed numbers, it is helpful first to change the mixed number into an improper fraction, and then use the correct procedure for fractions as previously described.

For example, to multiply $2\dfrac{1}{3} \times \dfrac{1}{4}$, first convert the mixed number to an improper fraction: $2\dfrac{1}{3} = \dfrac{(2 \times 3 + 1)}{3} = \dfrac{7}{3}$. Then multiply the numerators and multiply the denominators: $\dfrac{7}{3} \times \dfrac{1}{4} = \dfrac{7 \times 1}{3 \times 4} = \dfrac{7}{12}$.

Similarly, to add $4\dfrac{3}{8} + \left(-2\dfrac{7}{8}\right)$, first change the mixed numbers to improper fractions. The fractions have the same denominator, so subtract the numerators and keep the denominator of 8: $4\dfrac{3}{8} + \left(-2\dfrac{7}{8}\right) = \dfrac{35}{8} + \left(-\dfrac{23}{8}\right) = \dfrac{35 - 23}{8} = \dfrac{12}{8}$. Simplify by canceling the common factor of 4 to get $\dfrac{3}{2}$.

PRACTICE 11

Practice operations with mixed numbers in the following questions. Answers and explanations are located at the end of the chapter.

30. $11\dfrac{2}{3} \div 3 = ?$

31. $3\dfrac{1}{3} - 12\dfrac{5}{6} = ?$

32. Kafi wants to make bread stuffing. Her recipe calls for $4\dfrac{1}{2}$ cups of bread for 6 people. In order to make enough for 15 people, she needs $2\dfrac{1}{2}$ times as many cups of bread. How many cups of bread does she need?

Complex Fractions

Complex fractions are fractions whose numerator or denominator is also a fraction. To simplify these fractions, remember that the fraction bar means to divide. Rewrite the fraction as a division problem and follow the procedure for dividing fractions.

For example, to simplify $\dfrac{\frac{8}{15}}{4}$, rewrite it as division: $\dfrac{8}{15} \div 4 = \dfrac{8}{15} \times \dfrac{1}{4} = \dfrac{8}{60} = \dfrac{2}{15}$.

PRACTICE 12

Try simplifying these complex fractions. Answers and explanations are located at the end of the chapter.

33. $\dfrac{\frac{9}{5}}{\frac{3}{10}} = ?$

34. $\dfrac{\frac{2}{3}}{\frac{1}{2}} = ?$

DECIMALS

Decimal form is a convenient way to express a number because it is based on the powers of 10. This makes operations like addition, subtraction, multiplication, and division easier to perform. The GMAT occasionally tests your knowledge of this naming convention, so you should be familiar with it.

As an example, 5.092 is equivalent to 5 and 92 thousandths because the rightmost digit is three places after the decimal point.

PRACTICE 13

For the following set of statements, fill in the blank with the correct decimal place value word. Answers are located at the end of the chapter.

35. In the number 3.507, the 5 is in the _____ place.

36. In the number 17.624, the 2 is in the _____ place.

37. The decimal 9.003 represents 9 and 3 _____.

Equivalent Decimals

The first decimal place after the decimal point is known as the tenths place. Thus, we can convert fractions with 10 in the denominator to decimals ending in the tenths place. Here are some examples:

$$\frac{1}{10} = 0.1$$

$$\frac{3}{10} = 0.3$$

The second decimal place after the decimal point is the hundredths place. So we can convert fractions with 100 in the denominator to decimals ending in the hundredths place, as in the following example:

$$\frac{17}{100} = 0.17$$

Note that sometimes we must insert zeros after the decimal point to ensure that the digit is put into the correct decimal place.

$$\frac{4}{100} = 0.04$$

This pattern continues for all decimal places, as shown by the following examples:

$$\frac{248}{1,000} = 0.248$$

$$\frac{9}{1,000} = 0.009$$

$$\frac{5,478}{10,000} = 0.5478$$

$$\frac{8}{100,000} = 0.00008$$

Therefore, the number 3.5 is equivalent to any other decimal form of that number with trailing zeros; 3.5, 3.500, and 3.50000 are equivalent. Each represents 3 and 5 tenths. When adding, subtracting, or comparing decimals, it is often convenient to add trailing zeros, as the following chapters will demonstrate.

Conversions

To convert a decimal to a fraction or mixed number, just use the place value and then simplify if necessary. For example, the decimal 16.4 is equal to $16\frac{4}{10}$, or $16\frac{2}{5}$ simplified. To change a fraction to a decimal, recognize that a fraction bar means to divide. So to change $\frac{6}{15}$ to a decimal, divide 6 by 15 to get 0.4.

To change a mixed number to a decimal, separate and keep the whole number part; that is, the number to the left of the decimal point. Then divide the fractional part as described above. For example, the mixed number $12\frac{3}{4}$ is 12.75 because 3 divided by 4 is 0.75.

PRACTICE 14

Match each fraction on the left with its decimal equivalent on the right. Answers and explanations are located at the end of the chapter.

38. $3\frac{1}{5}$ A. 3.4

39. $\frac{3}{20}$ B. 3.20

40. $3\frac{3}{25}$ C. 0.15

41. $3\frac{2}{5}$ D. 3.12

Ordering

To order fractions, first convert the fractions to decimals by dividing and then order the decimal equivalents. Putting numbers in decimal form makes comparisons easy. Just rewrite each decimal to have the same number of places to the right of the decimal point. Then compare the numbers.

For example, to order the decimals {1.2, 1.07, 1.019} from least to greatest, rewrite the numbers as 1.200, 1.070, and 1.019. Since the whole number parts are the same, just order the decimal portion. With the trailing zeroes, it is evident that 200 > 70 > 19, so the correct order from least to greatest is 1.019, 1.07, 1.2.

PRACTICE 15

For each list, tell whether the fractions and decimals are in increasing order, decreasing order, or no order. Answers are located at the end of the chapter.

42. $\dfrac{3}{7}, \dfrac{2}{3}, \dfrac{3}{4}, \dfrac{5}{6}$

43. 7.5, 7.47, 7.08, 7.009

44. $-\dfrac{3}{4}, \dfrac{1}{8}, \dfrac{7}{16}, \dfrac{1}{2}$

45. −0.16, −0.42, 1.5, 1.83

Decimal Operations

ADDITION AND SUBTRACTION

To add or subtract decimal numbers, remember that it is imperative to *line up the decimal points*. This is the *first* step before performing addition or subtraction. Add trailing zeros if necessary to avoid careless mistakes.

For example, to add 2.509 to 234.6, first line up the decimal points as shown below. Two trailing zeros are added to the end of 234.6, and then addition is performed.

$$
\begin{array}{r}
234.600 \\
+\quad 2.509 \\
\hline
237.109
\end{array}
$$

▨ FLASHBACK ▨

The positive and negative arithmetic rules that you reviewed in chapter 2 with integers also apply to decimal numbers.

To subtract 5.908 from 3.7 (that is 3.7 − 5.908), recall that subtraction is the same as adding the opposite. Change the problem to read 3.7 + (−5.908). To add two numbers with different signs, subtract the number with the smaller absolute value from the number with the larger absolute value. The sign of the answer will be the sign of the number that has the larger absolute value. The final answer, −2.208, is negative because −5.908 is negative.

$$\begin{array}{r} 5.908 \\ -\,3.700 \\ \hline 2.208 \end{array}$$

The answer is −2.208
because −5.908 is negative.

PRACTICE 16

Use the number bank below to find the decimal sums and differences. Answers and explanations are located at the end of the chapter.

9.27	113.15	−2.16	17.96	10,172
11.315	22.9	1.3	7.16	9.24

46. −1.04 + 8.2

47. 12.7 + 100.45

48. 24 − 1.1

49. 7.9 − 10.06

MULTIPLICATION

To multiply decimal numbers, follow the steps below:

1. Multiply the numbers without regard to the decimal point and obtain a whole number product.

2. Count the number of digits that are to the right of the decimal point in *both* factors.

3. Move the decimal point in the product so that there are the same number of digits to the right of the decimal point as counted in step 2.

For example, to multiply 12.9 by 0.07, step 1 instructs you to multiply 129 by 7, which equals 903. In step 2, count the number of digits to the right of both decimal points. There is one digit in 12.9 and two digits in 0.07: $1 + 2 = 3$. In step 3, take the whole number product, 903, and alter it so that it has three digits to the right of the decimal point, making the answer 0.903.

FLASHBACK

Multiplication with negative numbers follows the same rule described in chapter 2.

PRACTICE 17

50. The product resulting from 3.098 times 1.02 has ____ digits to the right of the decimal point.

51. The product resulting from 1,254 times 234.003 has ____ digits to the right of the decimal point.

52. $1.002 \times 7.1 = ?$

53. $922 \times 0.06 = ?$

DIVISION

To divide decimal numbers, follow the steps below:

1. Set up the long division problem.

2. Count how many digits are to the right of the decimal point in the divisor (the number you are dividing by).

3. Move the decimal point in the dividend (the number you are dividing into) the amount from step 2.

4. Raise the newly placed decimal point up to the quotient.

5. Divide as usual as if there were no decimal points.

For example, to divide 0.39 by 2.6, look at the divisor: 2.6 has one digit to the right of the decimal point. Therefore, you move the decimal point one place to the right in the dividend. Move this new point position up to the quotient.

PRACTICE 18

54. $960 \div 0.08 = ?$

55. $5.67 \div 1.35 = ?$

SUMMARY

To review, here are five things about fractions you should take from this chapter:

1. To simplify a fraction, divide the numerator and the denominator by the greatest common factor.

2. To multiply fractions, multiply the numerator, multiply the denominator, and then simplify.

3. To divide fractions, change the division operation to multiplication, change the divisor (second) fraction to its reciprocal (or "flip"), and multiply.

4. To add or subtract fractions, change each fraction as needed so that they have a common denominator. Add or subtract the numerators and keep the denominator. Simplify if needed.

5. To change a fraction into a decimal, divide the numerator by the denominator.

Here are five things about decimals you should take from this chapter:

1. Decimals are a convenient form of numeration that can be used to compare numbers.

2. To change a decimal to a fraction, write it as such based on the place value of the digits. Then simplify the fractional part if necessary.

3. To add or subtract decimals, line up the decimal points in the addends and in the sum or difference.

4. To multiply decimals, multiply as whole numbers. Count the number of digits that appear to the right of the decimal point in the two factors. Move the decimal point in the product so that it has this number of digits to the right of the decimal point.

5. To divide decimals, move the decimal point in the dividend and quotient the number of places needed to make the divisor a whole number. Then divide as usual.

Practice Answers and Explanations

1.   1, 2, 3, 4, 6, 8, 12, 16, 24, 48

When you look for factors, start at 1 and stop when you see a number twice:

$48 \div 1 = 48$

$48 \div 2 = 24$

$48 \div 3 = 16$

$48 \div 4 = 12$

48 isn't divisible by 5.

$48 \div 6 = 8$

48 isn't divisible by 7.

The next number to check is 8, but it's already in our list. So, we're done!

2.   1, 7, 11, 77

When you look for factors, start at 1 and stop when you see a number twice:

$77 \div 1 = 77$

77 isn't divisible by 2, 3, 4, 5, or 6.

$77 \div 7 = 11$

77 isn't divisible by 8, 9, or 10.

The next number to check is 11, which is already in our list. Thus the factors of 77 are only 1, 7, 11, and 77.

3. $2 \times 2 \times 2 \times 3 \times 5$

The prime factorization of 120 is shown in the tree below.

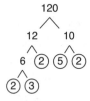

$120 = 2 \cdot 2 \cdot 2 \cdot 3 \cdot 5$

4. $2 \times 2 \times 2 \times 5$

The prime factorization of 40 is shown in the tree below.

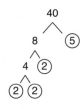

$$40 = 2 \cdot 2 \cdot 2 \cdot 5$$

5. 24

The prime factorization of 24 is $2 \times 2 \times 2 \times 3$ and of 96 is $2 \times 2 \times 2 \times 2 \times 2 \times 3$. The factors in common are $2 \times 2 \times 2 \times 3 = 24$.

6. 4

The prime factorization of 48 is $2 \times 2 \times 2 \times 2 \times 3$ and of 100 is $2 \times 2 \times 5 \times 5$. The factors in common are $2 \times 2 = 4$.

7. C

The Venn diagram is shown with common factors in the intersection of the circles. Multiply all factors shown in the diagram to get $2 \times 2 \times 2 \times 2 \times 3 \times 5 \times 5 = 1{,}200$.

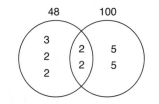

8. B

Look at the Venn diagram below. All of the factors of 24 are in the common intersection area because they are also factors of 96. The LCM is 96.

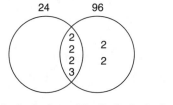

9. A

Since $12 \times 5 = 60$, 60 is a multiple of 12. The least common multiple is 60.

10. D

The prime factorization of 27 is $3 \times 3 \times 3$ and of 90 is $3 \times 3 \times 5 \times 2$. So the LCM is the product of the common multiples (3×3) and the leftovers ($3 \times 5 \times 2$). Thus, $3 \times 3 \times 3 \times 5 \times 2 = 270$.

11. True

$5 + 9 + 4 + 0 = 18$, which is divisible by 3.

12. False

$7 + 1 + 9 = 17$, which is not divisible by 9.

13. True

28 is divisible by 4.

14. True

1,550 is even and ends in a 0.

15. $\dfrac{14}{25}$

$$\frac{56}{100} \div \frac{4}{4} = \frac{14}{25}$$

16. $\dfrac{45}{60}$

$$\frac{45}{60} \div \frac{15}{15} = \frac{3}{4}$$

17. $\dfrac{4}{5}$

$$\frac{28}{35} \div \frac{7}{7} = \frac{4}{5}$$

18. $\dfrac{15}{63}$

$$\frac{5}{21} \times \frac{3}{3} = \frac{15}{63}$$

19. $\dfrac{4}{21}$

The key word *of* means to multiply: $\dfrac{1}{3} \times \dfrac{4}{7} = \dfrac{1 \times 4}{3 \times 7} = \dfrac{4}{21}$.

20. $\dfrac{25}{56}$

$$\dfrac{5}{8} \times \dfrac{5}{7} = \dfrac{5 \times 5}{8 \times 7} = \dfrac{25}{56}$$

21. $\dfrac{3}{11}$

The factor of 7 can be canceled in the denominator of the first factor and the numerator of the second factor.

22. $\dfrac{21}{2}$

Change the problem to multiplication and take the reciprocal of the divisor as follows: $7 \div \dfrac{2}{3} = \dfrac{7}{1} \times \dfrac{3}{2} = \dfrac{7 \times 3}{1 \times 2} = \dfrac{21}{2}$.

23. $\dfrac{2}{7}$

Change the problem to multiplication and take the reciprocal of the divisor. The factor of 12 can be canceled. Then multiply: $\dfrac{12}{7} \times \dfrac{2}{12} = \dfrac{1 \times 2}{7 \times 1} = \dfrac{2}{7}$.

24. $\dfrac{8}{15}$

Change the problem to multiplication and take the reciprocal of the divisor: $\dfrac{8}{9} \div \dfrac{5}{3} = \dfrac{8}{9} \times \dfrac{3}{5}$. The factor of 3 can be canceled, changing the 3 in the numerator to a 1 and the 9 in the denominator to a 3: $\dfrac{8}{9} \times \dfrac{3}{5} = \dfrac{8 \times 1}{3 \times 5} = \dfrac{8}{15}$.

25. $\dfrac{17}{24}$

Alter both fractions so they have a denominator of 24, the LCM of the denominators: $\dfrac{1}{12} + \dfrac{5}{8} = \dfrac{2}{24} + \dfrac{15}{24} = \dfrac{17}{24}$.

26. $-\dfrac{15}{21}$

Change $\dfrac{6}{7}$ to have a denominator of 21. Then add the fractions with different signs. This means subtracting and taking the sign of the number with the larger absolute value: $-\dfrac{6}{7} + \dfrac{3}{21} = -\dfrac{18}{21} + \dfrac{3}{21} = \dfrac{-18+3}{21} = -\dfrac{15}{21}$.

27. $\dfrac{8}{11}$

Eleven is a factor of 44: $11 \times 4 = 44$. So, $\dfrac{8}{11} = \dfrac{8}{11} \times \dfrac{4}{4} = \dfrac{32}{44}$, which has a greater numerator than $\dfrac{31}{44}$ and is therefore greater.

28. $\dfrac{8}{13}$

Multiply each fraction to get a common denominator of 65, the LCM of 5 and 13:

$$\dfrac{8}{13} \times \dfrac{5}{5} = \dfrac{40}{65}$$

$$\dfrac{3}{5} \times \dfrac{13}{13} = \dfrac{39}{65}$$

The greater fraction must be $\dfrac{8}{13}$, because after converting to a common denominator of 65 it has the greater numerator.

29. $\dfrac{15}{23}$

Making the numerators equal is the easiest way to compare this pair. Because 15 is 5×3, we can multiply as follows: $\dfrac{5}{8} = \dfrac{5}{8} \times \dfrac{3}{3} = \dfrac{15}{24}$. The greater fraction must be $\dfrac{15}{23}$, because it has the smaller denominator when the numerators are equal.

30. $\dfrac{35}{9}$

First change the mixed number to a fraction. Then alter the problem to multiply by the reciprocal of 3: $\dfrac{35}{3} \times \dfrac{1}{3} = \dfrac{35 \times 1}{3 \times 3} = \dfrac{35}{9}$.

31. $-\dfrac{57}{6}$

First change the mixed numbers to fractions: $3\dfrac{1}{3} = \dfrac{(9+1)}{3} = \dfrac{10}{3}$ and $-12\dfrac{5}{6} = \dfrac{-77}{6}$. Then alter the fractions so that each has 6 as the common denominator. Subtract and take the sign of the larger absolute value: $\dfrac{10}{3} - \dfrac{77}{6} = \dfrac{20}{6} - \dfrac{77}{6} = \dfrac{20-77}{6} = -\dfrac{57}{6}$.

32. 11.25 cups

Kafi wants to serve 15, but her recipe serves only 6. The fraction $\dfrac{15}{6}$ shows this comparison. When you divide 15 by 6, you get $2\dfrac{1}{2}$. Therefore, a recipe that serves 6 people, when multiplied by $2\dfrac{1}{2}$, will then serve 15 people. So all ingredient amounts must be multiplied by $2\dfrac{1}{2}$. To find the amount of bread needed, multiply: $4\dfrac{1}{2} \times 2\dfrac{1}{2} = \dfrac{9}{2} \times \dfrac{5}{2} = \dfrac{45}{4}$. This is equivalent to $11\dfrac{1}{4}$, or 11.25 cups of bread.

33. 6

Write the problem as a division problem: $\dfrac{9}{5} \div \dfrac{3}{10}$. Change the problem to multiply by the reciprocal. Cancel out the common factors of 3 and 5. Finally, multiply across to get the simplified answer: $\dfrac{9}{5} \times \dfrac{10}{3} = \dfrac{3}{1} \times \dfrac{2}{1} = 6$.

34. $\dfrac{4}{3}$

Write the problem as a division problem: $\dfrac{2}{3} \div \dfrac{1}{2}$. Change the problem to multiply by the reciprocal. Multiply across to get the simplified answer: $\dfrac{2}{3} \times \dfrac{2}{1} = \dfrac{4}{3}$.

35. Tenths

36. Hundredths

37. Thousandths

38. B

39. C

40. D

41. A

42. Increasing

43. Decreasing

44. Increasing

45. No order

46. 7.16

When you add two numbers with different signs, subtract the numbers and take the sign of the larger absolute value. Before subtracting, add a trailing zero to 8.2 so that the decimal point will be lined up correctly: $8.20 - 1.04 = 7.16$.

47. 113.15

Add a trailing 0 onto 12.7 to get 12.70 so that the numbers will be aligned with the decimal points lined up: $12.70 + 100.45 = 113.15$.

48. 22.9

Add a 0 in the tenths place to the whole number 24 to get 24.0. Now subtract, making sure that the decimal point is lined up: $24.0 - 1.1 = 22.9$.

49. −2.16

When you subtract, change the problem to addition and change the sign of the second number. The problem becomes $7.9 + (-10.06)$. When you add two numbers with different signs, subtract the smaller from the larger and keep the sign of the number with the larger absolute value. Thus, $10.06 - 7.90 = 2.16$, and this result will be negative since −10.06 is negative: −2.16.

50. 5

The number 3.098 has three digits to the right of the decimal point, and 1.02 has two digits: $3 + 2 = 5$.

51. 3

The number 1,254 has zero digits to the right of the decimal point, and 234.003 has three: $0 + 3 = 3$.

52. 7.1142

The product will have four digits to the right of the decimal point because the first factor has three digits, and the second factor has one digit to the right of the decimal point: $3 + 1 = 4$.

53. 55.32

The product will have two digits to the right of the decimal point because the first factor has zero digits, and the second factor has two digits to the right of the decimal point.

54. 12,000

There are two digits to the right of the decimal point in the divisor (0.08), so the decimal point is moved over two places to the right in the dividend (960). Two zeros are tacked onto the end of the dividend to make the number 96,000, and the decimal point's new position moves up. Thus, $96,000 \div 8 = 12,000$ because $96 \div 8 = 12$.

55. 4.2

Both the divisor and the dividend have two places to the right of the decimal point, so move the decimal point in both. The division is now $567 \div 135$. The figure below shows the long division.

$$
\begin{array}{r}
4.2 \\
1.35{\overline{\smash{\big)}\,5.67\,0}} \\
\underline{5.40} \\
27\,0 \\
\underline{27\,0} \\
0
\end{array}
\qquad 5.67 \div 1.35 = 4.2
$$

CHAPTER 3 TEST

Now that you have studied factors, multiples, fractions, and decimals, try the following set of questions. Use the chapter material, including the practice questions throughout, to assist you in solving these problems. The answer explanations that follow will provide additional help.

1. $6.002 - 3.7$

   (A) 5.965

   (B) 2.302

   (C) 3.005

   (D) 0.2302

   (E) 0.5965

2. What is the greatest common factor of 24 and 90?

   (A) 6

   (B) 2

   (C) 3

   (D) 180

   (E) 360

3. What is the prime factorization of 120?

   (A) $2 \times 3 \times 5$

   (B) $2 \times 5 \times 12$

   (C) $3 \times 4 \times 5$

   (D) $2^3 \times 3 \times 5$

   (E) $2^2 \times 3 \times 5$

4. Simplify: 2.8×4.002

   (A) 112.056

   (B) 6.802

   (C) 11.2056

   (D) 1.202

   (E) 1.429

5. Which order below shows the decimals from smallest to largest?

   (A) −3.05, −4.2, 1.5, 2.04, 2.009
   (B) −6.09, −2.6, 1.5, 2.009, 2.04
   (C) −7.12, −8.02, 0, 5.2, 10.4
   (D) 2.009, 2.04, 1.5, −4.2, −3.05
   (E) 2.04, 2.009, 1.5, −4.2, −3.05

6. What is $\frac{3}{4}$ of $\frac{2}{3}$?

   (A) $\frac{5}{7}$

   (B) $\frac{17}{12}$

   (C) $\frac{9}{8}$

   (D) $\frac{1}{2}$

   (E) $\frac{8}{9}$

7. Which of the following shows the fractions in increasing order?

   (A) $-\frac{1}{4}, -\frac{2}{5}, \frac{2}{3}, \frac{1}{2}$

   (B) $-\frac{2}{5}, -\frac{1}{4}, \frac{1}{2}, \frac{2}{3}$

   (C) $-\frac{1}{4}, -\frac{2}{5}, \frac{1}{2}, \frac{2}{3}$

   (D) $\frac{2}{3}, \frac{1}{2}, -\frac{1}{4}, -\frac{2}{5}$

   (E) $\frac{2}{3}, \frac{1}{2}, -\frac{2}{5}, -\frac{1}{4}$

8. What is the least common multiple of 54 and 32?

   (A) 2

   (B) 1

   (C) 108

   (D) 864

   (E) 8

9. The number 11,550 is divisible by

   (A) 5 only.

   (B) 3 only.

   (C) 2 only.

   (D) All of the above

   (E) None of the above

10. Which fraction is equivalent to $\frac{21}{56}$?

   (A) $\frac{3}{7}$

   (B) $\frac{7}{8}$

   (C) $\frac{3}{8}$

   (D) $\frac{42}{106}$

   (E) $\frac{11}{28}$

11. $-\frac{5}{12} \times \frac{6}{24} =$

   (A) $-\frac{5}{48}$

   (B) $\frac{5}{48}$

   (C) $\frac{10}{6}$

   (D) $\frac{1}{2}$

   (E) $-\frac{10}{6}$

12. $3\dfrac{5}{8} - 4\dfrac{1}{4} =$

    (A) $\dfrac{14}{8}$

    (B) $\dfrac{112}{25}$

    (C) $\dfrac{8}{14}$

    (D) $-\dfrac{5}{8}$

    (E) $-\dfrac{14}{8}$

13. $4.212 \div 2.34 =$

    (A) 18

    (B) 1.8

    (C) 1.08

    (D) 0.18

    (E) 9.85608

14. $\dfrac{16}{25} \div -\dfrac{4}{5} =$

    (A) $\dfrac{4}{5}$

    (B) $-\dfrac{4}{5}$

    (C) $\dfrac{12}{20}$

    (D) $-\dfrac{12}{20}$

    (E) $-\dfrac{5}{4}$

15. $17.6 \times 0.005 =$

    (A) 0.88

    (B) 8.8

    (C) 0.0088

    (D) 0.088

    (E) 3,520

16. Which of the following is *NOT* true?

    (A) $\dfrac{1}{4} < \dfrac{1}{3}$

    (B) $-\dfrac{2}{3} > -\dfrac{5}{6}$

    (C) $\dfrac{12}{15} = \dfrac{60}{75}$

    (D) $\dfrac{3}{4} < \dfrac{4}{6}$

    (E) $\dfrac{5}{6} \geq \dfrac{15}{18}$

17. Andrea needs $3\dfrac{3}{4}$ cups of flour to make 24 cupcakes. How much flour is needed to make 8 cupcakes?

    (A) $11\dfrac{1}{4}$

    (B) $1\dfrac{1}{4}$

    (C) 30

    (D) $\dfrac{15}{32}$

    (E) $1\dfrac{7}{8}$

18. In a bag of trail mix, $\frac{3}{8}$ of the mix is peanuts. How much of a 15-pound bag of trail mix is *NOT* peanuts?

    (A) 5.625 pounds
    (B) 40 pounds
    (C) 12 pounds
    (D) 7 pounds
    (E) 9.375 pounds

19. Adult admission to the movie theater is $6.75. The price of a ticket for a child under the age of 12 is $3.50. What is the total price for three adults and one child to attend the movie?

    (A) $17.25
    (B) $27.00
    (C) $23.75
    (D) $20.25
    (E) $206.00

20. Gloria's estate is to be divided evenly among her three children. One son, Miguel, is deceased; that portion is then to be divided among Miguel's five children. What fraction of Gloria's estate would each of Miguel's children receive?

    (A) $\frac{1}{3}$

    (B) $\frac{5}{3}$

    (C) $\frac{5}{15}$

    (D) $\frac{1}{15}$

    (E) $\frac{1}{5}$

Answers and Explanations

1. B

Add two zeroes onto the end of the decimal 3.7 so that the two numbers have the same number of digits to the right of the decimal point. Then line up your decimal points and subtract to get $6.002 - 3.700 = 2.302$.

2. A

The prime factors of 24 are $2^3 \times 3$. The prime factors of 90 are $2 \times 3^2 \times 5$. The common factors are $2 \times 3 = 6$, the greatest common factor. Choice (B) is a factor of both numbers but is not the greatest common factor. Choice (C) is also a factor of both numbers but, again, is not the greatest. Choice (D) is a multiple of 90. Choice (E) is the least common multiple of 24 and 90.

3. D

The number 120 can be broken down into prime factors as follows: $120 = 12 \times 10$; $10 = 2 \times 5$; $12 = 6 \times 2$; $6 = 2 \times 3$. This gives a total of three factors of 2, one factor of 3, and one factor of 5. Choice (A) is the prime factorization of 30: $2 \times 3 \times 5 = 30$. Choice (B) is a factorization of 120, but 12 is not prime. Choice (C) is a factorization of 60, and 4 is not prime. Choice (E) is the prime factorization of 60.

4. C

Multiply 4,002 by 28 to get 112,056. Because there are a total of four digits to the right of the decimal points in the factors, place the decimal point in the answer so that there are four places to the right of the decimal point: 11.2056.

5. B

Choice (B) shows the decimals arranged from smallest to largest. Even though the absolute value of -6.09 is greater than the absolute value of -2.6, $-6.09 < -2.6$ because they are negative numbers.

6. D

Remember, the key word *of* means to multiply. When you multiply these fractions, you can cancel a 3 from the numerator and the denominator, as well as canceling a 2 out of the numerator and the denominator. After canceling and multiplying across, the answer is $\frac{1}{2}$.

7. B

Increasing order shows the fractions ordered from smallest to largest. To make comparison easier, convert all the fractions to decimals. In choice (B), the numbers are: $\{-0.40, -0.25, 0.50, 0.67\}$. Because each number has the same number of digits to the right of the decimal point, it is easy to see that these numbers are ordered correctly.

8. D

The only common factor of 54 and 32 is 2. Make a Venn diagram as shown below; put the common factor of 2 in the intersection. Put all leftover factors in the outer circles and multiply all numbers in the diagram. The least common multiple is $3^3 \times 2 \times 2^4 = 864$. Choice (A) is the greatest common factor of 54 and 32. Choice (B) is a factor of every number. Choice (C) is a multiple of 54 but not a multiple of 32. Choice (E) is a factor of 32 but not of 54.

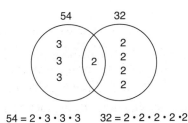

$$54 = 2 \cdot 3 \cdot 3 \cdot 3 \qquad 32 = 2 \cdot 2 \cdot 2 \cdot 2 \cdot 2$$

9. D

The number 11,550 is divisible by 2, 3, and 5. It is an even number, hence divisible by 2. The last digit is a 0; hence, it is divisible by 5. The sum of the digits is $1 + 1 + 5 + 5 + 0 = 12$, which is divisible by 3. Choices (A), (B), and (C) are all true.

10. C

Simplify the fraction by dividing each part by the GCF of 7: $\dfrac{21}{56} \div \dfrac{7}{7} = \dfrac{3}{8}$.

11. A

Cancel the common factor of 6 from the numerator and the denominator. Then multiply to get $-\dfrac{5}{2} \times \dfrac{1}{24} = \dfrac{-5 \times 1}{2 \times 24} = -\dfrac{5}{48}$. A negative number times a positive number is a negative number, so the answer is negative.

12. D

First change the mixed numbers to improper fractions: $3\dfrac{5}{8} = \dfrac{(24+5)}{8} = \dfrac{29}{8}$, and $4\dfrac{1}{4} = \dfrac{(16+1)}{4} = \dfrac{17}{4}$. Then change the second fraction to have the common denominator of 8: $\dfrac{17}{4} = \dfrac{34}{8}$. Subtract the numerators and keep the denominator: $\dfrac{29}{8} - \dfrac{34}{8} = \dfrac{29-34}{8} = -\dfrac{5}{8}$. The answer is negative because $\dfrac{34}{8}$ has the greater absolute value.

13. B

The divisor has two digits to the right of the decimal point, so move the decimal point in the dividend, 4.212, over two places right. Place this decimal point up to the quotient. Then divide as you normally would. The answer is 1.8.

14. B

Change the problem to multiplication by the reciprocal; that is, $\dfrac{16}{25} \times -\dfrac{5}{4}$. You can cancel out the common factors of 4 and 5 from a numerator and a denominator to get $-\dfrac{4}{5}$. A positive divided by a negative number is a negative number.

15. D

First multiply as if there were no decimal points: $176 \times 5 = 880$. Because there are a total of four digits to the right of the decimal point in the factors, there must be four digits to the right of the decimal point in the product. You must append a 0 before the 880 to get 0.0880.

16. D

Be careful! This problem is asking which of the statements is *not* true. You can see that $\dfrac{3}{4}$ is greater than $\dfrac{4}{6}$ by converting the fractions to decimal equivalents: $\dfrac{3}{4} = 0.75$, $\dfrac{4}{6} = 0.67$, and $0.75 > 0.67$. Therefore, choice (D) is *not* true. Because $\dfrac{1}{4}$, or 0.25 is less than $\dfrac{1}{3}$, or $0.\overline{3}$, choice (A) is true. Because $-\dfrac{2}{3} = -0.\overline{6}$ is greater than $-\dfrac{5}{6}$, or $-0.8\overline{3}$, (they are negative numbers), choice (B) is true. Because $\dfrac{12}{15} \times \dfrac{5}{5} = \dfrac{60}{75}$, choice (C) is true. The inequality in choice (E) is read as "greater than or equal to," and $\dfrac{5}{6} = \dfrac{15}{18}$ because $\dfrac{15}{18} \div \dfrac{3}{3} = \dfrac{5}{6}$. Therefore, choice (E) is true.

17. B

First set up the ratio of the values given: $\dfrac{24}{8}$. This problem is essentially asking you to take $3\dfrac{3}{4}$, or $\dfrac{15}{4}$, and divide by 3, because $24 \div 8 = 3$. Change division to multiplication by using the reciprocal: $\dfrac{15}{4} \div \dfrac{3}{1} = \dfrac{15}{4} \times \dfrac{1}{3} = \dfrac{15}{12}$. Now simplify by dividing out the common factor of 3 to get $\dfrac{5}{4} = 1\dfrac{1}{4}$ cups of flour.

18. E

The key word *of* means to multiply. Multiply $\dfrac{3}{8}$ by 15: $\dfrac{3}{8} \times \dfrac{15}{1} = \dfrac{45}{8}$. Then calculate $45 \div 8 = 5.625$ pounds of mix. Be sure to read the question carefully. This is the amount of mix that *is* peanuts. The amount of mix that is *not* peanuts is $15.000 - 5.625 = 9.375$.

19. C

Three adults and one child are buying tickets. The total price is $(3 \times 6.75) + 3.50$. Thus, $6.75 \times 3 = 20.25$, and $20.25 + 3.50 = \$23.75$.

20. D

Each of Gloria's children gets $\dfrac{1}{3}$ of the estate. Miguel's $\dfrac{1}{3}$ portion will be divided by 5. When you divide, you can multiply by the reciprocal of the divisor to get $\dfrac{1}{3} \times \dfrac{1}{5} = \dfrac{1}{15}$.

Ratios and Proportions

Now you will embark on the study of ratios, proportions, and the various applications of each. The highlights of this chapter include the concepts of ratios, rates, proportions, mixtures, and scale.

RATIOS

A **ratio** is a comparison of two or more quantities. Ratios usually appear in fraction form, but there are actually three different ways to write a ratio. A comparison of two different values represented by a and b can be written as $\frac{a}{b}$, $a{:}b$, or a to b. A ratio can be written using any values but is considered to be in its most simplified form if there are no common factors between the values and if the values are integers. Take the ratio 25 to 75 for instance. Since each number has a common factor of 25, the ratio can be reduced to 1 to 3 by dividing each number by 25. Therefore, this ratio can be written as 1 to 3, 1:3, or $\frac{1}{3}$.

When making a more complex comparison, such as $2\frac{1}{2}$ to $4\frac{1}{4}$, you can treat the ratio like a division problem to simplify. By writing the ratio as a fraction and changing each fraction to improper form, the ratio becomes $\frac{2\frac{1}{2}}{4\frac{1}{4}} = \frac{\frac{5}{2}}{\frac{17}{4}}$. Since the fraction bar means division, divide $\frac{5}{2}$ by $\frac{17}{4}$. Recall from chapter 3 that dividing by a number is the same as multiplying by its reciprocal: $\frac{5}{2} \times \frac{4}{17} = \frac{20}{34}$. This ratio reduces to $\frac{10}{17}$, 10:17, or 10 to 17 when the common factor of 2 is divided out of each number.

When using ratios to compare values, it is important to realize what type of ratio you are working with. In other words, find out if the ratio compares numbers that represent parts of a larger set or if the ratio includes a value that represents the entire set.

Here's an example. At a high school, seven out of every nine students are involved in extracurricular activities. What is the ratio of students that do not take part in extracurricular activities to the students that do take part in extracurricular activities?

The correct answer to this question is 2 to 7, 2:7, or $\frac{2}{7}$. Since seven out of every nine students take part in extracurricular activities, the 9 in the ratio represents the whole, or the total number of students at the school. (Keep in mind that there are probably more than nine students enrolled in this school and that you would have to multiply by a factor to find the actual number; however, this question does not ask us to find this number.) Since $9 - 7 = 2$, then 2 represents the part of the school that does not take part in these activities. The ratio then becomes 2 to 7.

The following problem is an example of a ratio comparing more than two quantities. An artist ordered cans of red paint, white paint, and green paint in the ratio 1:2:3, respectively. If she ordered a total of 12 cans of green paint, how many cans of white paint did she order?

Even though the ratio involves comparing three things, the same principles apply that were used when only two quantities were compared. Each number corresponds with the color of paint mentioned in the same order the numbers are listed. That means that the 1 corresponds with the cans of red paint, 2 corresponds with the cans of white paint, and 3 corresponds with the cans of green paint. Since the number in the original ratio that corresponds with green paint is 3 and the total number of cans of green paint is 12, the actual number of cans bought can be calculated as follows: $x \times 3 = 12, x = 12 \div 3, x = 4$. Therefore, each of the other numbers in the ratio can also be multiplied by 4 to find the actual number of cans purchased. Since we are looking for the number of cans of white paint, multiply 2 by 4 to get 8 cans of white paint. You can also use the proportion $\dfrac{\text{ratio of green cans}}{\text{number of green cans}} = \dfrac{\text{ratio of white cans}}{\text{number of white cans}}$. This proportion would be equal to $\dfrac{3}{12} = \dfrac{2}{x}$. We calculate: $\dfrac{3}{12} = \dfrac{2}{x}, \dfrac{1}{4} = \dfrac{2}{x}, x = 2 \times 4 = 8$.

Rates

A **rate** is a special type of ratio. Instead of relating a part to the whole or to another part, a rate relates one kind of quantity to a completely different kind. It is a comparison of two types of units. When we talk about rates, we usually use the word *per*, as in "miles per hour," "cost per item," etc. Since *per* means "for one" or "for each," we express the rates as ratios reduced to a denominator of 1. Some common examples of rates are miles per hour, feet per second, and miles per gallon.

REMEMBER THIS!

A rate with a denominator of 1 is called a **unit rate**. For example, if you traveled 100 miles in two hours, this would reduce to a unit rate of 50 miles in one hour, or 50 miles per hour.

SPEED

The most commonly tested rate on the GMAT is speed. This is usually expressed in miles or kilometers per hour. The relationship between speed, distance, and time is given by the following formula:

$$\text{speed} = \frac{\text{distance}}{\text{time}}$$

This can be rewritten in two ways:

$$\text{time} = \frac{\text{distance}}{\text{speed}}$$

$$\text{distance} = \text{speed} \times \text{time}$$

For instance, if you wanted to find the amount of time it would take to travel 660 miles while going at a rate of 60 miles per hour, you would use the formula and fill in 660 for your distance and 60 for your rate: $660 = 60t$. Divide both sides by 60 to get a time of 11 hours. In other words, it would take 11 hours to travel 660 miles going 60 miles per hour.

OTHER RATES

Speed is not the only rate that appears on the GMAT. For instance, you might get a word problem involving liters per minute or cost per unit. All rate problems, however, can be solved using the speed formula and its variants by conceiving of speed as "rate," and distance as "quantity."

For example, how many hours will it take to fill a 480-liter tank at a rate of 2 liters per minute?

Plug the numbers into a rate formula:

$$\text{time} = \frac{\text{quantity}}{\text{rate}}$$

$$time = \frac{480 \text{ liters}}{2 \text{ liters per minute}}$$

$$time = 240 \text{ minutes}$$

Now don't forget to calculate the answer in the units asked for in the question!

$$time = \frac{240}{60} = 4 \text{ hours}$$

Here's another example. If 350 widgets cost $20, how much will 1,400 widgets cost at the same rate?

Set up the proportion $\dfrac{\text{number of widgets}}{\text{cost}}$ as $\dfrac{350}{20} = \dfrac{1,400}{x}$.

Solving, you will find that $x = 80$. So 1,400 widgets will cost $80 at that rate.

You may be asked to solve a combined rate problem. In this type of problem, you are given two rates and you must find out how long a task will take if two entities are working together at the same time but at different rates. For example, if Kendra can mow the lawn in four hours and Tanya can mow the same lawn in six hours, how many hours would it take them to mow the lawn together? Use the formula: $\dfrac{ab}{a+b}$, where a and b represent the two amounts of time. So it would take $\dfrac{4 \times 6}{4+6} = \dfrac{24}{10} = \dfrac{12}{5} = 2\dfrac{2}{5}$ hours for Kendra and Tanya to mow the lawn together.

PRACTICE 1

Fill in the blank with the correct word, phrase, or symbols. Answers and explanations are located at the end of the chapter.

1. A ratio is a _____ of two or more quantities.

2. The ratio 4 to 10 can also be written as _____ or _____ when expressed in lowest terms.

3. How much time does it take to drive 300 miles at 60 miles per hour?

4. John can weed the garden in three hours. If Mary can weed the garden in two hours, how long will it take them to weed the garden together at this rate, working independently?

Proportion

A **proportion** is a comparison of two ratios. In other words, a proportion is two ratios set equal to each other. In the proportion $\frac{a}{b} = \frac{c}{d}$, a and d are identified as the **extremes**, and c and b are identified as the **means**. To solve a proportion, multiply the numerator from the first ratio by the denominator from the second ratio, then the denominator from the first ratio by the numerator of the second ratio, and set the values equal to each other. In other words, multiply the means and set it equal to the product of the extremes. After this step, divide each side of this new equation by the number with the variable to get your solution.

Note the following example:

$$\text{Solve for } x: \frac{6}{11} = \frac{x}{33}$$

Using cross multiplication, the equation becomes $6 \times 33 = x \times 11$. This simplifies to $198 = 11x$. Then divide each side of this new equation by 11. Thus, $x = 18$.

In word problems, proportions are set up so that corresponding units are either one above the other or directly across from one another.

Take the following example. The ratio of T-shirts to sweaters in a closet is 4:5. If there are 12 T-shirts in the closet, how many sweaters are there?

Set up a proportion to solve this question, being careful to line up the units. There are different ways you can approach this problem to get the correct answer. One possible proportion would be $\frac{4 \text{ T-shirts}}{5 \text{ sweaters}} = \frac{12 \text{ T-shirts}}{x \text{ sweaters}}$. Note that the label of T-shirts appears in the numerators and the label of sweaters appears in the denominators.

Another possible proportion would be $\frac{4 \text{ T-shirts}}{12 \text{ T-shirts}} = \frac{5 \text{ sweaters}}{x \text{ sweaters}}$, where the numbers corresponding with T-shirts appear on the left side and the values corresponding with sweaters appear on the right side. Either way, cross multiplying the means and the extremes results in the equation $4x = 60$. Therefore, $x = 15$. There are 15 sweaters in the closet.

An important concept to note is that ratios and proportions can be categorized as either **part-to-part** or **part-to-whole** comparisons. These problems involve different parts of a whole set, and the correct way to set up the proportion to solve the question depends on the question asked.

Take, for example, the following problem. Two numbers are in the ratio 4:1. If the sum of the numbers is 30, what is the value of the smaller number?

This is an example of a part-to-whole comparison, since the smaller number (the part) is the intended result and the total (or whole) of the two numbers is given. You want to find the smaller number and are given the sum of the two numbers. In the given ratio, the smaller number is 1 and the total, or whole, is 5 (since $4 + 1 = 5$). In other words, the whole in the ratio is represented by 5, and the part that represents the smaller number is represented by 1. Now set up your two ratios so you can cross multiply to get your solution:

$$\frac{\text{(smaller number)}}{\text{(whole)}} : \frac{\text{part}}{\text{whole}} = \frac{1}{5} = \frac{x}{30}$$

Cross multiply to get $5x = 30$. Divide each side by 5 to get $x = 6$. The smaller number is 6.

In a problem such as the one above, the ratios can also be expressed as the unknown number parts multiplied by x. Then you can write an equation to solve for the values. For instance, the above example can also be solved by writing the equation $4x + 1x = 30$, where $4x$ and $1x$ represent the two unknown number parts and 30 is the known sum. Since the equation can be simplified to $5x = 30$, dividing each side of the equation gives a result of $x = 6$. Therefore, the larger number is $4 \times 6 = 24$, and the smaller number is $1 \times 6 = 6$ (and $6 + 24 = 30$).

The following is an example of a part-to-part proportion problem. In a class, the ratio of students with red hair to black hair is 2:3. If there are six students with red hair, how many students have black hair in the class?

In this question, parts of the class are being compared (red hair to black hair), so set up a part-to-part proportion: $\dfrac{\text{red hair}}{\text{black hair}} = \dfrac{2}{3} = \dfrac{6}{x}$. Note that both numerators correspond with the number of students with red hair, and the denominators correspond with the number of students with black hair. It is important to use the labels associated with the values to help you set up the proportion correctly. Cross multiply to get $2x = 18$, and divide each side by 2 to get $x = 9$. Nine students have black hair.

PRACTICE 2

Try your hand at the following practice set of proportion questions. For each problem in the left-hand column, match the letter from the right-hand column that corresponds with the correct answer. Answers and explanations are located at the end of the chapter.

5. The ratio of voters who voted for the incumbent candidate versus the challenger was 5:2. If there were a total of 35 voters, how many votes did the incumbent get?

    A. 20

6. The sum of two numbers is 48. If the numbers are in the ratio 3:5, what is the smaller number?

    B. 25

7. A committee has 24 women. If the ratio of men to women on the committee is 5:6, how many men serve on the committee?

    C. 18

Mixtures

A **mixture** is a combination of two or more fluid quantities. Blends of juices, chemicals, and snack nuts are everyday examples of mixtures. Mixture problems on the GMAT will typically ask you to adjust one or more of the quantities in a mixture in order to arrive at a particular ratio.

For example, if a 75 mL chemical solution is 8% bromide, how much water must be added to create a 5% bromide solution? To solve the problem, first set up a proportion to determine the amount of bromide in the original solution:

$$\frac{8}{100} = \frac{x \text{ mL of bromide}}{75 \text{ mL of solution}}$$

$$x = 75\left(\frac{8}{100}\right)$$

$$x = 3\left(\frac{8}{4}\right)$$

$$x = 3(2)$$

$$x = 6 \text{ mL}$$

So there are 6 mL of bromide in the original solution. Notice that this quantity won't change: even after more water is added, the amount of bromide will still be 6 mL. What we need to find, then, is how many mL of solution there should be in order for those 6 mL of bromide to constitute 5% of the total volume. Because 5% really means 5 out of 100, this percentage can be expressed as the fraction $\frac{5}{100}$. This situation is something we can solve with a proportion:

$$\frac{5}{100} = \frac{6 \text{ mL of bromide}}{x \text{ total mL of solution}}$$

$$5x = 6 \times 100$$

$$x = \frac{6 \times 100}{5}$$

$$x = 6 \times 20$$

$$x = 120 \text{ mL}$$

In order for 6 mL to be 5% of the total volume, there needs to be 120 total mL of solution. We're not quite done yet, though. On the GMAT, always answer the question that was asked: we were asked how many mL of water must be *added,* not how many mL there must be total. To get a volume of 120 mL from 75 mL, 120 − 75 = 45 mL must be added.

In this problem, the amount of water changed while the amount of bromide stayed constant. Some problems on the GMAT will ask you to adjust both quantities in a mixture. Here's an example: A storekeeper sells almonds for $2.75 a pound and pecans for $4.50 a pound. If the storekeeper wants to create a mixture of almonds and pecans that costs $3.50 a pound, what fraction of the mixture should be almonds?

First, determine how much each pound of nuts is above or below the target price. Almonds cost $2.75 a pound, which is $0.75 short of the target price of $3.50. Pecans cost $4.50 a pound, which $1 above the target price. So think of it like this: each pound of almonds that the storekeeper adds to the mixture brings a "−0.75" to the mixture, while each pound of pecans the storekeeper adds brings a "+1" to the mixture. The storekeeper's goal, then, is to get these +1's and −0.75's to cancel out.

Adding 4 pounds of almonds will bring 4 × (−0.75) = −3 to the mixture. Then, adding 3 pounds of pecans will bring 3 × (+1) = +3 to the mixture, at which point the −3 and +3 will cancel out. Thus, there should be 4 pounds of almonds for every 3 pounds of pecans. In other words, in order for the mixture to have the desired price per pound, almonds and pecans must be in a 4:3 ratio, in which case almonds will be $\frac{4}{4+3} = \frac{4}{7}$ of the total nut mixture.

PRACTICE 3

Mixtures are a complicated topic, so practice is essential! Answers and explanations are located at the end of the chapter.

8. Cranberries constitute 15%, by weight, of a given berry mixture. If a bag of this berry mixture contains 160 grams, how many grams of the other types of berries must be removed from the bag in order for the mixture to be 20% cranberries?

9. Martha combined a detergent that was 30% bleach with a detergent that was 45% bleach to create a detergent that was 35% bleach. In the detergent that Martha created, what is the ratio of the 30% bleach detergent to the 45% bleach detergent?

Scale

How many times have you opened up a map to try to calculate the distance between two places and used a key such as 1 inch = 1 mile? This is just one example of a **scale**, where a smaller unit is often used to represent a much larger unit. The blueprints of a building or home, model cars, and model airplanes are just a few other examples of the use of scale.

REMEMBER THIS!

When working with scale models, the scale is often given as the ratio **model measurement:actual measurement**.

For example, if the scale of a model airplane is 1:25, then the actual airplane would be 25 times as large as the scale model. Therefore, if the length of the model airplane is 2 feet, then the length of the actual airplane is $2 \times 25 = 50$ feet. Another way to solve this problem is to set up the proportion $\dfrac{\text{model length}}{\text{actual length}} = \dfrac{1}{25} = \dfrac{2}{x}$. Then cross multiply to get $x = 50$ feet.

As mentioned above, proportions are often helpful when working with scale. Try this example that deals with a scale on a map. On a certain real estate map, 1 cm represents $\dfrac{1}{2}$ km. What distance, in kilometers, is represented by $2\dfrac{1}{2}$ cm?

To solve this problem, set up a proportion with the known values in the problem, being careful to line up the units either across from one another or directly above one another. A possible proportion could be $\dfrac{\text{cm}}{\text{km}} = \dfrac{1 \text{ cm}}{\frac{1}{2} \text{ km}} = \dfrac{2\frac{1}{2} \text{ cm}}{x \text{ km}}$.

Cross multiply the values in the proportion to get $1x = \dfrac{1}{2} \times 2\dfrac{1}{2}$. Change to improper fractions to get $x = \dfrac{1}{2} \times \dfrac{5}{2}$, which is equal to $\dfrac{5}{4}$, or $1\dfrac{1}{4}$ km.

PRACTICE 4

The following question set provides practice in the use of scale. Fill in each answer blank with the expression that best answers the question. Answers and explanations are located at the end of the chapter.

10. If the scale model of a boat measures six inches and the model has a scale of 1:20, then the actual boat measures _____ feet.

11. The actual height of a train engine is 12 feet. If a scale model of the train is built and is 12 inches high, then the scale used to build the model is _____.

12. The scale on a map is 1 cm = 5 km. If the actual distance between two cities is 37.5 km, then the cities are _____ cm away from each other on the map.

RATIO AND PROPORTION WORD PROBLEMS USING VARIABLES

Many times a question or answer choices on a test may contain a series of variables that make the question seem more difficult than it really is. To solve this type of question, simply use labels just as you would in a question that contained numbers.

The following is an example of a question where you can use this strategy. Celine can paint n tiles in m minutes. Working at this rate, how many tiles can she paint in one hour?

Since you are not given any numerical values, your answer will have to include the variables m and n. Set up a proportion as if you had numerical values. Rate is found by dividing the total number of tiles by the number of minutes, or $\dfrac{n \text{ tiles}}{m \text{ minutes}}$. Since there are 60 minutes in 1 hour (your given value), set up the proportion using minutes: $\dfrac{n \text{ tiles}}{m \text{ minutes}} = \dfrac{x \text{ tiles}}{60 \text{ minutes}}$. Cross multiply to get the equation $60n = mx$. Since you are looking for x (the question asks for number of tiles), divide each side of the equation by m to get $x = \dfrac{60n}{m}$. This equation is your correct answer.

Another strategy to use in this type of question is to replace the letters with numbers of your choice and try evaluating to make sure you have the correct variable expression. Suppose Celine can paint 10 tiles in 2 minutes, which is a rate of 5 tiles in 1 minute. If she can paint 5 tiles in 1 minute, then she can paint $5 \times 60 = 300$ tiles in 1 hour. If you are checking to see if your variable expression is correct, then plugging the numerical values into the expression $\frac{60n}{m}$ would simplify to $\frac{60 \times 10}{2} = \frac{600}{2} = 300$ tiles in 1 hour, which is the correct solution.

PRACTICE 5

The following TRUE/FALSE questions ask you to use the skills just presented on similar figures and word problems using variables. Remember, repetition is the key to mastery. Answers and explanations are located at the end of the chapter.

13. **T   F**   If the cost of three notebooks is equal to d dollars, then the cost of f notebooks can be represented by the expression $\frac{3f}{d}$.

14. **T   F**   A manufacturer ships bottles of a certain beverage in shipments that contain c cases per shipment and b bottles per case. Each shipment sold earns the manufacturer s dollars of revenue. On a day in which the manufacturer earns R dollars of total revenue through selling shipments of this beverage, the number of bottles that the manufacturer shipped can be expressed as $\frac{Rcb}{s}$.

SUMMARY

In this chapter, you reviewed and practiced many skills and concepts pertaining to the important principles of ratios, rates, and proportions. Here are five important things about ratios and proportions that you should take away from this lesson:

1.   A ratio is a comparison of two quantities.

2.   A rate is a comparison of different units and uses the key word *per.*

3.   A unit rate is a rate with a denominator of 1.

4.   A proportion is a comparison of two ratios; some are part-to-part, and others are part-to-whole.

5.   You can use proportions to help you solve real-world applications of ratios, such as mixtures, scale, and various word problem situations.

Practice Answers and Explanations

1. Comparison

A ratio is a *comparison* of two or more quantities.

2. 4:10, $\dfrac{2}{5}$

The ratio 2 to 5 can also be written as 2:5, or $\dfrac{2}{5}$ in lowest terms.

3. 5 hours

$$\text{Time} = \frac{\text{distance}}{\text{speed}}$$

$$\text{Time} = \frac{300}{60}$$

$$\text{Time} = 5 \text{ hours}$$

4. 1.2 hours

Set John's time per unit of work as a and Mary's time per unit of work as b.

$$\frac{ab}{a+b} = \frac{3 \times 2}{3+2} = \frac{6}{5} \text{ hours}$$

5. B

Set up the part-to-whole proportion $\dfrac{5}{7} = \dfrac{x}{35}$, and then cross multiply and divide to get $x = 25$. Or set up the equation $5x + 2x = 35$, which turns into $7x = 35$. Divide both sides by 7 to find that $x = 5$. Then multiply 5×5 (the larger number) to get the same answer of 25.

6. C

Set up the part-to-whole proportion using the given smaller number: $\dfrac{3}{8} = \dfrac{x}{48}$. Then cross multiply and divide to get $x = 18$. Or set up the equation $5x + 3x = 48$ and calculate as follows: $8x = 48$, $x = 6$. Multiply 6×3 (the smaller number) to get the same answer of 18.

7. A

Set up the part-to-part proportion and cross multiply and divide to get $x = 20$.

8. 40 grams

Set up a proportion to determine the initial weight of the cranberries in the mixture, using the fraction $\dfrac{15}{100}$ for 15%:

$$\frac{x \text{ grams of cranberries}}{160 \text{ total grams}} = \frac{15}{100}$$

$$x = 160\left(\frac{15}{100}\right)$$

$$x = 160\left(\frac{3}{20}\right)$$

$$x = 8 \times 3 = 24 \text{ grams}$$

There are 24 grams of cranberries, and we want those 24 grams to be 20% of the total mixture. Set up another proportion for the desired mixture:

$$\frac{20}{100} = \frac{24 \text{ grams of cranberries}}{x \text{ total grams}}$$

$$20x = 24 \times 100$$

$$x = \frac{24 \times 100}{20}$$

$$x = 24 \times 5 = 120 \text{ grams}$$

Thus, there should be 120 total grams in the mixture. Since we started with 160 grams, $160 - 120 = 40$ grams of berries other than cranberries need to be removed.

9. 2:1

Martha makes a detergent that's 35% bleach. Each part of the 30% bleach detergent she adds is −5% below the mark ($30 - 35 = -5$), and each part of the 45% bleach detergent she adds is +10% above the mark ($45 - 35 = +10$). In order for the −5's and +10's to cancel out, Martha has to add two parts of the 30% bleach for every one part she adds of the 45% bleach: $(2 \times -5) + (1 \times +10) = -10 + 10 = 0$. Therefore, the 30% bleach and the 45% bleach detergents are in a 2:1 ratio.

10. 10 feet

First set up a proportion using the scale and the length of the boat: $\frac{1}{20} = \frac{6}{x}$. Cross multiply to get $x = 120$ inches. Be careful to note what units the question is asking for! Divide by 12 to find the length in feet: $120 \div 12 = 10$ feet.

11. 1:12

Be careful to pay attention to the units being used. Since 12 inches is equal to 1 foot, use feet when comparing. The scale can be expressed as model measurement:actual measurement. Since the model is 1 foot long and the actual is 12 feet long, the scale is 1:12.

12. 7.5 cm

Use a proportion and line up the corresponding units: $\dfrac{1 \text{ cm}}{5 \text{ km}} = \dfrac{x \text{ cm}}{37.5 \text{ km}}$. Cross multiply to get $5x = 37.5$. Divide each side by 5 to get $x = 7.5$. They are about 7.5 cm apart on the map.

13. False

Set up a proportion using the given information. Since three notebooks cost d dollars, you can write the proportion: $\dfrac{3}{d} = \dfrac{f}{x}$. The variable x represents the amount we are looking for, so cross multiply and solve for x: $3x = fd$, $x = \dfrac{fd}{3}$.

14. True

Calculate the number of shipments sold by dividing the total revenue, R, by the revenue per shipment, s: $\dfrac{R}{s}$. Once you know the number of shipments, multiply this by the number of cases per shipment, c, and the number of bottles per case, b, to get the total number of bottles in the shipments that were sold: $\dfrac{R}{s} \times c \times b = \dfrac{Rcb}{s}$.

CHAPTER 4 TEST

Try the following questions to see what you have learned about ratios and proportions. Following the questions are complete answer explanations to help you assess your understanding.

1. A ratio is in reduced form if there are no common factors between the numbers in the ratio and the numbers are

   (A) irrational.

   (B) operations.

   (C) integers.

   (D) decimals.

   (E) fractions.

2. Which of the following is *NOT* equivalent to the ratio 8 to 6?

   (A) $\dfrac{4}{3}$

   (B) $\dfrac{6}{8}$

   (C) 4:3

   (D) $\dfrac{16}{12}$

   (E) 32:24

3. The ratio of dogs to cats in a show is 9 to 11. If the show allows only dogs and cats, what is the ratio of cats to the total animals at the show?

   (A) 9 to 11

   (B) 9 to 20

   (C) 11 to 9

   (D) 11 to 20

   (E) 20 to 9

4. Solve for x: $\dfrac{17}{x} = \dfrac{51}{6}$

   (A) 2.8

   (B) 2

   (C) 3

   (D) 5.6

   (E) 51

5. After completing $\dfrac{7}{10}$ of his math homework assignment, Josh has 15 more questions to complete. What is the total number of questions in this assignment?

   (A) 17

   (B) 21

   (C) 25

   (D) 32

   (E) 50

6. In a certain county, two out of three households have two or more telephones. If there are approximately 210,000 households in the county, how many have less than two telephones?

   (A) 7,000

   (B) 14,000

   (C) 21,000

   (D) 70,000

   (E) 140,000

7. Steven types at a rate of 44 words per minute. At this rate, how many words can he type in eight minutes?

   (A) 352

   (B) 5.5

   (C) 6

   (D) 176

   (E) 358

8. Chelsea feeds her dog 32 ounces of dog food once a day. At this rate, how many days will a 40-pound bag of dog food last?

(A) 20

(B) 24

(C) 32

(D) 40

(E) 48

9. A factory cleans its machinery with a solution that is 87% water and the remainder vinegar. If the factory manager starts with 260 L of a 40% vinegar solution, how much water must the manager add to the existing solution to attain the proper vinegar concentration for cleaning the machinery?

(A) 104 L

(B) 120 L

(C) 470 L

(D) 540 L

(E) 800 L

10. The model of a car is built in the ratio 1:40. If the actual length of the car is 10 feet, what is the length of the model, in inches?

(A) 3 inches

(B) 4 inches

(C) 10 inches

(D) 40 inches

(E) 400 inches

11. On a road map, the distance between two cities is approximately 14 inches. If the actual mileage between the two cities is 70 miles, then what is the scale used on the map?

(A) 1 mile = 5 inches

(B) 1 inch = 14 miles

(C) 1 inch = 5 miles

(D) 1 mile = 70 inches

(E) 1 inch = 70 miles

12. A scale replica of a building is 18 inches tall. If the actual height of the building is 36 feet, then the scale used between the model and the actual building is 1 inch = _____.

    (A) 18 inches

    (B) 1.5 feet

    (C) 2 feet

    (D) 18 feet

    (E) 24 feet

13. A photographer wishes to enlarge a picture that is $2\frac{1}{2}$ inches wide by 3 inches long to have a new width of 10 inches. What will be the length of the enlargement?

    (A) 3 inches

    (B) 6 inches

    (C) 8 inches

    (D) 10 inches

    (E) 12 inches

14. If the cost of r pencils is t cents, what is the cost of x pencils?

    (A) $\dfrac{tx}{r}$

    (B) $\dfrac{r}{tx}$

    (C) $\dfrac{t}{rx}$

    (D) $\dfrac{rt}{x}$

    (E) $\dfrac{xr}{t}$

15. Peter works *h* hours per day, *d* days per week. If he earns *c* dollars per hour, what is his total pay for one week?

   (A) cdh

   (B) $\dfrac{cd}{h}$

   (C) $\dfrac{cd}{d}$

   (D) $\dfrac{d}{ch}$

   (E) $\dfrac{c}{dh}$

16. Todd rides his bike *x* miles in *y* hours. How far does he ride in *z* hours?

   (A) $\dfrac{xz}{y}$

   (B) $\dfrac{x}{yz}$

   (C) xyz

   (D) $\dfrac{2}{xy}$

   (E) None of these

Answers and Explanations

1. C

By definition, a ratio is in reduced, or simplest, form if there are no common factors between the numbers in the ratio and the numbers in the ratio are integers.

2. B

Be careful about the order of the numbers used in a ratio. The ratio 8 to 6 can be written in a variety of equivalent forms, including answer choice (A), choice (C), choice (D), and choice (E). The only answer choice that is *not* equivalent is $\dfrac{6}{8}$.

3. D

Because the label *dogs* is mentioned first in the sentence, the first number listed corresponds with the number of dogs in the show. Thus, 9 corresponds with the number of dogs, and 11 corresponds with the number of cats. The total number of animals would then be represented by the value $9 + 11 = 20$. Since the question asks for the ratio of cats to the total number of animals in the show, the final ratio is 11 to 20.

4.   B

To solve this proportion, cross multiply the means and the extremes and set them equal to each other. Then divide to solve the equation. Cross multiplying gives the equation $102 = 51x$. Divide each side by 51 to get $x = 2$.

5.   E

Set up a proportion to solve this question. Since Josh has completed $\dfrac{7}{10}$ of the assignment, 7 represents the part he has finished and 10 represents the whole assignment. This makes $10 - 7 = 3$, which represents the part he still needs to complete. Since he still has 15 questions to complete, then set up the proportion $\dfrac{\text{part}}{\text{whole}} = \dfrac{3}{10} = \dfrac{15}{x}$. Cross multiply to get $3x = 150$. Divide each side by 3 to get $x = 50$. There are a total of 50 questions on his assignment.

6.   D

Because two out of three households have two or more telephones, one out of every three households has fewer than two telephones. Set up the proportion $\dfrac{\text{part}}{\text{whole}} = \dfrac{1}{3} = \dfrac{x}{210{,}000}$, and cross multiply to get $210{,}000 = 3x$. Divide each side of the equation by 3 to get $x = 70{,}000$. Thus, 70,000 households in this county have fewer than two telephones.

7.   A

Since Steven types at a rate of 44 words per 1 minute, multiply 44 by 8 to get 352 words in 8 minutes. Another way to solve this problem is to set up the proportion $\dfrac{\text{words}}{\text{minute}} = \dfrac{44 \text{ words}}{1 \text{ minute}} = \dfrac{x \text{ words}}{8 \text{ minutes}}$. Cross multiply to get $352 = x$.

8.   A

Look closely at the units your problem asks for. First convert 40 pounds to ounces. Since there are 16 ounces in 1 pound, multiply 40 by 16 to get 640 ounces. She uses 32 ounces per day, so divide the total number of ounces by the ounces per day to figure out how many days the bag will last: $\dfrac{640 \text{ ounces}}{32 \text{ ounces per day}} = 20 \text{ days}$.

9. D

The manager needs to mix a solution that is $100 - 87 = 13\%$ vinegar. First, calculate the amount of vinegar in the initial solution: 40% of 260 L is 104 L of vinegar. Since the manager is only adding water to the existing solution, the amount of vinegar will not change. Now calculate the total volume of solution needed such that 104 L vinegar represents 13% of the total volume. Set up a proportion, where x equals the total amount of solution needed: $\dfrac{104}{x} = \dfrac{13}{100}$. Now cross multiply to solve:

$$(104)(100) = (13)(x)$$
$$10{,}400 = 13x$$
$$\dfrac{10{,}400}{13} = x$$
$$800 = x$$

The manager needs a total of 800 L of the solution in order to attain the needed concentration, so she must add $800 - 260 = 540$ L of water to the existing solution.

10. A

Since the ratio of the model to the actual car is 1:40, set up the proportion $\dfrac{\text{model}}{\text{actual}} = \dfrac{1}{40} = \dfrac{x}{10}$. Cross multiply to get $10 = 40x$. Divide each side of the equation by 40 to get 0.25 feet. To convert to inches, multiply 0.25 by 12 inches to get 3 inches.

11. C

Set up the proportion $\dfrac{1 \text{ inch}}{14 \text{ inches}} = \dfrac{x \text{ miles}}{70 \text{ miles}}$. Cross multiply to get the equation $70 = 14x$. Divide each side of the equation by 14 to get $x = 5$. Therefore, 1 inch is equal to 5 miles.

12. C

Set up the proportion $\dfrac{\text{model}}{\text{actual}} = \dfrac{1}{x} = \dfrac{18 \text{ inches}}{36 \text{ feet}}$. Cross multiply to get $36 = 18x$. Divide each side of the equation by 18 to get $x = 2$ feet.

13. E

Set up the proportion $\dfrac{\text{width}}{\text{length}} = \dfrac{2\frac{1}{2}}{3} = \dfrac{10}{x}$. Cross multiply to get $2.5x = 30$. Divide each side of the equation by 2.5 to get $x = 12$ inches.

14. A

Since the cost of r pencils is t cents, then the cost of one pencil is $\dfrac{t \text{ cents}}{r \text{ pencils}}$, or $\dfrac{t}{r}$.

Therefore, the cost of x pencils would be $\dfrac{t}{r} \times x$, which is equal to $\dfrac{tx}{r}$. Another approach to this question is to substitute values for the variables and see which answer choice matches the evaluated solution. Suppose that $r = 5$ pencils, $t = 50$ cents, and $x = 6$ pencils. In this case, 5 pencils would cost 50 cents, so each pencil would cost $50 \div 5 = 10$ cents. Then the cost of 6 pencils would be $10 \times 6 = 60$ cents. The answer choice that would also give a value of 60 cents with these same values plugged in for the variables is answer choice (A): $\dfrac{(50)(6)}{5} = 60$.

15. A

Since Peter works h hours per day, d days per week, he works $h \times d$, or dh, hours per week. If he makes c dollars per hour, multiply this number by his total number of hours, or $c \times dh$. The expression becomes cdh. Another approach to this problem is to substitute values for the variables and see which answer choice results in the evaluated result. Suppose that $h = 8$ hours, $d = 5$ days, and $c = 10$ dollars per hour. In this case, Peter would work 8 hours a day, 5 days a week, or $8 \times 5 = 40$ hours per week. If he then made \$10 per hour, his total pay for the week would be $40 \times \$10 = \$400$. The answer choice that would also give a value of \$400 with these same values plugged in for the variables is answer choice (A).

16. A

Set up the proportion $\dfrac{x \text{ miles}}{y \text{ hours}} = \dfrac{? \text{ miles}}{z \text{ hours}}$. Cross multiply to get $xz = y \times ?$ Divide each side of the equation by y to get the expression $\dfrac{xz}{y}$.

Percents

Percents are used often in everyday life. Any time you shop at a sale, you work with a percentage off of the original price of merchandise. Many institutions give test results as percentages. Budget reports often break down expenses or revenues based on percentages. Health-conscious consumers are concerned with the percentage of fats or carbohydrates in various foods. You can solve percent problems with methods similar to those described in chapter 4. This chapter will also introduce you to additional methods.

WORKING WITH PERCENTS

Converting between Decimals and Percents

A **percent** is a special ratio that compares a numerical quantity to 100. Forty-five percent (45%) is the same as $\frac{45}{100}$ and the same as 0.45. Because of this relationship to 100, it is easy to convert a percent number to a decimal.

REMEMBER THIS!

- To change a *percent to a decimal,* remove the percent symbol (%) and divide by 100.

- To change a *decimal to a percent,* just multiply by 100.

Because of our place value number system, to change a percent to a decimal, you just have to move the decimal point two places to the left and remove the percent symbol (%). For example, 56% is 0.56, 230% is 2.30, and 4% is 0.04.

To change a decimal to a percent, simply move the decimal point two places to the right and add the percent symbol %. For example, 0.76 is 76%, 1.34 is 134%, and 0.06 is 6%.

Converting between Fractions and Percents

Remember that a percent is a ratio, or fraction, that compares a numerical quantity to 100. To convert the fraction $\frac{a}{b}$ to a percent, you can use a variable to represent the unknown percent and set up a proportion, $\frac{x}{100} = \frac{a}{b}$, and cross multiply to solve for the variable x. For example, to change $\frac{4}{5}$ to a percent, set up the proportion $\frac{x}{100} = \frac{4}{5}$. Cross multiply to get $5x = 4 \times 100$, or $5x = 400$. Divide both sides by 5 to get $x = 80$, or 80 percent.

To convert from a percent into a fraction, just put the given percent over 100, remove the percent symbol (%), and simplify if needed. For example, to convert 68% to a fraction, simply place 68 over 100: $\frac{68}{100}$. Divide the numerator and denominator by 4 to simplify the fraction: $\frac{68}{100} \div \frac{4}{4} = \frac{17}{25}$.

If the percent is a decimal, such as 43.2 percent, the fraction will be $\frac{43.2}{100}$. First multiply the fraction by $\frac{10}{10}$ to clear the decimal point from the numerator: $\frac{43.2}{100} \times \frac{10}{10} = \frac{432}{1,000}$. Now simplify the fraction by dividing the numerator and the denominator by 8, the greatest common factor. Therefore, 43.2% = $\frac{432}{1,000} \div \frac{8}{8} = \frac{54}{125}$.

PRACTICE 1

In the following exercise, match each item in the left column with its equivalent value in the right column. Answers are located at the end of the chapter:

1. 13%   A. $\frac{3}{10}$

2. 30%   B. 0.13

3. 1.3% C. $\dfrac{8}{10}$

4. 0.8% D. $\dfrac{8}{1,000}$

5. 0.08% E. 0.013

6. 80% F. 0.0008

The Percent of a Number

You can think of a percent as a part-whole relationship. If you are asked to find the percent of a number, you are trying to find the part of the whole number that is represented by the given percent.

REMEMBER THIS!

- The key word *of* in mathematics usually means multiply.
- The key word *is* in mathematics means equals.

The equation "part is percent times number" can be used to solve problems of this type. For example, to find 18 percent of 250, change 18 percent to a decimal and then multiply by 250: $0.18 \times 250 = 45$.

You may be asked to find a missing percent, such as in this question: 252 is what percent of 600? Set up a simple equation, substituting an equal sign for *is* and a multiplication sign for *of*: $252 = 600x$. Divide both sides by 600 to get 0.42, or 42 percent. Note that when using the equation method, the percent is expressed as a decimal number.

Another type of problem may give you the part and the percent and ask you to find the whole number. For example, 26 percent of some number is 105.3. What is the number? Again, set up a simple equation: $0.26x = 105.3$. Divide both sides by 0.26 to get $x = 405$.

An alternate method, which you may prefer, is to set up a proportion $\dfrac{\text{part}}{\text{whole}} = \dfrac{x}{100}$ and cross multiply to find the missing term. The part is associated with the word *is*, and the whole is associated with the word *of*. For example, if asked, "What percent of 600 is 114?" set up the proportion $\frac{114}{600} = \frac{x}{100}$. Cross multiply to get $600x = 11,400$. Divide both sides by 600 to get 19, which is 19 percent. As you can see, when using the proportion method, the percent is not expressed as a decimal.

PRACTICE 2

The key to mastering percents is practice! Use the following bank of answers to solve the problems below. Answers and explanations are located at the end of the chapter.

65%	45	65	30
85%	30%	450	0.85%

7. What is 26 percent of 250?

8. The number 629 is what percent of 740?

9. The quantity 11.25 is 25 percent of what number?

10. What is 200 percent of 15?

There are many examples of the percent relationship of part-to-whole. For example, a company's expense budget may be represented in the following circle graph.

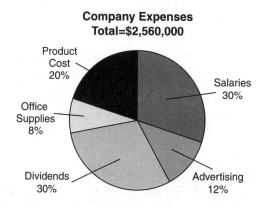

Company Expenses
Total=$2,560,000

The whole is the total expenses, and each slice of the circle graph is a part of the total. To find the amount of money allocated to advertising, use the percent value (12%) and total budget allocation given in the graph (2,560,000) and set up a proportion: $\frac{12}{100} = \frac{x}{2,560,000}$. Cross multiply to get $100x = 30,720,000$. Divide both sides by 100 to get the expense related to advertising: $307,200.

Sometimes a salesperson earns a percentage commission from the sale of items. The commission is a percentage of the selling price. Find the amount of this commission by multiplying the percent, written as a decimal, by the selling price.

For example, Rita earns a 5 percent commission on each pair of shoes she sells. If she sells 10 pairs of $15 shoes each day, how much commission will she earn after five working days? At this rate, Rita will sell 50 pairs of shoes (10 each day for five working days) at $15 each for a total in sales of (50)(15) = $750. Her commission is 5 percent of this amount, or (0.05)(750) = $37.50.

Try the following percentage word problems to test your understanding. Answers and explanations are located at the end of the chapter.

PRACTICE 3

11. The standard tip percentage for a waitress is 15 percent. What is the tip amount on a meal total of $32?

12. Joe earns a 3 percent commission for every home he sells. What is his commission on a $132,000 home?

13. Of the 50,000 commuters to the city, 60 percent of them use public transportation. How many commuters use public transportation?

14. In the following chart, what is the percentage of people who wear a shoe size of 9 or larger?

Shoe Size	Number of People
6	10
7	15
8	25
9	20
10	10

PERCENT APPLICATIONS

Percent Increase or Decrease

At times, you may be interested in how much an amount has changed, either as an increase or a decrease. For instance, stock price values are examined in this manner. Likewise, a company might track a change in sales or fixed costs, or a club might track a change in attendance at meetings. The government and news organizations keep a close watch on the change in the number of unemployed or uninsured citizens. All of these examples could be solved as percent increase or decrease applications.

REMEMBER THIS!

Percent increase or decrease is calculated as $\dfrac{\text{change}}{\text{original amount}} = \dfrac{\text{percent}}{100}$.

It is important to realize that the part is the change that occurs and the whole is the starting amount. The new amount does not enter into the formula to calculate the percent. The new amount is used only to calculate the change from the original. For example, to find the percent decrease in attendance at a town board meeting where attendance went from 125 people to 50 people, first calculate the change in attendance: $125 - 50 = 75$. Set up the proportion $\dfrac{75}{125} = \dfrac{x}{100}$. Cross multiply to get $125x = 7{,}500$. Divide both sides by 125 to get $x = 60$, or 60 percent.

You can also solve percent increase or decrease problems by setting up an equation such as this:

$$\text{change} = \text{percent} \times \text{original}$$

The above example would be set up as $75 = 125x$. For this equation, you divide both sides by 125 to get $x = 0.60$, which is also 60 percent.

PRACTICE 4

Use the percentage bank of answers to find the missing percents. (Percents are rounded to the nearest tenth.) Answers and explanations are located at the end of the chapter.

60%	14%	56%	25%	5.6%	4%
16.7%	5%	20%	10.3%	24%	73%

15. What is the percent increase from 25 to 39?

16. What is the percent decrease from 90 to 85?

17. What is the percent decrease from 24 to 20?

18. What is the percent increase from 125 to 200?

19. The stock price of Buyer's Choice rose from $12.50 to $15.00 per share. What was the percentage increase?

20. The total number of teams at a weekly trivia competition went from 25 to 19 due to a location change. What was the percentage decrease?

Sales and Sales Tax

The retail world of buying and selling is filled with examples of percentage use. When merchandise goes on sale, the discount is represented as a percent decrease, where the change in price is the amount of money saved. When merchandise is sold, usually a sales tax is involved that is calculated as a percent—a percent increase to the original price.

For example, if you purchase a computer for 35 percent off the retail price of $1,000, what is the sale price? The discount (change in price) equals 0.35 times the original price; that is, discount = (0.35)(1,000). Multiply to get the discount of $350. This is the change in price, so the sale price is 1,000 − 350 = $650.

Here's another example. Hockey sticks normally sell for $129.99. They are on sale now for 20 percent off this price. There is also a 6 percent sales tax. What will be the total price paid for one hockey stick?

This is a two-step problem. First you calculate the sale price, and then you calculate the tax, which will be added to the sale price. The discount is (0.20)(129.99) = $26.00, rounded to the nearest penny. The sale price is thus 129.99 − 26.00 = $103.99. For step two, calculate the tax on the sale price. The tax is (0.06)(103.99) = $6.24. The total price paid is the sale price plus the tax: 103.99 + 6.24 = $110.23.

There is an alternate, shortcut method to calculating sale prices. If you think of the original price as 100 percent, then the percentage savings is one part of the original price, and the price paid is the other part of the original price. Therefore, if an item is on sale for 35 percent off the original price, you pay 65 percent of the original price. If an item is 20 percent off, you pay 80 percent of the original price. Likewise, to find the price that you will pay with sales tax, first understand that you will pay the sale price plus the sales tax. If the sales tax is 7 percent, then you pay 107 percent of the sale price to the cashier; if the sales tax is 4 percent, you pay 104 percent of the sale price.

PRACTICE 5

Practice is essential for understanding mathematics. Try the following sales tax exercises. Answers and explanations are located at the end of the chapter.

21. What is the sales tax on a $289 portrait purchase if the sales tax percentage is 7 percent?

22. Lara purchases a new coat for 30 percent off of the original price of $160. What is the sale price?

23. A camera, originally priced at $350, is on sale for 25 percent off. There is a 4 percent sales tax. What will be the purchase price, including sales tax?

24. Josh pays $3,450 for a piano. This price reflects a sale discount of 20 percent. What was the original price of the piano?

Simple Interest Rates

Banks use interest rates in the form of percentages to award interest to savings accounts and to charge interest on loans. **Simple interest** is calculated by multiplying the amount of principal (or money) that is saved or borrowed, by the rate and time. Therefore, we get the following formula, where I is the interest charged or paid out, p is the principal amount, r is the percentage rate written as a decimal, and t is the time in years:

$$I = prt$$

For example, to find the simple interest earned on $1,700 at 8 percent interest for three years, set up the formula $I = prt$. Plugging in the values, you get $I = (1,700)(0.08)(3)$, or interest = $408. Note that when you use the simple interest formula, you change the percent to a decimal equivalent.

Here's another example. If Keisha borrows $450 at an interest rate of 17 percent for 18 months, how much will she have paid in simple interest at the end of the 18 months? First remember to convert the 18 months to years: 18 months = 1.5 years. Then compute the interest owed: $I = (450.00)(0.17)(1.5)$, or $I = \$114.75$.

PRACTICE 6

Fill in the blanks for the formula $I = prt$.

25. In the simple interest formula, I represents the _____.

26. In the simple interest formula, p represents the _____.

27. In the simple interest formula, r represents the _____.

28. In the simple interest formula, t represents the _____.

Often with simple interest problems, you want to find the total amount of money that is either earned (in the case of an investment) or owed (in the case of a loan). To find this, you add the original principal to the interest:

$$\text{total} = p + prt$$

Compound Interest Rates

In the real world, simple interest is normally used for a single period of less than a year, such as 30 or 60 days, because it is calculated on the original amount only. If your interest accumulated annually, you'd get a very different sum.

Compound interest is interest that accumulates on the original amount *and* all money that accumulated during each period. Think of compound interest as a series of back-to-back simple interest calculations.

If you recall our first simple interest rate example, the total interest you received on $1,700 at 8 percent interest for three years was $408, so you'd end up with a total of $2,108. If you compounded the interest annually instead, you'd get more out of your investment: First you figure out 8 percent interest on original principal ($1,700) in one year. So using the formula $I = prt$, that's (1,700)(0.08)(1) (or 1,700 × 0.08). So you get $136. Then you add that to your $1,700 to get $1,836, and calculate 8 percent interest on that amount for one year, which is 146.88. Then you add that amount to $1,836 to get $1,982.88, and calculate 8 percent interest on that amount for one year, which is $158.63. Add all that interest together (136 + 146.88 + 158.63) and you get a total compound interest of $441.51, and your investment total would be $2,141.51.

So all those calculations look a little like this, if p represents your original principal and r represents the rate:

Year	Balance
Now	p
1	$p + rp$
2	$(p + rp) + (p + rp)$
3	$(p + rp) + (p + rp) + (p + rp)$

But we don't want to have to do all those calculations, expecially on an investment that's compounded annually over 30 years! The formula for compound interest is $A = p(1 + r)^t$, where A represents the final amount and t represents the time in years. So using the previous example one more time:

$A = 1,700(1 + 0.08)^3$

$A = (1,700)(1.259712)$

$A = 2,141.51$

Try your hand at these types of problems below. Answers and explanations are located at the end of the chapter.

PRACTICE 7

29. Elisabeth borrows $14,000 for a new car. The simple interest is 7 percent, and she borrows the money for five years. How much interest will she repay after the five years?

30. Michael invests $2,500 in a certificate of deposit (CD) that pays 11 percent simple interest for 42 months. How much will the CD be worth in total, including interest, after the 42-month maturation date?

31. Ando keeps $5,000 in a savings account that pays 2.33 percent compound interest. How much will he have in his bank account at the end of five years?

SUMMARY

Here are six important things about percents you should take from this chapter:

1. Percents are special ratios that compare a number to 100.

2. Percents are a part-whole relationship where the part is a percentage of the whole.

3. For percent increase and decrease, the part is the amount of change that occurred, and the whole is the original amount.

4. Sales problems are percent decrease problems. Tax is a percent increase problem.

5. The formula for finding simple interest is $I = prt$, where I is the interest, p is the principal, r is the percentage rate (written as a decimal), and t is the time in years.

6. The formula for finding compound interest is $A = p(1 + r)^t$, where A represents the final amount, p represents the principal amount, r represents the annual percentage rate, and t represents the time in years.

Practice Answers and Explanations

1. **B**

2. **A**

$$\frac{30}{100} = \frac{3}{10}$$

3. **E**

4. **D**

$$\frac{0.8}{100} = \frac{8}{1,000}$$

5. **F**

6. **C**

7. **65**

Multiply 0.26 by 250 to get 65.

8. **85%**

Set up the equation $629 = 740x$. Divide both sides by 740 to get $x = 0.85$, which is 85 percent.

9. **45**

Set up the proportion $\frac{11.25}{x} = \frac{25}{100}$. Cross multiply to get $25x = 1,125$. Divide both sides by 25 to get 45.

10. 30

200% of 15 = 200% × 15. Changing 200% to a decimal, you get 2 × 15 = 30.

11. $4.80

The tip amount is 15 percent of the total meal cost. The key word *of* means to multiply. Thus, 0.15 × $32.00 = $4.80.

12. $3,960

The commission earned is 3 percent of the sale price. The key word *of* means to multiply. Thus, 0.03 × $132,000 = $3,960.

13. 30,000

Since 60 percent of the total commuters use public transportation, multiply: 0.60 × 50,000 = 30,000.

14. 37.5%

Use a proportion, $\frac{\text{part}}{\text{whole}} = \frac{\text{percent}}{100}$. The part is the sum of the number of people who wear size 9 or size 10, or 20 + 10 = 30. The whole is the total number of people: 10 + 15 + 25 + 20 + 10 = 80. Fill in the missing amounts: $\frac{30}{80} = \frac{x}{100}$. Cross multiply to get 3,000 = 80x. Divide each side by 80 to get 37.5 percent.

15. 56%

Percent increase is found by using the proportion $\frac{\text{change}}{\text{original amount}} = \frac{\text{percent}}{100}$. The change is 14(39 − 25), and the original number is 25. By substitution, $\frac{14}{25} = \frac{x}{100}$. Cross multiply to get 1,400 = 25x. Divide both sides by 25 to get 56 percent.

16. 5.6%

The change is 5 (90 − 85), and the original number is 90. By substitution, $\frac{5}{90} = \frac{x}{100}$. Cross multiply to get 500 = 90x. Divide both sides by 90 to get 5.6 percent, rounded to the nearest tenth.

17. 16.7%

The change is 4 (24 − 20), and the original number is 24. By substitution, $\frac{4}{24} = \frac{x}{100}$. Cross multiply to get 400 = 24x. Divide both sides by 24 to get 16.7 percent, rounded to the nearest tenth.

18. 60%

The change is 75 (200 − 125), and the original number is 125. By substitution, $\dfrac{75}{125} = \dfrac{x}{100}$. Cross multiply to get 7,500 = 125x. Divide both sides by 125 to get 60 percent.

19. 20%

The change in stock price is $15.00 − $12.50 = $2.50. The original price is $12.50. By substitution, $\dfrac{2.50}{12.50} = \dfrac{x}{100}$. Cross multiply to get 250 = 12.5x. Divide both sides by 12.5 to get 20 percent.

20. 24%

The change in the number of teams is 25 − 19 = 6. The original number is 25. By substitution, $\dfrac{6}{25} = \dfrac{x}{100}$. Cross multiply to get 600 = 25x. Divide both sides by 25 to get 24 percent.

21. $20.23

The sales tax is 7 percent of the purchase price of $289. Multiply to find the sales tax: 289.00 × 0.07 = $20.23.

22. $112

Since the coat is 30 percent off, Lara will pay 100% − 30% = 70% of the original price. Multiply 0.70 by the price of $160: 160.00 × 0.70 = $112.

23. $273

The discount is 25 percent of the $350.00 price: 0.25 × 350.00 = $87.50. The sale price is thus 350.00 − 87.50 = $262.50. The tax is 4 percent of this price, so multiply: 0.04 × 262.50 = $10.50. Add this to the sale price to get the total purchase price: 262.50 + 10.50 = $273.00.

24. $4,312.50

Use the fact that Josh paid 100% − 20% = 80% of the original price for the piano. Now use a variable, x, to represent the original price. Set up the equation, which shows that 80 percent of the original is $3,450: 0.80x = 3,450. Divide both sides by 0.80 to get $4,312.50.

25. **Interest** (earned or owed)

26. **Principal amount** (invested or borrowed)

27. **Percentage rate**

28. **Time, in years**

29. **$4,900**

This problem asks for the interest that will be paid. Use the formula $I = prt$. Interest = $14,000 \times 0.07 \times 5 = \$4,900$.

30. **$3,462.50**

This problem asks for the total worth of the investment, including the interest. Use the formula total $= p + prt$. Since the period is 42 months, first convert this to years: $42 \div 12 = 3.5$ years. Total = $2,500.00 + (2,500.00 \times 0.11 \times 3.5) = \$2,500.00 + \$962.50 = \$3,462.50$.

31. **$5,610.25**

Use the formula $A = p(1 + r)^t$. So total $= 5,000(1 + 0.0233)^5$. So total $= 5,000(1.12205) = \$5,610.25$.

CHAPTER 5 TEST

In this chapter, you have reviewed the key concepts of percents and have tried various types of problems. Use the chapter material, including the practice questions throughout, to assist you in solving these problems. The answer explanations that follow will provide additional help.

1. Which of the following is equivalent to 58 percent?

   (A) $\dfrac{5}{8}$

   (B) $\dfrac{29}{50}$

   (C) $\dfrac{14}{25}$

   (D) $\dfrac{8}{5}$

   (E) None of the above

2. Change $\dfrac{3}{8}$ to a percent.

   (A) 38%

   (B) 3.8%

   (C) 37.5%

   (D) 0.375%

   (E) 375%

3. Change 12.5 percent to a decimal.

   (A) 125

   (B) 12.5

   (C) $\dfrac{1}{8}$

   (D) $\dfrac{12}{5}$

   (E) 0.125

4. The number 1.2 is equivalent to what percent?

   (A) 120%

   (B) 1.2%

   (C) 12%

   (D) 0.012%

   (E) 20%

5. Which of the following sets is in increasing order?

   (A) $\{2.5, 25\%, \frac{3}{4}, 85\%\}$

   (B) $\{25\%, \frac{3}{4}, 85\%, 2.5\}$

   (C) $\{25\%, 2.5, \frac{3}{4}, 85\%\}$

   (D) $\{25\%, 85\%, \frac{3}{4}, 2.5\}$

   (E) None of the above

6. A county census determined that 41 percent of the population was 30 years old or younger. If there are 230,000 people in the county, how many are 30 years old or younger?

   (A) 560,976

   (B) 94,300

   (C) 230,041

   (D) 89,700

   (E) 589,744

7. What is 62 percent of 434?

   (A) 269.08

   (B) 700

   (C) 2,690.8

   (D) 70

   (E) 2.6908

8. What percent of 500 is 90?

    (A) 5.56%
    (B) 0.18%
    (C) 55.6%
    (D) 18%
    (E) 90%

9. What is 82 percent of 112?

    (A) 82
    (B) 91.84
    (C) 30
    (D) 20.16
    (E) 0.7321

10. Forty-five percent of the college students at the local university are not registered to vote. If the student population is 8,500 students, how many students are not registered to vote?

    (A) 4,000
    (B) 450
    (C) 4,500
    (D) 4,675
    (E) 3,825

11. Of the 200 cars in the used car sales lot, 80 are white. What percent of the cars are white?

    (A) 40%
    (B) 80%
    (C) 120%
    (D) 0.40%
    (E) 12%

12. The number of people enrolled at the health spa rose from 240 to 310. What is the percent increase, to the nearest percent?

    (A) 70%

    (B) 77%

    (C) 29%

    (D) 23%

    (E) 31%

13. What is the percent decrease from 72 to 64, to the nearest percent?

    (A) 11%

    (B) 12%

    (C) 8%

    (D) 89%

    (E) 17%

14. Using the graph for stock prices below, what was the percent increase in stock share price from 2002 to 2003?

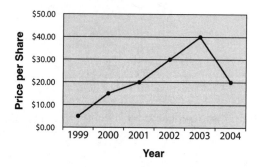

Stock Price per Share

    (A) 10%

    (B) 25%

    (C) 33.3%

    (D) 75%

    (E) 50%

15. What is the percent increase in sales, to the nearest percent, if last year's sales were 12,000 and this year's sales are 25,000?

    (A) 48%
    (B) 13%
    (C) 108%
    (D) 10.8%
    (E) 52%

16. A tent has a sale price of $450. This price reflects a 25 percent discount. What was the original price of the tent?

    (A) $475
    (B) $425
    (C) $1,800
    (D) $600
    (E) $180

17. What is the sales tax on a $49 cell phone purchase if the sales tax percentage is 7 percent?

    (A) $56.00
    (B) $7.00
    (C) $34.30
    (D) $5.60
    (E) $3.43

18. All novels at the convenience store are discounted 20 percent. There is a 4 percent sales tax on books. What is the total purchase price of a book listed at $14.95, including tax?

    (A) $12.44
    (B) $11.96
    (C) $3.59
    (D) $12.56
    (E) $11.36

19. Given a tax amount of $7.80 on a snowboard, priced at $130.00, what is the sales tax percentage?

    (A) 7.8%

    (B) 0.06%

    (C) 6%

    (D) 0.078%

    (E) 60%

20. Using the bar graph below, approximately what percentage of the day is spent sleeping?

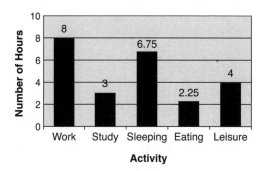

Time Allocation per Average Day

    (A) 6.75%

    (B) 28%

    (C) 33.3%

    (D) 12.5%

    (E) 8%

21. Robert borrows $75,000 at 5.5 percent simple interest for his new home mortgage. If the mortgage is held for 30 years, how much total will he spend on the loan and interest?

    (A) $198,750

    (B) $123,750

    (C) $12,375

    (D) $87,375

    (E) $165

22. Rhonda invests $3,500 in a savings account that pays 7 percent compound interest. How much will she have in her account after 36 months, if no other deposits or withdrawals are made?

    (A) $612.50

    (B) $7,350.00

    (C) $3,710.00

    (D) $4,287.65

    (E) $42,125.00

Answers and Explanations

1. B

Change 58 percent to a fraction and then simplify by dividing by the common factor of 2: $\dfrac{58}{100} \div \dfrac{2}{2} = \dfrac{29}{50}$.

2. C

Set up a proportion: $\dfrac{3}{8} = \dfrac{x}{100}$, where x is the percent. Cross multiply to get $8x = 300$. Divide both sides by 8 to get $x = 37.5$ percent. If your answer choice was (A), you thought that $\dfrac{3}{8}$ meant 38 percent, which is incorrect; 38 percent is equal to $\dfrac{38}{100} = \dfrac{19}{50}$. In choice (B), 3.8 percent is equal to 0.038, or $\dfrac{38}{1,000} = \dfrac{19}{500}$. Choice (D) is the decimal equivalent of $\dfrac{3}{8}$: $3 \div 8 = 0.375$. The percent is found by multiplying this decimal by 100. If you chose (E), you may have converted the fraction to a decimal, 0.375, and then mistakenly interpreted this to be 375 percent.

3. E

To change a percent to a decimal, just move the decimal point two places to the left to get 0.125.

4. A

To change a decimal to a percent, just move the decimal point two places to the right, adding a trailing 0, to get 120 percent.

5. B

Change each of the numerical values to a decimal to compare them: $25\% = 0.25$, $\frac{3}{4} = 0.75$, and $85\% = 0.85$. It is easier now to see that $0.25 < 0.75 < 0.85 < 2.5$.

6. B

The problem states that 41 percent of the population is 30 years or younger. The key word *of* means to multiply: $0.41 \times 230{,}000 = 94{,}300$.

7. A

Change 62 percent to a decimal and multiply: $0.62 \times 434 = 269.08$.

8. D

Set up an equation, stating that part = percent × whole. Use the variable x to represent the percent, written as a decimal: $90 = 500x$. Divide both sides by 500 to get $x = 0.18$, or 18 percent.

9. B

Change 82 percent to a decimal and multiply: $0.82 \times 112 = 91.84$.

10. E

This is an application of percent based on the part-whole relationship. Change 45 percent to a decimal and then multiply by the whole student body of 8,500: $0.45 \times 8{,}500 = 3{,}825$.

11. A

Set up a proportion using $\frac{\text{part}}{\text{whole}} = \frac{\%}{100}$, where 80 is the part and 200 is the whole. Use the variable x for the percent: $\frac{80}{200} = \frac{x}{100}$. Cross multiply to get $200x = 8{,}000$. Divide both sides by 200 to get $x = 40$ percent.

12. C

Use the proportion $\frac{\text{change}}{\text{original amount}} = \frac{\text{percent}}{100}$. The change in enrollment is $310 - 240 = 70$. The original amount is 240. Let x represent the percent increase: $\frac{70}{240} = \frac{x}{100}$. Cross multiply to get $240x = 7{,}000$. Divide both sides by 240 to get $x = 29.17$, or 29 percent.

13. A

Use the proportion $\dfrac{\text{change}}{\text{original amount}} = \dfrac{\text{percent}}{100}$. The change is $72 - 64 = 8$. The original amount is 72. Let x represent the percent decrease: $\dfrac{8}{72} = \dfrac{x}{100}$. Cross multiply to get $72x = 800$. Divide both sides by 72 to get $x = 11.11$, or 11 percent.

14. C

Read the values for the stock price for 2002 and 2003. These values are \$30 and \$40, respectively. Use the proportion $\dfrac{\text{change}}{\text{original amount}} = \dfrac{\text{percent}}{100}$. The change is $40 - 30 = 10$. The original amount is 30. Let x represent the percent increase: $\dfrac{10}{30} = \dfrac{x}{100}$. Cross multiply to get $30x = 1{,}000$. Divide both sides by 30 to get $x = 33.3$ percent.

15. C

Use the proportion $\dfrac{\text{change}}{\text{original amount}} = \dfrac{\text{percent}}{100}$. The change is $25{,}000 - 12{,}000 = 13{,}000$. The original amount is 12,000. Let x represent the percent increase: $\dfrac{13{,}000}{12{,}000} = \dfrac{x}{100}$. Cross multiply to get $12{,}000x = 1{,}300{,}000$. Divide both sides by 12,000 to get $x = 108.33$, or 108 percent.

16. D

If the tent is on sale for 25 percent off, then the sale price is $100\% - 25\% = 75\%$ of the original price. Use the variable x to represent the original price of the tent, remembering that the part (the sale price) is a percent (75 percent) of the whole: $450 = 0.75x$. Divide both sides by 0.75 to get $x = \$600$.

17. E

If the sales tax percentage is 7 percent, then the sales tax is 7 percent, or 0.07, of the purchase price. The key word *of* means to multiply: $0.07 \times 49.00 = \$3.43$.

18. A

The novels are discounted 20 percent, so the buyer will be charged $100\% - 20\% = 80\%$ of the listed price, and $0.80 \times 14.95 = \$11.96$. Because sales tax is added to the price, the buyer will pay $100\% + 4\% = 104\%$ of the sale price: $1.04 \times 11.96 = \$12.44$.

19. C

The sales tax is a part of the purchase price. Use the proportion $\dfrac{\text{change}}{\text{original amount}} = \dfrac{\%}{100}$.

The part is the $7.80 tax amount, the whole is the $130.00 purchase price, and x will represent the sales tax percentage: $\dfrac{7.80}{130.00} = \dfrac{x}{100}$. Cross multiply to get $130x = 780$.

Divide both sides by 130 to get $x = 6$ percent.

20. B

Use the proportion $\dfrac{\text{part}}{\text{whole}} = \dfrac{\%}{100}$. The part is the hours spent sleeping, or 6.75, the whole is a 24-hour day, and x represents the percentage: $\dfrac{6.75}{24} = \dfrac{x}{100}$. Cross multiply to get $24x = 675$. Divide both sides by 24 to get $x = 0.28125$, or 28 percent.

21. A

For this problem, you are asked to find the total he will spend on the loan and the interest. Use the simple interest formula: total $= p + prt$, where p is the principal borrowed (75,000), r is the percentage rate (5.5 percent, or 0.055), and t is the time (30 years). Total $= 75,000 + 75,000 \times 0.055 \times 30$, or total $= 75,000 + 123,750 = \$198,750$.

22. D

This problem asks for the total worth of the investment, including the interest. Since the period is 36 months, first convert this to years: $36 \div 12 = 3$ years. Use the formula total $= p(1 + r)^t$, where p is the principal investment (3,500), r is the rate (7 percent, or 0.07), and t is the time in years (3). Total $= 3,500(1 + 0.07)^3 = (3,500)(1.225043) = \$4,287.65$.

Statistics and Probability

This chapter will review the concepts of statistics and probability. You will learn about new concepts, including measures of central tendency, such as mean, median, mode, and range; overlapping sets; different types and uses of statistical graphs; probability; counting problems; and sequences.

STATISTICS AND PROBABILITY

In this section, we'll talk about a variety of topics dealing with statistical analysis: averages, median, mode, range, and standard deviation, as well as the basics of probability.

Measures of Central Tendency: Mean, Median, Mode, and Range

Measures of central tendency are values that are examined from a set of data to make predictions and draw conclusions about that set of data as a whole. Four of the most common measures that we use are mean, median, mode, and range.

MEAN

The **mean** of a set of numbers is the sum of the numbers in the set divided by the total number of values in the set.

$$\frac{\text{sum of all values}}{\text{number of values}} = \text{average (arithmetic mean)}$$

For example, find the mean of the set {8, 9, 22, 14, 12}. First find the sum by adding the numbers: $8 + 9 + 22 + 14 + 12 = 65$. Since there are five numbers in the set, the mean can be found by dividing the sum of 65 by 5. The mean is $65 \div 5 = 13$.

Here's another example. Over the course of five hours, a storm passed over City X. In the first hour, 3 inches of rain fell. In the second, 1.5 inches fell. In the remaining three hours, 4 inches, 2.5 inches, and 1 inch fell, respectively. What was the average rainfall per hour for the five hours of the storm?

$$\frac{3+1.5+4+2.5+1}{5}$$
$$= \frac{12}{5}$$
$$= 2.4$$

Another variation of a problem that involves the mean is a question where one or more values from the data set are unknown, but the mean is identified.

Take the following example. In a certain greenhouse, 35 seedbeds are planted with pumpkin seeds. On average, 24 seeds are planted in each of these beds. How many seeds, in total, were planted? Now we are looking for the sum of all values.

$$\frac{\text{sum of all values}}{\text{number of values}} = \text{mean}$$

$$\frac{x}{35} = 24$$
$$x = 24 \times 35$$

The total number of seeds is 840.

In another example, let's say that Michelle received an 88, 84, 79, and 93 on her first four science exams. What does she need on her fifth exam to have an exam average (arithmetic mean) of 88?

There are a few different ways to approach this problem. One is to find the total number of points Michelle has earned so far and to compare that number with the amount of points she needs to have a mean of 88. The sum of her first four tests is $88 + 84 + 79 + 93 = 344$ points. The number of points she needs to have an 88 average over five exams is $88 \times 5 = 440$. Since the number of points she needs is 440 and the number of points she has earned so far is 344, subtract to find the points she needs on the fifth test: $440 - 344 = 96$.

If you call the fifth test score the unknown x, this proportion is written as $\dfrac{88+84+79+93+x}{5}=88$. Simplifying by adding the known values gives the equation $\dfrac{344+x}{5}=88$. Since 88 can also be represented as $\dfrac{88}{1}$, cross multiply to get the equation $344 + x = 440$. Subtract 344 from each side of the equation to get $x = 440 - 344 = 96$. Either method results in a fifth exam grade of 96.

It can save you a lot of work if you know that in the case of evenly spaced numbers, the average is equal to the middle term (called the median, which we'll discuss below). Numbers that are **evenly spaced** are the same distance apart. For example, consecutive integers like 6, 7, and 8 are evenly spaced, as are consecutive multiples of 4 (4, 8, 12, 16, and 20) or even just numbers that are apart by the same amount (4, 7, 10, 13, and 16).

Here's an example dealing with evenly spaced numbers. What is the average of 5, 6, 7, 8, and 9? We do not have to use the average formula. These numbers are evenly spaced, so the average is equal to the middle term. The middle term is 7, so the average is 7.

Notice that this is the same amount we would have reached if we had used the average formula:

$$\text{average} = \frac{5+6+7+8+9}{5}$$
$$\text{average} = \frac{35}{5}$$
$$\text{average} = 7$$

REMEMBER THIS!

While it is true that in any group of evenly spaced terms, the average is equal to the median, the opposite is not necessarily true. In other words, if you know that the average of a group of terms is equal to their median, you cannot infer that the numbers are evenly spaced.

However, it is clearly far preferable to solve the problem without doing that work!

Take another example: what is the average of −5, −2, 1, 4, and 7? While it might not be immediately obvious, these numbers are evenly spaced—they are all 3 apart. Thus, the average is equal to the median, which is 1.

MEDIAN

The **median** of a set of data is the middle number when the values are listed in order from smallest to largest.

In lists containing an odd number of values, one value is located directly in the middle of the list.

For example, find the median of the following set of numbers: {20, 65, 34, 21, 55, 89, 38, 41, 76}. First list the numbers in order from smallest to greatest: 20, 21, 34, 38, 41, 55, 65, 76, 89. Since there are nine numbers in the list, the fifth number, 41, is in the middle. The number 41 is the median of the data set.

If the list has an even number of values, the average of the two middle values is the median.

For example, find the median of 6, 3, 10, 7, 8, and 1. First we must arrange the numbers in numerical order. Doing so gives us the group 1, 3, 6, 7, 8, and 10. The two middle numbers are 6 and 7, and their average is 6.5. Thus, the median of this group is 6.5.

MODE

The **mode** of a set of data is the number that occurs the most in the data set. Sometimes we encounter a list where no number occurs more than any other; in this case, we say there is **no mode**. There is also the case when two or more values occur the same number of times. If two values occur the same number of times and they occur more than any other number in the list, the set is considered to be **bimodal**, meaning it has two modes. It is also possible to have more than two modes in a set of data.

Find the mode in each data set:

8, 9, 10, 4, 5, 8, 8	The mode is 8.
2, 20, 18, 66, 3, 14, 23	There is no mode for this set.
−1, 9, 10, −1, 5, 77, 10	Both −1 and 10 appear the most often. This set is bimodal.

RANGE

The **range** of a set of numbers is the difference between the largest value in the list and the smallest value in the list. Take the following data set: 34, 54, 22, 84, 90, 55, 60, and 23. The range of this set would be $90 - 22 = 68$, since 90 is the largest value in the set and 22 is the smallest.

PRACTICE 1

Try the following matching exercises to polish your skills finding the mean, median, mode, and range. Answers and explanations are located at the end of the chapter.

1. The mean of the set {9, 7, 8, 14, 22, 12}   A. 27

2. The mode of the set {22, 33, 91, 45, 33, 76, 87}   B. 13

3. The range of the set {101, 105, 112, 123, 98, 96}   C. 12

4. The sum of the median and the range of the set {1, 4, 9, 8, 5}   D. 36

5. The median of the set {24, 53, 32, 39, 33, 61}   E. 33

Standard Deviation

Like mean, mode, median, and range, **standard deviation** describes sets of numbers. It is a measure of how spread out a set of numbers is (how much the numbers deviate from the mean). The greater the spread, the higher the standard deviation.

You'll never actually have to calculate the standard deviation on test day, but to help you understand how it works, here's how it's calculated:

1. Find the average (arithmetic mean) of the set.

2. Find the differences between the mean and each value in the set.

3. Square each of the differences.

4. Find the average of the squared differences.

5. Take the positive square root of the average.

Again, you will not have to actually do this on the test—which, as you'll see, is good news! Still, let's see it worked out so that you'll begin to understand the process.

Find the standard deviation of 4, 7, and 13. First we find the average of the terms.

$$\frac{4+7+13}{3} = 8$$

Next we find the difference between each term and the average.

$$8 - 4 = 4$$
$$8 - 7 = 1$$
$$8 - 13 = -5$$

Then we square each of those differences.

$$4^2 = 16$$
$$1^2 = 1$$
$$-5^2 = 25$$

Now we find the average of those squared terms.

$$\frac{16 + 1 + 25}{3} = 14$$

Finally, we find the square root of that average.

$$\sqrt{14} \approx 3.5$$

Here's another example. The following chart shows high temperatures, in degrees Fahrenheit, in two cities over five days. Which city had the greater standard deviation in high temperatures?

September	1	2	3	4	5
City A	54	61	70	49	56
City B	62	56	60	67	65

Even without calculating the standard deviations, you can see that City A has the greater spread in temperatures and, therefore, the greater standard deviation in high temperatures.

If you were to go ahead and calculate the standard deviations following the steps described above, you would find that the standard deviation in high temperatures for City A = $\sqrt{50.8} = 7.1$, while the same for City B = $\sqrt{14.8} = 3.8$.

As you can see, this is an intensive process. Thus, the test simply will not *ever* make you actually calculate the standard deviation of a group of terms. Ever!

The main way in which standard deviation is tested is conceptually, usually in the Data Sufficiency section of the test, so rather than simply memorize the previous steps, it's more useful to think through what standard deviation actually means. The exercise below will help you understand how standard deviation works.

Here is one small group of terms: 5, 10, 15. Their standard deviation is worked out for you below.

$$\text{Average} = \frac{5+10+15}{3} = 10$$

$$\sqrt{\frac{(5-10)^2 + (10-10)^2 + (15-10)^2}{3}}$$

$$= \sqrt{\frac{(-5)^2 + (0)^2 + (5)^2}{3}}$$

$$= \sqrt{\frac{25+0+25}{3}}$$

$$= \sqrt{\frac{50}{3}}$$

Standard deviation = approximately 4.08.

Overlapping Sets

A **set** is simply a collection of things called **members**. The members of a set can be anything—numbers, places, people, things, or even other sets. In addition to the types of data sets we've seen in dealing with statistics, you'll also encounter sets on the GMAT in questions that involve overlapping sets.

There are a number of ways to answer overlapping set questions. One is to use the formula for overlapping sets:

total = group 1 + group 2 − both + neither

Another common way is by using a Venn diagram, which involves circles that partially overlap with quantities of items drawn in the appropriate places. Finally, you can also draw out a table.

Let's look at an example question and solve it by using these three methods.

Of the 150 employees at Company X, 80 are full-time, and 100 have worked at Company X for at least a year. There are 20 employees at Company X who aren't full-time and haven't worked at Company X for at least a year. How many full-time employees of Company X have worked at the company for at least a year?

First, we need to determine the number of employees who are both full-time and have worked at the company for at least one year. Using the overlapping sets formula, we calculate as follows:

$$\text{total} = \text{group 1} + \text{group 2} - \text{both} + \text{neither}$$
$$150 = 80 + 100 - \text{both} + 20$$
$$150 = 200 - \text{both}$$
$$50 = \text{both}$$

Using a Venn diagram, we first draw the diagram, labeling the categories.

Total = 150

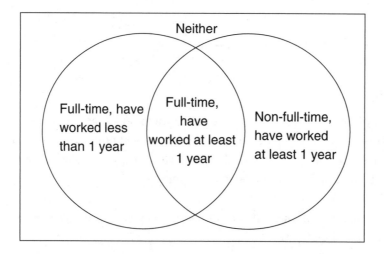

Directly below the circles, write 80 and 100, respectively. Write 20 to represent the "neither" category. We know that 100 employees are in the "at least 1 year" circle. This means that $150 - 100 = 50$ employees are outside of it. Of these, we know that 20 fall into the "neither" category. So $50 - 20 = 30$ employees must fall into the "full-time, have worked less than 1 year" category. Now we know that $80 - 30 = 50$ employees fall into the "full-time, have worked at least 1 year" category. So the answer is 50.

Using a chart, we first fill in what we are given in the question stem and place an x in the box to represent the number we are looking for.

	Less Than 1 Year	At Least 1 Year	Total
Full-time		x	80
Non-full-time	20		
Total		100	150

Then we determine the other numbers (and the answer) using simple addition and subtraction.

	Less Than 1 Year	At Least 1 Year	Total
Full-time	**30** $(80 - 50)$	$x =$ **50** $(100 - 50)$	80
Non-full-time	20	**50** $(70 - 20)$	**70** $(150 - 80)$
Total	**50** $(150 - 100)$	100	150

PRACTICE 2

6. Of the 90 members of a club, 35 are female and the rest male. 10 males are less than 50 years old, and 60 members are at least 50 years old. How many female members are under 50 years old?

Statistical Graphs

Many types of **statistical graphs** are used to display data. Although it is rare to see questions based on charts or graphs in the Quantitative section of the GMAT, such visual displays of data are common on the Integrated Reasoning section. Some of the most common types of statistical graphs are the bar graph, the line graph, the circle graph, and the scatter plot.

BAR GRAPHS

Bar graphs are used to compare data. They can be drawn as horizontal bars or vertical bars. The graph below compares the price of a popular video game from four different stores.

Using the graph above, answer the following question: How much more does a video game cost at Video Village than at Games Plus?

By reading the above graph, we see that the price of the video at Video Village is $65, and the price at Games Plus is $47. Since the question asks for the difference in price, subtract the two values: $65 − 47 = $18.

LINE GRAPHS

A **line graph** is used to show a trend that occurs over time. Take, for example, the following graph that shows stock prices for a certain company over one month.

Using the information in the graph, answer the following question: Between which two weeks did the price of the stock almost double?

You are looking for an increase in price. The price for week 3 was $22, and the price for week 4 was $40. Since $22 times 2 is equal to $44, which is close to $40, then between these two weeks the price of the stock almost doubled.

CIRCLE GRAPHS

A **circle graph** is used to show parts of a whole. Percents are often shown by a circle graph; always make sure that any percents used in a circle graph add up to 100 percent.

FLASHBACK

To review the steps for calculating with **percent**, refer to chapter 5: Percents.

The following graph shows the breakdown of the participation in extracurricular activities at a middle school. Each student can be a member of only one club.

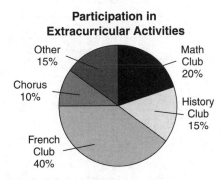

**Participation in
Extracurricular Activities**

Other 15%

Math Club 20%

Chorus 10%

History Club 15%

French Club 40%

From the information in the graph above, how many students participate in the history club if a total of 420 students take part in an extracurricular activity?

Since 15 percent of the students participate in the history club, find 15 percent of 420. Use the proportion $\dfrac{x}{420} = \dfrac{15}{100}$. Cross multiply to get $100x = 6{,}300$. Divide each side of the equation by 100 to get $x = 63$. Sixty-three students participate in the history club.

SCATTER PLOTS

Much like a line graph, a scatter plot is used to show trends in data. In this type of graph, however, the data points are not connected. Instead, the general trend of the data points is examined. The more the data in the graph appears to form a straight line, the stronger the relationship is between the two variables.

The following is an example of a scatter plot that shows the relationship between the number of assignments completed and the student averages from a certain academic class.

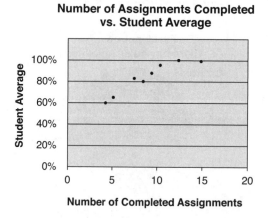

Number of Assignments Completed vs. Student Average

Specific information about the data can be determined from the graph. For example, the greatest number of assignments completed is 15, and the person who completed 15 assignments has approximately a 98 percent average.

Usually, one of three conclusions can be made based on a scatter plot. The first is a positive trend, or positive correlation: when the x-values increase, the y-values also increase. As you can see from the graph above, the relationship between the number of assignments completed and the student average is positive. The more assignments completed, the higher the student average; the less assignments completed, the lower the student average.

The second type of trend is a negative trend, or negative correlation: the *y*-values decrease as the *x*-values increase. An example of a negative correlation might be the cost of a ticket for a show and the number of tickets sold. As the price increases, the number of tickets purchased may decrease.

A third possibility is that no correlation, or relationship, exists in the data graphed. The figure below shows what each type of correlation looks like on a graph.

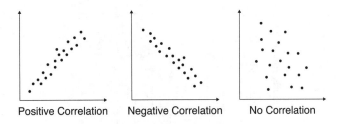

Positive Correlation   Negative Correlation   No Correlation

PRACTICE 3

For questions 7–9 match the information with the best choice of graph. Answers and explanations are found at the end of the chapter.

    A. Bar graph   B. Line graph   C. Circle graph

7. The Wood family's monthly budget

Rent	40%
Food	35%
Utilities	15%
Other	10%

8. The high temperature each day for five days

Monday	61°
Tuesday	59°
Wednesday	60°
Thursday	54°
Friday	72°

9. The number of employees at four companies

    Company A   450
    Company B   300
    Company C   490
    Company D   110

10. Based on the scatter plot below, a person with five years of experience makes how much per hour? _____

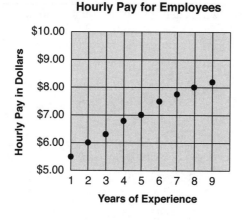

Hourly Pay for Employees

PROBABILITY

The concept of **probability** falls under the category of arithmetic, but for the most part, it is an advanced topic that is not necessary to master early in the learning process. Still, it's good to learn at least the basics of probability.

Probability refers to the likelihood of events with a finite number of outcomes. For example, we can talk about the probability of getting a certain result in a coin flip or a die toss. The probability of an event (E) is defined as follows:

$$P(E) = \frac{\text{the number of ways (E) can occur}}{\text{the total number of possible outcomes}}$$

The **outcome set**, also known as the **sample space**, is the list of all possible outcomes. For example, the outcome set when flipping a coin is {heads, tails} because these are the only possible outcomes. The probability that you will get tails when flipping a coin is $P(\text{tails}) = \frac{1}{2}$, since there is one way to get tails out of two possible outcomes.

REMEMBER THIS!

- The probability of an event that *cannot* happen, or an impossible event, is 0.
- The probability of an event that is *certain* to happen is 1.
- All other simple probabilities are between 0 and 1.

Take this problem as an example. What is the probability of rolling a 3 or a 4 on a single toss of a fair die?

$$\frac{\text{the number of ways (E) can occur}}{\text{the total number of possible outcomes}} = \frac{2}{6} = \frac{1}{3}$$

Let's look at another example. In a bag, there are seven green marbles, four blue marbles, and three red marbles. What is the probability of randomly drawing a red marble from the bag?

$$\frac{\text{the number of ways (E) can occur}}{\text{the total number of possible outcomes}} = \frac{3}{14}$$

Independent Event Probability

Many hard probability questions involve finding the probability of a certain outcome after multiple repetitions of the same experiment or different experiments, or involve combining probabilities of independent separate events.

Let's say that a certain machine has two components, A and B. Component A works one-third of the time. Component B works one-fourth of the time. If both components must work for the machine to operate, what is the probability that the machine operates?

When two events occur completely independently of one another, to find the probability of their combined occurrence, multiply their individual probabilities. Here, we'll multiply $\frac{1}{3}$ by $\frac{1}{4}$ to get $\frac{1}{12}$. The final answer is $\frac{1}{12}$.

Here's another problem. A bill will be passed only if Senator Anders, Senator Bryson, and Senator Carter all vote yes. The probability that Senator Anders will vote yes is $\frac{2}{7}$. The probability that Senator Bryson will vote yes is $\frac{1}{3}$. The probability that Senator Carter will vote yes is $\frac{7}{9}$. What is the probability that the bill will pass?

This problem is very similar to the previous one. To find the probability, we'll multiply each of the individual probabilities: $\frac{2}{7} \times \frac{1}{3} \times \frac{7}{9} = \frac{2}{27}$. The bill has only a $\frac{2}{27}$ chance of passing.

Let's look at one more. If Alison flips a fair coin three times, what is the probability that she will get heads on all three flips?

The probability of getting heads on a fair coin is $\frac{1}{2}$. To get three heads in a row, the likelihood is $\frac{1}{2} \times \frac{1}{2} \times \frac{1}{2} = \frac{1}{8}$.

Compound Probability

Compound probability occurs when a problem asks for the chance of more than one outcome to occur. The key word used in most compound probability questions is *or*.

The formula for compound probability is the following:

$$P(A \text{ or } B) = P(A) + P(B) - P(A \text{ and } B)$$

Mutually exclusive events are situations that cannot occur at the same instance. For these events, P(A and B) from the formula above is 0.

Two examples of compound probability problems are finding the probability of getting a 3 or a 6 when rolling a die and finding the probability of selecting a red card or a 5 from a standard deck of 52 cards.

In the first example, the probability of rolling a 3 is $\frac{1}{6}$, the probability of rolling 6 is $\frac{1}{6}$, and the probability of rolling both a 3 *and* a 6 (mutually exclusive events) is $\frac{0}{6}$. Thus, the probability is $P(3 \text{ or } 6) = \frac{1}{6} + \frac{1}{6} - \frac{0}{6} = \frac{2}{6} = \frac{1}{3}$.

In the second example, the probability of selecting a red card is $\frac{26}{52}$, the probability of selecting a 5 is $\frac{4}{52}$, and the probability of selecting a red card that is *also* a 5 is $\frac{2}{52}$. Thus, the probability is $P(\text{red card or a 5}) = \frac{26}{52} + \frac{4}{52} - \frac{2}{52} = \frac{28}{52} = \frac{7}{13}$. In this example, these two events could occur at the same time. In other words, there is a possibility that a card chosen could be a red 5 (such as the 5 of hearts or 5 of diamonds). Since each of those cards fits both categories of being red and being a 5, they cannot be counted twice. Therefore, the chance that one of those two cards is selected— $P(A \text{ and } B) = \frac{2}{52}$ —was subtracted out.

PRACTICE 4

Fill in the blank with the solution that best answers the question. Answers and explanations are located at the end of the chapter.

11. When rolling one die, the probability of rolling a 6 is _____.

12. When spinning the spinner below, the probability of getting section B is _____.

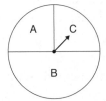

13. When selecting a card from a standard deck, the probability of choosing a 2 or a face card (jack, queen, or king) is _____.

14. When rolling one die, the probability of rolling a 3 or an odd number is _____.

15. If a bag contains only five red, six purple, and two green balls, then P(pink ball) is _____.

Independent and Dependent Events

More complex situations occur in probability problems when more than one event is taking place at the same time or when one event is taking place right after another. In these circumstances, the probabilities of each event are multiplied together to get the final likelihood of occurrence.

REMEMBER THIS!

The key word used often in **independent and dependent events** is *and*, which indicates that the probabilities should be multiplied together.

INDEPENDENT EVENTS

Independent events are two or more events that will occur without the outcome of one affecting the outcome of the other. Put another way, the probability of the second event will be the same regardless of the outcome of the first event. An example of two independent events is rolling a die and flipping a coin. No matter what was rolled on the die, the probability of getting heads or tails on the coin is the same. Another example would be selecting a card from a deck, replacing the card, and then selecting the next card. In this case, the key word *replace* or the phrase *with replacement* indicates that the events are independent. Since the first card is replaced, there are still 52 cards to choose from when selecting the next card. The probabilities are the same each time.

Try this exercise with two independent events: A bag contains three red marbles, five blue marbles, and two green marbles. A marble is selected at random, replaced, and then another marble selected. What is P(red, blue)?

This question is asking you to find the probability of pulling out a red marble first and then a blue marble second. Since the marble is selected and then replaced, there are still the same 10 marbles to choose from in the bag. Therefore, the events are independent of each other. The probability of selecting a red marble first is $\frac{3}{10}$, and the probability of selecting a blue marble second is $\frac{5}{10}$. Thus, P(red, blue) = $\frac{3}{10} \times \frac{5}{10} = \frac{15}{100}$, or $\frac{3}{20}$.

DEPENDENT EVENTS

Dependent events are situations where the outcome of the first event *does* affect the probability of the second event. These events are much like the ones mentioned above, but there is no replacement. For example, find the probability of selecting two kings from a standard deck of cards *without replacement*. The probability of selecting a king is $\frac{4}{52}$. Since the first king is not replaced, the probability of selecting a second king is $\frac{3}{51}$. After the first king is selected and not put back in the deck, there are only three kings left and a total of 51 cards. Thus, the probability of selecting two kings from a deck without replacement is $\frac{4}{52} \times \frac{3}{51} = \frac{12}{2,652}$, or $\frac{1}{221}$.

Take another look at the exercise from above but now with two dependent events. A bag contains three red marbles, five blue marbles, and two green marbles. A marble is selected at random, not replaced, and then another marble is selected. What is the probability of P(red, blue)?

Since the marble is selected and then not replaced, there will be only nine marbles left in the bag for the second draw. Therefore, the events are dependent on each other. The probability of selecting a red marble first is $\frac{3}{10}$, and the probability of selecting a blue marble second is $\frac{5}{9}$. Thus, P(red, blue) $\frac{3}{10} \times \frac{5}{9} = \frac{15}{90}$, or $\frac{1}{6}$.

Don't take chances with your skills in probability! The following practice set will build additional skill in finding the probability of independent and dependent events.

PRACTICE 5

Answer TRUE or FALSE to each of the following statements. Answers and explanations are located at the end of the chapter.

16. **T   F**   If two cards are drawn from a standard deck with replacement, the probability of drawing a king and then a queen is $\frac{16}{2,704}$, or $\frac{1}{169}$.

17. **T   F**   When rolling a die and flipping a coin, the probability P(5, tails) is $\frac{1}{8}$.

18. **T   F**   If two cards are drawn from a standard deck without replacement, the probability of drawing a king and then a queen is $\frac{12}{2,652}$, or $\frac{1}{221}$.

19. **T   F**   A bag contains three red, five blue, and four white marbles. If a marble is drawn from the bag, not replaced, and then another is drawn, then P(white, blue) is $\frac{5}{33}$.

The Counting Principle

Sometimes when you are given many options, the number of possible choices can seem unlimited. However, when the number of choices in a situation is known, the actual number of possibilities can be calculated. For example, when ordering a sandwich at a deli, you may have three choices of condiments, four choices of bread, and five choices of meat, or main ingredient, for the sandwich. To find the total number of possible sandwich combinations, multiply the number of choices in each category together: $3 \times 4 \times 5 = 60$ different sandwiches. Multiplying the number of choices together is a concept called the **counting principle**. This strategy is also used when solving the next two types of situations presented: permutations and combinations.

Permutations

A **permutation** of objects is the number of possible arrangements for that set of objects. With permutations, it's all about order. Every time the order changes, a new permutation of the objects is formed.

For example, if six different books are placed on a shelf, there are six choices for the first spot on the shelf, five choices for the second, four for the third, three for the fourth, two for the fifth, and only one book left for the sixth. Thus, the total number of arrangements for those six books can be represented by an operation that looks like this: $6! = 6 \times 5 \times 4 \times 3 \times 2 \times 1 = 720$. This is known as 6 factorial. The **factorial** of a whole number is the product of that whole number and each of the natural numbers less than the number. It is written as $n! = n \times (n - 1) \times (n - 2) \times \ldots \times 1$.

In other words, the number of permutations of n objects taken n at a time is the following:

$$_nP_n = n!$$

But sometimes not all of the objects are considered for each different arrangement. In this case, n represents the total number of objects you have to choose from, and r is the number of objects actually selected to be arranged. The formula for the permutation of n objects taken r at a time is the following:

$$_nP_r = \frac{n!}{(n-r)!}$$

For example, if there are seven runners in a race, how many different orders are possible for first, second, and third place? In this case, there are a total of seven runners, but you are finding only the number of permutations of three of them at a time. Using the above formula, we calculate as follows:

$$_nP_r = \frac{n!}{(n-r)!}$$

$$= {_7P_3} = \frac{7!}{(7-3)!} = \frac{7!}{4!} = \frac{7 \times 6 \times 5 \times 4 \times 3 \times 2 \times 1}{4 \times 3 \times 2 \times 1}$$

$$= \frac{7 \times 6 \times 5 \times \cancel{4} \times \cancel{3} \times \cancel{2} \times \cancel{1}}{\cancel{4} \times \cancel{3} \times \cancel{2} \times \cancel{1}}$$

$$= 7 \times 6 \times 5$$

$$= 210 \text{ ways seven runners can place first, second, or third}$$

A faster way to think through this is by using the counting principle. There are three different places (first, second, third) to be considered. Since there are seven choices for first place, then six choices for second place, then five choices for third place, the number of arrangements is $7 \times 6 \times 5 = 210$.

Combinations

With combinations, the order is not important. The grouping of objects changes the number of combinations that exist. A **combination** is the total number of groupings of a set of objects. The formula for the number of combinations of n objects taken r at a time is the following:

$$_nC_r = \frac{n!}{r!(n-r)!}$$

Note that $_nC_n$ is always equal to 1. There is only one way to select *all* the members of a group or committee.

For example, if you were selecting three people from a group of ten to form a committee, the order of the members of the committee is not important; each person, whether picked first, second, or third, will end up being on the committee. Thus, the key words for combinations include *choose* and *committee*.

In this example, if there are ten people to choose from for a committee of three, how many different combinations could be formed? Using the above formula, we calculate as follows:

$$_nC_r = \frac{n!}{r!(n-r)!}$$

$$= {}_{10}C_3 = \frac{10!}{3!(10-3)!} = \frac{10!}{3!7!}$$

$$= \frac{10 \times 9 \times 8 \times 7 \times 6 \times 5 \times 4 \times 3 \times 2 \times 1}{3 \times 2 \times 1 \times (7 \times 6 \times 5 \times 4 \times 3 \times 2 \times 1)}$$

$$= \frac{10 \times 9 \times 8 \times \cancel{7} \times \cancel{6} \times \cancel{5} \times \cancel{4} \times \cancel{3} \times \cancel{2} \times \cancel{1}}{3 \times 2 \times 1 \times (\cancel{7} \times \cancel{6} \times \cancel{5} \times \cancel{4} \times \cancel{3} \times \cancel{2} \times \cancel{1})}$$

$$= \frac{10 \times 9 \times 8}{3 \times 2 \times 1} = \frac{720}{6}$$

$$= 120 \text{ ways the committee could be formed}$$

A faster way to think this through is by using the counting principle. Start with the fact that there are three people to be chosen from a total of ten. There are ten, then nine, then eight choices for the three people. Divide this result by the number of permutations, or orders, of the three people, since order does not matter in combinations. In this way, the number of combinations can be found just using $\frac{10 \times 9 \times 8}{3 \times 2 \times 1} = \frac{720}{6} = 120$.

PRACTICE 6

Practice makes perfect when enhancing your skills with counting problems. Work with the next set of practice problems to help in this area. Answers and explanations are at the end of the chapter.

20. If you have five shirts, four pairs of pants, and three pairs of shoes, how many different outfits can you make using one shirt, one pair of pants, and one pair of shoes?

21. Find $_4P_4$.

22. How many different arrangements of five students can be made in a row of three desks?

23. Find $_5C_3$.

24. How many different four-person committees can be formed from a total of eight people?

SEQUENCES

In grade school, your math teacher might have given you a sequence of numbers and asked you to find the pattern. For example, what is the pattern that relates the numbers in the sequence 4, 7, 10, 13, 16? Each number in this sequence is the previous number plus 3, and the first number is 4.

On the GMAT, the sequence above would be expressed like this: $a_n = a_{n-1} + 3$ for all $n > 1$, and $a_1 = 4$. In **sequence notation**, a_n represents the "nth" term in the sequence, while a_{n-1} represents the "$(n-1)$th" term, or the term that comes immediately before a_n in the sequence. For example, when $n = 2$, the equation reads: $a_2 = a_{2-1} + 3 = a_1 + 3$. Since we were told that $a_1 = 4$, it follows that $a_2 = a_1 + 3 = 4 + 3 = 7$, and 7 is indeed the second term in the sequence.

Sequences on the GMAT can have more complicated patterns than the ones you saw in school. For example, if $a_{n-1} = 3a_n + 6$ for all $n > 1$ and $a_1 = 36$, what is a_3? To solve this problem, you'll need to find a_2, then a_3. First, let $n = 2$:

$$a_{n-1} = 3a_n + 6$$

$$a_{2-1} = 3a_2 + 6$$

$$a_1 = 3a_2 + 6$$

Since $a_1 = 36$, plug that value in for a_1 and solve for a_2:

$$36 = 3a_2 + 6$$

$$30 = 3a_2$$

$$10 = a_2$$

You can now find a_3. Use the original sequence equation and let $n = 3$:

$$a_{n-1} = 3a_n + 6$$

$$a_{3-1} = 3a_3 + 6$$

$$a_2 = 3a_3 + 6$$

And now plug in the value of a_2, which is 10, and solve from there:

$$10 = 3a_3 + 6$$

$$4 = 3a_3$$

$$\frac{4}{3} = a_3$$

PRACTICE 7

As always, repetition is the key to mastery. Solidify your understanding of sequences with these practice problems.

25. If $a_n = a_{n-1} + a_{n-2}$ for all $n > 2$, $a_1 = 2$, and $a_2 = 4$, what is a_5?

26. If $a_n = 2(a_{n-1})^2 - 10$ for all $n > 1$ and $a_1 = 1$, was is a_3?

SUMMARY

Here are five main ideas about statistics that you should take from this chapter:

1. The arithmetic mean is the average of a set of numbers.

2. The median is the middle number in an ordered list.

3. The mode is the number that appears most often.

4. The range is the difference between the highest and lowest values in a set.

5. Being able to read and interpret data in graphs is an important skill to have; some of the most common graphs used are bar graphs, line graphs, circle graphs, and scatter plots.

Here are five key concepts about probability that you should take from this chapter:

1. The probability of an event (E) is $P(E) = \dfrac{\text{the number of ways event E can occur}}{\text{the total number of possible outcomes}}$.

2. In probability, the word *or* is a key word for addition, and the word *and* is a key word for multiplication.

3. There are many different types of counting problems. To work with them, multiply out the total number of choices you have to find the total number of possible outcomes.

4. A permutation is a special type of counting problem where the order is important; it uses the formula $_nP_r = \dfrac{n!}{(n-r)!}$.

5. A combination is a special type of counting problem where the order does not matter; it uses the formula $_nC_r = \dfrac{n!}{r!(n-r)!}$.

Lastly, here are two important concepts about sequences that you should take from this chapter:

1. A sequence is a list of numbers in which each term is based upon the previous term(s).

2. In sequence notation, a_n represents the "*n*th" term in the sequence, a_{n-1} represents the "$(n-1)$th" term, and so on.

Practice Answers and Explanations

1. C

$$\frac{9+7+8+14+22+12}{6} = 12$$

2. E

The number 33 appears the most.

3. A

$$123 - 96 = 27$$

4. B

$$5 + 8 = 13$$

5. D

The median of a set with an even number of terms is equal to the average of the two middle terms, 33 and 39.

6. 20

The chart below shows both information gathered from the question, as well as information calculated using simple addition and subtraction (in bold).

	Female	Male	Total
Under 50	**20** $(30 - 10)$	10	**30** $(90 - 60)$
At least 50	**15** $(35 - 20)$	**45** $(55 - 10)$	60
Total	35	**55** $(90 - 35)$	90

First you determine how many people total are under 50 by subtracting 60 from 90, which equals 30. Then you subtract the number of males under 50, which we know from the question is 10, from the total of club members under 50, which gives you 20 females under 50 years old.

7. C

A circle graph shows parts of a whole. The percents must add up to 100 percent.

8. B

A line graph shows a trend over a period of time.

9. A

A bar graph is used to compare different things.

10. $7

The point directly above 5 years on the x-axis is also directly to the right of $7 on the y-axis. A person with 5 years' experience makes $7 per hour.

11. $\dfrac{1}{6}$

There is one side with a 6 out of six possible sides to a die.

12. $\dfrac{1}{2}$

One section is labeled with a B; however, this section is twice as big as the other two sections. Since it takes up $\dfrac{1}{2}$ of the spinner, the probability is $\dfrac{1}{2}$.

13. $\dfrac{16}{52}$ or $\dfrac{4}{13}$

The probability of a 2 is $\dfrac{4}{52}$, and the probability of a face card is $\dfrac{12}{52}$. Remember, P(A or B) = P(A) + P (B) − P(A and B). Since these events are mutually exclusive, their probability is $\dfrac{4}{52} + \dfrac{12}{52} = \dfrac{16}{52} = \dfrac{4}{13}$.

14. $\dfrac{3}{6}$ or $\dfrac{1}{2}$

The probability of rolling a 3 is $\dfrac{1}{6}$, and the probability of rolling an odd number is $\dfrac{3}{6}$. Remember, P(A or B) = P(A) + P (B) − P(A and B). Since 3 is an odd number, the events are mutually inclusive. Therefore, the probability is $\dfrac{1}{6} + \dfrac{3}{6} - \dfrac{1}{6} = \dfrac{3}{6} = \dfrac{1}{2}$.

15. $\dfrac{0}{13}$ or 0

Since there are no pink balls in the bag, the event is impossible, and the probability is 0.

16. True

With replacement, P(king, queen) = $\dfrac{4}{52} \times \dfrac{4}{52} = \dfrac{16}{2,704} = \dfrac{1}{169}$

17. False

P(5, tails) = $\dfrac{1}{6} \times \dfrac{1}{2} = \dfrac{1}{12}$

18. False

Without replacement, P(king, queen) = $\dfrac{4}{52} \times \dfrac{4}{51} = \dfrac{16}{2,652}$.

19. True

With replacement, P(white, blue) $= \dfrac{4}{12} \times \dfrac{5}{11} = \dfrac{20}{132} = \dfrac{5}{33}$.

20. 60

Use the counting principle to find the total number of possibilities. Multiply the choices together: $5 \times 4 \times 3 = 60$ different outfits.

21. 24

$$_4P_4 = 4 \times 3 \times 2 \times 1 = 24$$

22. 60

Since the order is important, this problem is a permutation. Arranging five students in a row with three desks can be expressed as $_5P_3 = 5 \times 4 \times 3 = 60$.

23. 10

$$_5C_3 = \frac{5 \times 4 \times 3}{3 \times 2 \times 1} = \frac{60}{6} = 10$$

24. 70

Choosing a four-person committee from eight people can also be expressed as $_8C_4 = \dfrac{8 \times 7 \times 6 \times 5}{4 \times 3 \times 2 \times 1} = \dfrac{1,680}{24} = 70$.

25. 16

In this sequence, each number (a_n) is the sum of the two numbers that immediately precede it $(a_{n-1}$ and $a_{n-2})$. Given $a_1 = 2$ and $a_2 = 4$, calculate the value of each number up to a_5:

$a_3 = a_2 + a_1 = 4 + 2 = 6$

$a_4 = a_3 + a_2 = 6 + 4 = 10$

$a_5 = a_4 + a_3 = 10 + 6 = 16$

26. 118

Given $a_1 = 1$, use the definition of the sequence to compute each term up to a_3:

$a_2 = 2(a_1)^2 - 10 = 2(1)^2 - 10 = 2 - 10 = -8$

$a_3 = 2(a_2)^2 - 10 = 2(-8)^2 - 10 = 2(64) - 10 = 128 - 10 = 118$

CHAPTER 6 TEST

Try the following questions to test your knowledge of statistics and probability. Answer explanations are provided at the conclusion of the chapter to help you assess your understanding of the concepts.

1. The daily snowfall amounts, in inches, for a certain city over a period of five days were 12, 2, 1, 0, and 5. What was the mean snowfall in this period, in inches?

   (A) 0

   (B) 1

   (C) 2

   (D) 4

   (E) 6

2. Five students working at summer jobs make the following amounts per hour: $6.50, $6.00, $7.25, $5.50, and $7.00. What is the range in pay per hour?

   (A) $1.00

   (B) $1.50

   (C) $1.75

   (D) $2.25

   (E) $3.25

3. Given the following set of data, which of the following is *TRUE*?

   {3, 5, 11, 12, 17, 18, 5, 20, 5, 22, 3}

   I.   The mean is equal to the mode.

   II. The median is greater than the mean.

   III. The mode is less than the range.

   (A) I only

   (B) II only

   (C) III only

   (D) II and III only

   (E) I, II, and III

Use the graph below to answer questions 4 and 5.

The graph below shows the number of automobiles sold at a dealership by salesperson.

4. According to the bar graph above, how many automobiles were sold by Tad?

   (A) 25

   (B) 30

   (C) 35

   (D) 40

   (E) 50

5. What is the ratio of the number of automobiles sold by Jarvis to the number of automobiles sold by Ellen?

   (A) 1:2

   (B) 2:3

   (C) 3:4

   (D) 1:1

   (E) 2:1

Use the graph below to answer questions 6 and 7.

The graph below shows the enrollment at a college from 1998 to 2004.

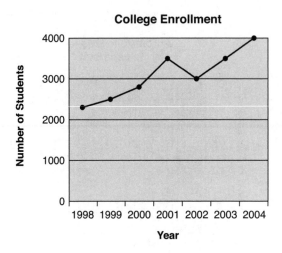

6. How many more students were enrolled at the college in 2004 than in 1999?

   (A) 500
   (B) 1,000
   (C) 1,500
   (D) 2,000
   (E) 2,500

7. Between which two years did the greatest increase in enrollment occur?

   (A) 1998 and 1999
   (B) 1999 and 2000
   (C) 2000 and 2001
   (D) 2002 and 2003
   (E) 2003 and 2004

Use the graph below to answer questions 8 and 9.

The following circle graph shows the breakdown of summer activities of certain students.

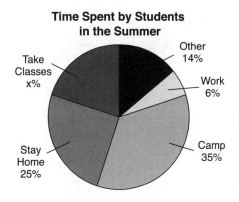

Time Spent by Students in the Summer

8. According to the graph, what percent of students attended classes during the summer?

    (A) 1%

    (B) 10%

    (C) 15%

    (D) 20%

    (E) 25%

9. If 300 students participated in this study, how many either worked or went to a camp?

    (A) 41

    (B) 82

    (C) 123

    (D) 143

    (E) 105

10. What type of correlation is shown in the scatter plot below?

  (A) Positive
  (B) Negative
  (C) No correlation
  (D) Choices A, B, and C
  (E) None of these

11. The following scatter plot shows the relationship between the hours spent studying and the grade on the exam.

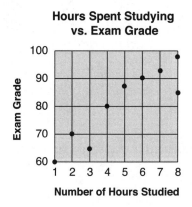

According to the graph, how many hours did a person spend studying if she received a 90 on the exam?

  (A) 4
  (B) 5
  (C) 6
  (D) 7
  (E) 8

12. According to the bar graph, how many of the given categories did *NOT* see an increase of at least 25 percent in 1987–88 over 1982–83?

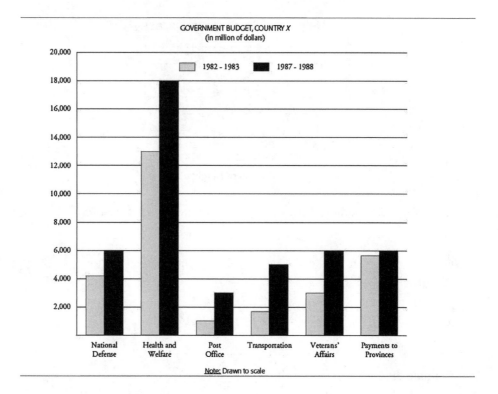

(A) 0

(B) 1

(C) 2

(D) 3

(E) 6

13. The bar graph below shows the results after students in a class were measured for their heights.

Heights of Students in a Class

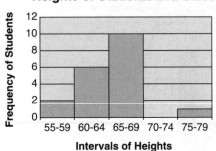

Intervals of Heights

According to the graph, how many total students were measured?

(A) 10

(B) 17

(C) 18

(D) 19

(E) 21

14. Evaluate $_7P_3$.

    (A) 10

    (B) 21

    (C) 35

    (D) 120

    (E) 210

15. Evaluate $_{10}C_2$.

    (A) 10

    (B) 20

    (C) 45

    (D) 90

    (E) 100

16. At an ice cream shop, Kerensa can choose from eight flavors of ice cream, three toppings, and two types of cones. If she selects one flavor of ice cream, one topping, and one type of cone, how many different combinations can she make?

    (A) 12

    (B) 13

    (C) 24

    (D) 36

    (E) 48

17. A bag contains six red, four blue, ten orange, and three yellow candies. What is P(red or yellow)?

    (A) $\dfrac{3}{23}$

    (B) $\dfrac{23}{23}$

    (C) $\dfrac{10}{23}$

    (D) $\dfrac{9}{23}$

    (E) $\dfrac{9}{46}$

18. A coin is tossed, the result is noted, and then the coin is tossed again. What is P(heads, heads)?

    (A) $\dfrac{1}{4}$

    (B) $\dfrac{1}{2}$

    (C) $\dfrac{2}{3}$

    (D) 1

    (E) None of these

19. A cooler of cold drinks contains six bottles of cola, eight bottles of orange drink, four bottles of root beer, and three bottles of water. If a drink is selected, not replaced, and then another selected, what is P(orange drink, cola)?

(A) $\dfrac{48}{441}$

(B) $\dfrac{4}{35}$

(C) $\dfrac{14}{41}$

(D) $\dfrac{10}{41}$

(E) $\dfrac{40}{441}$

20. How many ways can two students be selected from seven to be representatives on the student council?

(A) 9

(B) 14

(C) 21

(D) 42

(E) 84

21. In the sequence $a_{n-2} = a_n + a_{n-1}$, where $n > 2$, $a_1 = 100$, and $a_2 = 90$, what is a_4?

(A) 80

(B) 50

(C) 10

(D) −70

(E) −100

22. At a town picnic, there is a basket containing 240 granola bars. 80% of the granola bars are chewy, and the others are all crunchy. There are two flavors available: chocolate and peanut. 35% of the granola bars are chocolate, and the rest are peanut. 75% of the chewy granola bars are peanut. How many crunchy peanut granola bars are in the basket?

   (A) 12
   (B) 24
   (C) 36
   (D) 48
   (E) 84

Answers and Explanations

1. D

The mean can be found by finding the sum of the numbers in the set and then dividing by the total number of elements in the set. The sum of the set is 20. Since there are 5 numbers, divide 20 by 5 to get a mean of 4. Choice (A) is the lowest number in the list, not the mean. Choice (B) is too small to be the mean of the set. Choice (C) is the median of the set but not the mean. Choice (E) is too large to be the mean of the set.

2. C

The range in pay can be found by subtracting the smallest amount from the largest amount: $7.25 − 5.50 = $1.75.

3. C

For this set of data, the mean is 11, the median is 11, the mode is 5, and the range is 19. Therefore, the only true statement is statement III—the mode is less than the range: 5 < 19. Choice (A) is incorrect because the mean is 11 and the mode is 5, which are not equal. Choice (B) is incorrect because both the median and mean are 11. The median is not greater than the mean; they are equal. Thus, choices (D) and (E) are incorrect because statement I and statement II are false.

4. B

Since the height of Tad's bar reaches 30 on the vertical axis, he sold 30 automobiles.

5. A

Jarvis sold 25 automobiles, and Ellen sold 50. Therefore, the ratio is 25:50, which can be simplified to 1:2 when each number is divided by 25.

6. C

The enrollment at the college in 1999 was 2,500; the enrollment in 2004 was 4,000. To find the difference, subtract: 4,000 − 2,500 = 1,500.

7. C

The greatest increase occurs between the years 2000 and 2001. Here, the enrollment went from 2,800 to 3,500, an increase of 700 students.

8. D

Since the percents in a circle graph need to add up to 100 percent, add the known percents and subtract that sum from 100: $14\% + 6\% + 35\% + 25\% = 80\%$, and $100\% - 80\% = 20\%$.

9. C

Because 6 percent worked and 35 percent went to a camp, add 6 percent and 35 percent to get 41 percent. Now find 41 percent of 300 by using the proportion $\dfrac{x}{300} = \dfrac{41}{100}$. Cross multiply to get $100x = 12,300$, and divide each side of the equation by 100 to get $x = 123$. Recall from chapter 5 that you can also multiply $0.41 \times 300 = 123$ to find the percent of a number.

10. B

Since the series of points in the graph has a trend that decreases as you move to the right on the horizontal axis, this is an example of a negative correlation.

11. C

First, find 90 on the vertical axis. Then look directly to the right until you get to the point at that height. This point is directly above the number 6 on the horizontal axis. Therefore, a person who received a 90 studied for six hours.

12. B

What we're actually looking for is the number of categories that showed an increase of *less than* 25 percent. Since there is a note below the graph that says it is drawn to scale, we can estimate figures directly from the graph. Therefore, we see that *National Defense* grew from about 4.2 billion to about 6 billion, which is an increase of about 1.8 billion. That's nearly 2 billion, which is half of 4 billion, which is a percent change increase closer to 50 percent than 25 percent! (To roughly calculate the percent change increase, we'd divide 1.8 billion by 4.2 billion, which equals 0.428 or 43 percent.) So rule out *National Defense. Health and Welfare* grew from about 13 billion to 18 billion, an increase of about 5 billion. Again, 5 billion is more than 25 percent of 13 billion, so *Health and Welfare* is out. And we can also see that *Post Office, Transportation,* and *Veterans' Affairs* saw increases of more than 25 percent. That leaves us with *Payments to Provinces.* The increase was slight, obviously less than a 25 percent increase; therefore, the answer is that only one category did NOT see at least a 25 percent increase, making choice (B) the correct answer.

13. D

To find the total number of students, add the heights of each of the bars: $2 + 6 + 10 + 0 + 1 = 19$.

14. E

The expression $_7P_3 = 7 \times 6 \times 5 = 210$.

15. C

The expression $_{10}C_2 = \dfrac{10 \times 9}{2 \times 1} = \dfrac{90}{2} = 45$.

16. E

Use the counting principle to multiply the total number of choices together: $8 \times 3 \times 2 = 48$ different combinations.

17. D

The bag holds a total of 23 candies. Because there are six red and three yellow, the probability of P(red or yellow) is $\dfrac{6}{23} + \dfrac{3}{23} = \dfrac{9}{23}$.

18. A

The probability of getting heads on the coin is always $\dfrac{1}{2}$. Therefore, the probability of getting heads first and then heads again is $\dfrac{1}{2} \times \dfrac{1}{2} = \dfrac{1}{4}$.

19. B

The cooler holds a total of 21 bottles. If an orange drink is removed and not replaced, then only 20 bottles are left in the cooler the second time a drink is chosen. Therefore, the P(orange drink, cola) is equal to $\dfrac{8}{21} \times \dfrac{6}{20} = \dfrac{48}{420} = \dfrac{4}{35}$.

20. C

This problem is a combination situation. Since you are looking for two students to be selected from seven and the order does not matter, evaluate $_7C_2 = \dfrac{7 \times 6}{2 \times 1} = \dfrac{42}{2} = 21$.

21. A

First, solve the sequence for a_n so it's easier to read: $a_n = a_{n-2} - a_{n-1}$. Next, use the given values $a_1 = 100$ and $a_2 = 90$ to compute the numbers of the sequence up to a_4:

$a_1 = 100$

$a_2 = 90$

$a_3 = a_{3-2} - a_{3-1} = a_1 - a_2 = 100 - 90 = 10$

$a_4 = a_{4-2} - a_{4-1} = a_2 - a_3 = 90 - 10 = 80$

Be careful and methodical when computing sequences. Choice (C), 10, is a_3, and choice (D), –70, is a_5, not a_4. Choice (E) is what a_4 would be if a_n equaled $a_{n-1} - a_{n-2}$, not $a_{n-2} - a_{n-1}$.

22. A

This question combines overlapping sets and percents. First, 80% of 240 total bars is $240 \times 0.8 = 192$, so there are 192 total chewy granola bars. Of these 192 chewy granola bars, 75% are peanut, so this makes $192 \times 0.75 = 144$ chewy peanut granola bars. The problem also states that 35% of the total granola bars are chocolate, so $240 \times 0.35 = 84$. The question asks for the number of crunchy peanut granola bars, so we can use x to represent this number. Use a chart to organize the given information:

	Chewy	**Crunchy**	**Total**
Chocolate			84
Peanut	144	x	
Total	192		240

Then determine the other numbers (including the value of x) using addition and subtraction:

	Chewy	**Crunchy**	**Total**
Chocolate	**48** (192 – 144)	**36** (84 – 48)	84
Peanut	144	**12** (156 – 144)	**156** (240 – 84)
Total	192	**48** (240 – 192)	240

Each column and row adds up to the total, so you can confirm that the calculations are correct. The number of crunchy peanut granola bars in the basket is 12.

CHAPTER 7

Powers and Roots

Exponents are a way to write very small and very large numbers in a shortened fashion, which can save both time and space. This chapter will review the concepts of exponents and provide various practice exercises to help you refine your skills.

EXPONENTS

Some of the topics we will cover in this chapter include exponents as powers, the laws of exponents, negative exponents, fractional exponents (otherwise known as **radicals** and **roots**), and scientific notation.

Exponents As Powers

Using exponents is a way to write repeated multiplication more efficiently. They are used when a factor being multiplied several times is the same. The **exponent** or **power** is the total number of times a base is used as a factor.

The number or expression that appears below the exponent is called the **base number** or **base expression**. The exponent is always written in smaller type and sits a little above and to the right of the base number. For example, in the numerical expression 6^4, 6 is considered the base number and 4 the exponent. As stated above, the exponent in the expression tells you how many times to use the base number as a factor. In the expression 6^4, 6 should be used as a factor 4 times: $6^4 = 6 \times 6 \times 6 \times 6 = 1,296$.

When an expression is written out showing all of its factors, as above, this is called the **expanded form** of the expression.

Sometimes a number or expression has no exponent. If there is no exponent written with a base number or variable, the exponent is equal to 1. For example, the numerical expression 6 actually means 6^1.

In another special case, any base expression to the 0 power is equal to 1. For example, the expressions 5^0, 101^0, and $12,045^0$ all equal 1.

When simplifying expressions containing exponents, evaluating the exponent(s) is an early step in the order of operations. In fact, you would evaluate exponents directly after simplifying within any parentheses or other grouping symbols in the expression.

FLASHBACK!

PEMDAS from chapter 1 helps you remember the correct order of operations: **P**arentheses, **E**xponents, **M**ultiplication and **D**ivision, **A**ddition and **S**ubtraction.

Let's look at some examples of problems involving exponents.

Evaluate $(-3) - (2)^3 + 1$. No expressions contained within the parentheses need to be simplified, so your first step is to evaluate the exponent of 3 on the base number of 2: $2^3 = 2 \times 2 \times 2 = 8$. Notice that the exponent belongs only to the base it is directly next to. The expression becomes $-3 - 8 + 1$. Perform subtraction next to get $-11 + 1$. Then add to get a final result of -10.

Evaluate $3^4 \times 4^3$. First evaluate the exponents using expanded form to help visualize the operation: $3^4 = 3 \times 3 \times 3 \times 3 = 81$, and $4^3 = 4 \times 4 \times 4 = 64$. Now multiply: $81 \times 64 = 5,184$.

Evaluate $(7)^2$, $(-7)^2$, and $-(7)^2$. The first expression $(7)^2$ is equal to $7 \times 7 = 49$. The second expression $(-7)^2$ is equal to $(-7) \times (-7) = 49$. However, the third expression $-(7)^2$ is equal to $-[(7) \times (7)] = -49$. Since the negative is not within the parentheses, it is not raised to the second power. The expression reads as the opposite of 7 to the second power. Using the correct order of operations leads to an answer of -49 instead of 49.

PRACTICE 1

Use the bank of numbers below to answer each question. Answers and explanations are located at the end of the chapter.

10   108   4   14   16   −15   25   32   17   21   81

1. The expression 2^5 is equal to _____.

2. In the expression 16^{14}, the base number is _____.

3. In the expression 7^4, 7 should be used as a factor _____ times.

4. The expression $(-4)^2 + 5^0$ is equal to _____.

5. The expression $2^2 \times 3^3$ is equal to _____.

Multiplying Like Bases

When working with exponents, there are shortcuts to simplifying expressions. Understanding expanded form will help you comprehend and apply the different laws of exponents.

One pattern occurs when you are multiplying exponents and the base numbers are the same. These are called **like bases.** In the example $2^3 \times 2^5$, 2 is the common base number, or the like base. When writing the expressions out in expanded form, 2^3 is equal to $2 \times 2 \times 2$, and 2^5 is equal to $2 \times 2 \times 2 \times 2 \times 2$. So the expression $2^3 \times 2^5$ becomes $(2 \times 2 \times 2) \times (2 \times 2 \times 2 \times 2 \times 2)$. Since 2 is used as a factor eight times, this expression can be rewritten as 2^8. Notice that the exponents of 3 and 5 were added together to get an exponent of 8. Thus, when multiplying like bases, add the exponents.

Dividing Like Bases

A pattern also occurs when dividing exponents where the base expressions are the same. For example, in the expression $\dfrac{5^6}{5^4}$, 5 is the common base for each expression. Recall that the fraction bar means division. Write both the numerator and denominator in expanded form and cancel out the same number of factors from each. The expression becomes $\dfrac{5^6}{5^4} = \dfrac{5 \times 5 \times 5 \times 5 \times 5 \times 5}{5 \times 5 \times 5 \times 5} = \dfrac{\cancel{5} \times \cancel{5} \times \cancel{5} \times \cancel{5} \times 5 \times 5}{\cancel{5} \times \cancel{5} \times \cancel{5} \times \cancel{5}}$. Notice that four pairs of factors of 5 can be canceled from the numerator and denominator, leaving only 5×5 in the numerator. The simplified expression is then equal to 5^2, or 25. As in the generalization for multiplication, compare the original exponents with the result to determine the rule. Since the original exponents were 6 and 4 and the result was an exponent of 2, the exponents were subtracted when the like bases were divided.

REMEMBER THIS!

- To *multiply* with like bases, *add* the exponents: $a^m \times a^n = a^{m+n}$.
- To *divide* with like bases, *subtract* the exponents: $\dfrac{a^m}{a^n} = a^{m-n}$.

PRACTICE 2

Answer TRUE or FALSE for the following questions. Answers and explanations are located at the end of the chapter.

6. **T F**   The expression $\dfrac{6^7}{6^2}$ is equivalent to 6^9.

7. **T F**   When multiplying $10^2 \times 10^4$, the result is equivalent to 10^6.

8. **T F**   The expression $2^5 \times 5^2$ is equivalent to 10^7.

9. **T F**   The expression $\dfrac{5^3 \times 5^5}{5^4}$ simplifies to 5^4.

Operations with Powers

RAISING A POWER TO A POWER

Another situation you might encounter is raising an exponent, or power, to another power. An example of this is the expression $(2^3)^4$. In this type of problem, use expanded form to help visualize your operation. Since the exponent of 4 is outside of the parentheses, it implies that $(2^3)^4 = (2^3) \times (2^3) \times (2^3) \times (2^3)$. In other words, the base of 2^3 is being used as a factor four times. By adding the exponents of the like bases as explained above, the result is 2^{12}. Since raising the exponents of 3 to the fourth power gave a resulting exponent of 12, you can see that the original exponents were multiplied together to simplify the expression.

RAISING A PRODUCT OR QUOTIENT TO A POWER

When a base expression contains more than just one variable or constant and is then raised to another power, this is called **raising a product to a power**. An example is $(3x^4)^3$, where the entire expression $3x^4$ is raised to the third power. The good news is that the same principle mentioned previously also applies to this example. The catch is that you need to remember to multiply each base number or variable's exponent by 3. Keep in mind that the bases here are 3 and x^4. Thus, $(3x^4)^3$ becomes $3^3 x^{4 \times 3}$, which simplifies to $27x^{12}$ using the power-to-a-power multiplication rule.

The product-to-a-power principle is also used if an expression contains a fraction. In this case, both numerator and denominator are raised to the exponent using these same rules. For example, in the expression $\left(\dfrac{3^2}{2}\right)^3$, the exponent of 3 needs to be applied to the base in the numerator of 3^2 and the base in the denominator of 2. The simplified expression would be $\left(\dfrac{3^2}{2}\right)^3 = \dfrac{(3^2)^3}{(2)^3} = \dfrac{3^6}{2^3} = \dfrac{729}{8}$. The rules for raising a power to a power and raising a product to a power were both used to simplify this expression.

REMEMBER THIS!

- To raise an exponent to another power, multiply the exponents: $(a^m)^n = a^{m \times n}$.

- To raise a product to a power, raise each base number and/or variable to that power: $(a^m b^n)^t = a^{m \times t} b^{n \times t}$.

- To raise a fraction to a power, raise both the numerator and denominator to that exponent and simplify the expression: $\left(\dfrac{a}{b}\right)^m = \dfrac{a^m}{b^m}$.

PRACTICE 3

Match each question in the left column with the correct answer choice from the right column. Answers and explanations are located at the end of the chapter.

10. $(8^3)^5 =$

    A. $512x^{12}$

11. $(8x^5)^3 =$

    B. 8^{15}

12. $(8^4)(8^2)^3 =$ C. 8^6

13. $\left(\dfrac{8^3}{8^2}\right)^6 =$ D. $512x^{15}$

14. $(8x^4)^3 =$ E. 8^{10}

Negative Exponents

Working with negative exponents can be a challenge. A common misconception is that the negative sign on the exponent makes the base number negative—not the case! A base expression raised to a negative exponent is equal to the *reciprocal* of the base raised to a positive exponent. To evaluate a negative exponent, first take the reciprocal of the base. Then make the exponent positive and evaluate. For example:

$$5^{-3} = \frac{1}{5^3} = \frac{1}{125}.$$

An exponent that is negative in the numerator will be positive in the denominator. In the same fashion, an exponent that is negative in the denominator will be positive in the numerator. Take a look at the following examples.

Simplify $\dfrac{2^{-3}}{4^{-2}}$. First rewrite the expression with positive exponents by taking the reciprocal of any base with a negative exponent. In this case, the expression becomes $\dfrac{4^2}{2^3}$. Notice that when the bases switched between the numerator and denominator, the signs of the exponents also switched. Now simplify by evaluating the exponents:

$$\frac{4^2}{2^3} = \frac{4 \times 4}{2 \times 2 \times 2} = \frac{16}{8} = 2.$$

Simplify $\dfrac{5^{-2} \times 2^2}{2^{-3}}$. First rewrite the expression with positive exponents by taking the reciprocal of any base with a negative exponent. The expression becomes $\dfrac{2^2 \times 2^3}{5^2}$. Multiply in the numerator by adding the exponents to get $\dfrac{2^5}{5^2}$. Simplify the expression by evaluating the exponents: $\dfrac{2^5}{5^2} = \dfrac{32}{25}.$

REMEMBER THIS!

To simplify an expression with negative exponents, remember that $a^{-m} = \dfrac{1}{a^m}.$

Try another example of a problem dealing with negative exponents and a variable. If $x^{-3} = \dfrac{1}{27}$, what is the value of x? Since 3^3 is equal to 27, then 3^{-3} is equal to $\dfrac{1}{3^3} = \dfrac{1}{27}$. Therefore, $x = 3$.

PRACTICE 4

Try the following set of problems to assess your understanding of negative exponents. Answers and explanations are located at the end of the chapter.

15. Simplify: $\dfrac{3^{-4}}{4^{-1}}$

16. Simplify: $\dfrac{6^{-2} \times 4^2}{6^2}$

17. If $x^{-5} = \dfrac{1}{32}$ what is the value of x^2?

Scientific Notation

A common application of exponents is **scientific notation**. Scientific notation is often used to write very large or very small numbers more efficiently. To write a number in scientific notation, place a decimal within the nonzero digits of the number to create a number between 1 and 10. Then multiply this number by a factor of 10, where the exponent of 10 is the number of places the decimal point has moved.

For example, to change the number 6,400,000 to scientific notation, write the nonzero digits as a number between 1 and 10 and drop the zeros. The number becomes 6.4. Then multiply this number by 10 raised to an exponent; the exponent is the number of places the decimal has to move to get between the 6 and the 4. By counting from the ones place of 6,400,000 to the space between 6 and 4, we find that the decimal moved six places to the left.

$$6,400,000$$
$$\underbrace{}$$
$$6 \text{ places}$$

Therefore, 6,400,000 written in scientific notation is equal to 6.4×10^6.

Because the number in the example above was greater than 1, the exponent of 10 in scientific notation was positive. If the number being converted is less than 1, the exponent of 10 will be negative. For instance, take the number 0.00000045 and follow the same procedure as above. Write the nonzero digits as a number between 1 and 10 and drop the zeros to get 4.5. Now multiply this value by 10 raised to a power, where the exponent is the total number of places that the decimal point moved. Since the decimal point must move seven places to the left to arrive at the original number, the exponent is −7.

$$0.\underbrace{00000045}_{7 \text{ places}}$$

Therefore, $0.00000045 = 4.5 \times 10^{-7}$.

You can also convert from scientific notation to standard notation. If converting 2.3×10^4 to standard notation, for example, write the first factor of 2.3 and then move the decimal four places to the right. Add zeros as placeholders where necessary. Thus, the number becomes 23,000 in standard notation.

Note that if the exponent were negative in scientific notation, the decimal would move that number of places to the left instead of the right. Remember that a negative exponent indicates a number less than 1. For example, $5.4 \times 10^{-3} = 0.0054$ in standard notation.

REMEMBER THIS!

To convert a number to **scientific notation**, first use the nonzero digits to make a number between 1 and 10. Then multiply by a factor of 10 to a power, where the power is the number of places the decimal moved. If the number is less than 1, the exponent is negative; if the number is greater than 1, the exponent is positive.

PRACTICE 5

Answer TRUE or FALSE for each of the following. Answers and explanations are located at the end of the chapter.

18. **T F**   The number 9,000,000 is written as 9.0×10^9 in scientific notation.

19. **T F**   The number 0.00086 is written as 8.6×10^{-4} in scientific notation.

20. **T F**   The number 6.5×10^5 is equal to 650,000 in standard notation.

ROOTS AND FRACTIONAL EXPONENTS

The study of roots and fractional exponents begins with the concept of **perfect squares**.

Perfect Squares

Perfect squares are numbers that result from multiplying two of the same integers together. Following are some examples:

$$1 \times 1 = 1$$
$$2 \times 2 = 4$$
$$3 \times 3 = 9$$
$$4 \times 4 = 16$$
$$5 \times 5 = 25$$

Therefore, the perfect squares listed above are 1, 4, 9, 16, and 25. Other perfect squares can be generated in the same way. In each of these cases, the pattern is the same: $1^2 = 1$, $2^2 = 4$, $3^2 = 9$, $4^2 = 16$, and $5^2 = 25$. The square of the integer is equal to the perfect square.

The symbol for a **square root** is $\sqrt{}$, known as the **radical sign**. The number under the radical sign is called the **radicand**.

Finding the square root of a number, or a radicand, is the opposite of finding the square of a number. To find the square root of a number, find the integer that you would multiply by itself to equal the number. For example, since $4^2 = 4 \times 4 = 16$, then $\sqrt{16} = 4$. Four is the square root of 16. In addition, since $10^2 = 10 \times 10 = 100$, then $\sqrt{100} = 10$. Ten is the square root of 100.

The root of a number can also be written as an exponent. However, when the root of a base number is involved, the exponent is in fraction form. For any square root, the fractional exponent is always $\frac{1}{2}$, where the root (or index) is 2 and the power is 1. Here are some examples:

$$25^{\frac{1}{2}} = \sqrt{25} = 5$$
$$81^{\frac{1}{2}} = \sqrt{81} = 9$$
$$169^{\frac{1}{2}} = \sqrt{169} = 13$$

Fractional exponents other than $\frac{1}{2}$ are also used. The numerator of the fraction is the **power** of the base number, and the denominator is the **root** of the base number. Because of this fact, fractional exponents can be written as $a^{\frac{x}{y}} = (\sqrt[y]{a})^x$. In the case of $4^{\frac{5}{2}}$, for instance, take the square root of 4 and then raise that result to the power of 5: $4^{\frac{5}{2}} = (\sqrt{4})^5 = 2^5 = 32$.

Square Roots That Are Not Perfect Squares

As you probably could predict, not all radicands are perfect squares. If the radicand is not the product of a number and itself, then the square root is irrational.

FLASHBACK

Revisit chapter 1 to review the different sets of numbers, including **irrational numbers**.

But just like fractions, most radicals can be expressed in a reduced, or simplified form, even if they are not perfect squares. To simplify radicals, look for the perfect square factors of the number in the radical. In other words, find the largest perfect square that divides evenly into the radicand without a remainder. Take, for example, the square root of 8, or $\sqrt{8}$. Since 8 is the product of 4 and 2, then $\sqrt{8} = \sqrt{4} \times \sqrt{2}$. Because the square root of 4 is equal to 2, this expression can be simplified to $2 \times \sqrt{2}$ or $2\sqrt{2}$. Four is the largest perfect square factor of 8, and simplifying this factor reduces the radical to simplest radical form.

For another example, simplify $\sqrt{54}$. Since the largest perfect square factor of 54 is 9, express $\sqrt{54}$ as $\sqrt{9} \times \sqrt{6}$. The square root of 9 is 3, so $\sqrt{54} = 3\sqrt{6}$.

An additional twist to simplifying radicals is when the problem involves a coefficient, or a number in front of the radical. In this situation, simplify the radicand as explained above and then multiply the coefficient by any number taken out of the radical. For example, take the expression $5\sqrt{44}$. Since the largest perfect square factor of 44 is 4, the expression becomes $5 \times \sqrt{4} \times \sqrt{11}$. The square root of 4 is 2, so the expression is $5 \times 2 \times \sqrt{11}$, which simplifies to $10\sqrt{11}$.

Always keep in mind that a radical is in simplest form if there are no perfect square factors contained in the radicand.

PRACTICE 6

Express each of the following in simplest form. Answers and explanations are located at the end of the chapter.

21. $\sqrt{144} =$

22. $289^{\frac{1}{2}} =$

23. $16^{\frac{3}{2}} =$

24. $\sqrt{72} =$

25. $2\sqrt{24} =$

Operations with Radicals

ADDITION AND SUBTRACTION

Adding and subtracting radicals is very much like adding and subtracting with fractions or variables—you need to have like terms. In the case of radicals, you must have the same radicand to add and subtract instead of a common denominator. If the terms being combined do not have the same radicand to begin with, simplify each term to see if a common radicand is possible. Then add only the terms with this common radicand.

Here is an example: $4\sqrt{3} + 5\sqrt{3} = 9\sqrt{3}$. Since each term has a common radicand of 3, add the coefficients of 4 and 5 and keep the radical the same.

Here's another example: $4\sqrt{2} - \sqrt{8} = 4\sqrt{2} - 2\sqrt{2} = 2\sqrt{2}$. Since the terms do not have the same radicand, the square root of 8 is reduced to $2\sqrt{2}$. Now subtract the coefficients and keep the radical to get an answer of $2\sqrt{2}$.

In this problem, $\sqrt{6} + 2\sqrt{11}$, these terms cannot be combined. Each term is in simplest form with no common radicand between them.

▒ **REMEMBER THIS!** ▒▒▒

To add or subtract radicals, be sure to have the same radicand for all terms. If the radicands are not the same and all are in simplest form, the radicals cannot be combined (e.g., $\sqrt{2} + \sqrt{5}$ cannot be combined).

MULTIPLICATION AND DIVISION

When multiplying and dividing radicals, no common radicand is necessary. Multiply (or divide) coefficients with coefficients and radicals with radicals. Use the examples below as a reference.

In this calculation, $2\sqrt{5} \times 3\sqrt{3} = 6\sqrt{15}$, the coefficients of 2 and 3 are multiplied to get a coefficient of 6. The radicands of 5 and 3 are multiplied to get a radicand of 15.

In this example, $\dfrac{15\sqrt{10}}{5\sqrt{2}} = 3\sqrt{5}$, because 15 divided by 5 is 3, the coefficient of the result is 3. Since 10 divided by 2 is 5, the radicand of the solution is 5.

Now let's look at $2\sqrt{16} \times 7\sqrt{9} = (2 \times 4) \times (7 \times 3) = 8 \times 21 = 168$. Since 16 and 9 are both perfect squares, each is converted to its square root and then multiplied by its coefficient. These two results are then multiplied together to get a final answer of 168.

An important thing to note at this point is that any radical in simplest form *cannot* be written with a radical in the denominator of a fraction. To take care of this, you need to do a procedure called **rationalizing the denominator**.

Take an example such as $\dfrac{3}{\sqrt{2}}$. To rationalize the denominator, multiply both the denominator and numerator by $\sqrt{2}$. When doing this, you are really just multiplying the fraction by 1. But performing this simple operation will take the radical out of the denominator by creating a perfect square within the radical sign: $\dfrac{3}{\sqrt{2}} \times \dfrac{\sqrt{2}}{\sqrt{2}} = \dfrac{3\sqrt{2}}{\sqrt{4}} = \dfrac{3\sqrt{2}}{2}$. Since there are no common factors between the coefficients of 3 and 2 and the denominator is rational, the expression is simplified.

Similarly, any radicand that is a fraction needs to be rationalized. In the radical $\sqrt{\dfrac{4}{3}}$, divide the fraction into numerator and denominator by placing each number under its own radical sign and simplifying: $\sqrt{\dfrac{4}{3}} = \dfrac{\sqrt{4}}{\sqrt{3}} = \dfrac{2}{\sqrt{3}}$. Notice that since 4 is a perfect square, the square root is an integer. Now rationalize the denominator by multiplying by $\frac{\sqrt{3}}{\sqrt{3}}: \frac{2}{\sqrt{3}} \times \frac{\sqrt{3}}{\sqrt{3}} = \frac{2\sqrt{3}}{3}$. This fraction is simplified.

REMEMBER THIS!

A radical is in simplified form if:

- there are no perfect square factors of the radicand other than 1.
- there are no fractions under the radical sign.
- there are no radicals in the denominator of any fraction.

PRACTICE 7

Complete each of the following with the best answer in simplest radical form. Answers and explanations are located at the end of the chapter.

26. The sum of $6\sqrt{5} + 2\sqrt{45}$ is _____.

27. The difference of $12\sqrt{6} - 10\sqrt{6}$ is _____.

28. The product of $2\sqrt{7} \times 12\sqrt{2}$ is _____.

29. The quotient $\frac{24\sqrt{6}}{8\sqrt{2}}$ is equal to _____.

30. The expression $\frac{7}{\sqrt{2}}$ written in simplest form is _____.

31. The expression $\sqrt{\dfrac{5}{6}}$ written in simplest form is _____.

SUMMARY

Here are five things about exponents, powers, and roots that you should take from this chapter:

1. Any nonzero base to the exponent of 1 is equal to itself; any nonzero base to the exponent of 0 is equal to 1.

2. When multiplying like bases, add the exponents; when dividing like bases, subtract the exponents.

3. Remember that radicals are in simplest form if they contain no perfect square factors, there are no fractions under the radical, and there are no radicals in the denominator of any fraction.

4. When adding and subtracting radicals, be sure to have the same radicand before combining. A common radicand is not necessary for multiplying and dividing.

5. Use scientific notation to express very large and very small numbers. This notation is always a number between 1 and 10 multiplied by an appropriate power of 10.

Here is a summary of the rules that govern exponents and radicals:

Exponent Rules

- $a^b \times a^c = a^{b+c}$
- $\dfrac{a^b}{a^c} = a^{b-c}$
- $(a^b)^c = a^{b \times c}$
- $(a^b)(c^b) = (a \times c)^b$
- $a^{-b} = \dfrac{1}{a^b}$

Radical Rules

- $\sqrt{ab} = \sqrt{a} \times \sqrt{b}$
- $\sqrt{\dfrac{a}{b}} = \dfrac{\sqrt{a}}{\sqrt{b}}$
- $\sqrt{a+b} \neq \sqrt{a} + \sqrt{b}$
- $\sqrt{a-b} \neq \sqrt{a} - \sqrt{b}$
- $\left(\sqrt{a}\right)^2 = a$
- $a^{\frac{1}{2}} = \sqrt{a}$
- $a^{\frac{b}{c}} = \sqrt[c]{a^b}$

Practice Answers and Explanations

1. **32**

2. **16**

3. **4**

4. **17**

$(-4)^2 + 5^0 = 16 + 1 = 17$

5. **108**

$2^2 \times 3^3 = 4 \times 27 = 108$

6. **False**

Subtract the exponents of 7 and 2 to get 6^5.

7. True

When multiplying and the bases are the same, add the exponents.

8. False

Since the bases are not the same, this problem has to be evaluated using the order of operations. The result is $32 \times 25 = 800$, which is not equal to 10^7.

9. True

Since the bases are the same, add the exponents in the numerator to get $\dfrac{5^8}{5^4}$. Subtract the exponents to complete the division: 5^4.

10. B

11. D

12. E

13. C

14. A

15. $\dfrac{4}{81}$

Since there are negative exponents, take the reciprocal of the bases and evaluate using positive exponents: $\dfrac{3^{-4}}{4^{-1}} = \dfrac{4^1}{3^4} = \dfrac{4}{81}$.

16. $\dfrac{1}{81}$

Take the reciprocal of the base with the negative exponent and evaluate using the positive exponents: $\dfrac{6^{-2} \times 4^2}{6^2} = \dfrac{4^2}{6^2 \times 6^2} = \dfrac{4^2}{6^4} = \dfrac{16}{1,296} = \dfrac{1}{81}$.

17. 4

Since $x^{-5} = \dfrac{1}{32}$, then $x^5 = 32$. Thus, $x = 2$ because $2^{-5} = \dfrac{1}{2^5} = \dfrac{1}{32}$. This question asks for x^2, so $2^2 = 4$.

18. False

The number $9,000,000$ is equal to 9.0×10^6.

19. True

20. True

21. 12

$12 \times 12 = 144$

22. 17

The radical $\sqrt{289} = 17$ since $17 \times 17 = 289$.

23. 64

With a fractional exponent, the numerator is the power and the denominator is the root. Thus, $16^{\frac{3}{2}} = (\sqrt{16})^3 = 4^3 = 64$.

24. $6\sqrt{2}$

Since $72 = 36 \times 2$, then $\sqrt{72} = \sqrt{36} \times \sqrt{2} = 6\sqrt{2}$.

25. $4\sqrt{6}$

Since $\sqrt{24} = \sqrt{4} \times \sqrt{6} = 2\sqrt{6}$, multiply 2 by $2\sqrt{6}$ to get $4\sqrt{6}$.

26. $12\sqrt{5}$

First convert $2\sqrt{45}$ into simplified form: $2\sqrt{45} = 2 \times \sqrt{9} \times \sqrt{5} = 2 \times 3 \times \sqrt{5} = 6\sqrt{5}$. Then combine like terms: $6\sqrt{5} + 6\sqrt{5} = 12\sqrt{5}$.

27. $2\sqrt{6}$

Because the terms already have the same radicand, subtract the coefficients and keep the radical the same: $12\sqrt{6} - 10\sqrt{6} = 2\sqrt{6}$.

28. $24\sqrt{14}$

Multiply the coefficients together and then the radicals to get the answer: $2\sqrt{7} \times 12\sqrt{2} = 2 \times 12 \times \sqrt{7} \times \sqrt{2} = 24\sqrt{14}$.

29. $3\sqrt{3}$

Divide coefficient by coefficient, radical by radical: $\dfrac{24\sqrt{6}}{8\sqrt{2}} = \dfrac{24}{8} \times \dfrac{\sqrt{6}}{\sqrt{2}} = 3\sqrt{3}.$

30. $\dfrac{7\sqrt{2}}{2}$

To express this in simplest form, multiply both the numerator and denominator by $\sqrt{2}$ so no radical is left in the denominator.

31. $\dfrac{\sqrt{30}}{6}$

First express the numerator and denominator as separate radicals: $\sqrt{\dfrac{5}{6}} = \dfrac{\sqrt{5}}{\sqrt{6}}$. Then multiply both the numerator and denominator by $\sqrt{6}$ so no radical is left in the denominator: $\dfrac{\sqrt{5}}{\sqrt{6}} \times \dfrac{\sqrt{6}}{\sqrt{6}} = \dfrac{\sqrt{30}}{6}.$

CHAPTER 7 TEST

Try the following questions to test your knowledge of powers, roots, and exponents. Assess your progress by using the complete answer explanations that follow the test. Turn back to the appropriate section(s) in the lesson portion of the chapter for more help and clarification of the key concepts.

1. $5^4 =$

   (A) 9

   (B) 20

   (C) 25

   (D) 125

   (E) 625

2. $13^0 - (-2)^3 =$

   (A) -7

   (B) 1

   (C) 7

   (D) 9

   (E) 21

3. The formula for the surface area of a cube is $SA = 6e^2$, where e represents the length of an edge. What is the surface area, in square inches, of a cube with an edge length of 5 inches?

   (A) 25

   (B) 31

   (C) 60

   (D) 125

   (E) 150

4. Multiply: $3^2 \times 2^3$

   (A) 6^5

   (B) 6^6

   (C) 81

   (D) 2^6

   (E) 72

5. Simplify: $(5^2)^3$

(A) 5^1

(B) 5^5

(C) 5^6

(D) 5^8

(E) 5^{12}

6. Simplify: $(2y^3)^5$

(A) $10y^8$

(B) $10y^{15}$

(C) $2y^8$

(D) $2y^{15}$

(E) $32y^{15}$

7. Simplify: $(6^2)(6^2)^4$

(A) 6^2

(B) 6^8

(C) 6^{10}

(D) 6^{12}

(E) 6^{16}

8. Simplify: $\left(\dfrac{4^8}{4^7}\right)^5$

(A) 4^5

(B) 4^6

(C) 4^{13}

(D) 4^{15}

(E) 4^{20}

9. Evaluate: $\dfrac{3^{-2}}{2^{-3}}$

   (A) $\dfrac{8}{9}$

   (B) $\dfrac{9}{8}$

   (C) 1

   (D) −1

   (E) $\dfrac{2}{3}$

10. Simplify: $\dfrac{5^2 \times 2^{-2}}{5^{-2}}$

   (A) $\dfrac{1}{4}$

   (B) $\dfrac{625}{4}$

   (C) $\dfrac{4}{625}$

   (D) 5

   (E) 4

11. If $x^{-3} = \dfrac{1}{27}$, then what is the value of x ?

   (A) 27

   (B) 9

   (C) 3

   (D) $\dfrac{1}{3}$

   (E) $\dfrac{1}{27}$

12. The distance between two planets in a solar system is 750,000,000 miles. What is this distance written in scientific notation?

   (A) 0.75×10^7

   (B) 7.5×10^7

   (C) 7.5×10^8

   (D) 0.75×10^6

   (E) 75.0×10^8

13. What is the value of 6.02×10^{-6} in standard notation?

    (A) 6,020,000
    (B) 602,000,000
    (C) 0.0000602
    (D) 0.00000602
    (E) 0.000000602

14. $25^{\frac{3}{2}} =$

    (A) 25
    (B) 37.5
    (C) 50
    (D) 125
    (E) 150

15. Express in simplest radical form: $\sqrt{48}$

    (A) $\sqrt{24}$
    (B) $4\sqrt{3}$
    (C) $3\sqrt{4}$
    (D) $2\sqrt{6}$
    (E) $6\sqrt{4}$

16. $(9\sqrt{81})^2 =$

    (A) 18
    (B) 81
    (C) 162
    (D) 1,458
    (E) 6,561

17. $\sqrt{28} + 3\sqrt{7} =$

    (A) $\sqrt{38}$

    (B) $7\sqrt{7}$

    (C) $3\sqrt{35}$

    (D) $4\sqrt{7}$

    (E) $5\sqrt{7}$

18. $(8\sqrt{3})(4\sqrt{2}) =$

    (A) $12\sqrt{5}$

    (B) 32

    (C) $32\sqrt{5}$

    (D) $32\sqrt{6}$

    (E) None of these

19. Express $\dfrac{11}{\sqrt{7}}$ in simplest radical form.

    (A) $\sqrt{4}$

    (B) $11\sqrt{7}$

    (C) $\dfrac{11\sqrt{7}}{7}$

    (D) $\dfrac{7}{\sqrt{7}}$

    (E) $\dfrac{11\sqrt{7}}{77}$

20. Express $\sqrt{\dfrac{12}{7}}$ in simplest radical form.

    (A) $12\sqrt{7}$

    (B) $7\sqrt{12}$

    (C) $\dfrac{12\sqrt{7}}{7}$

    (D) $\dfrac{84}{\sqrt{7}}$

    (E) $\dfrac{2\sqrt{21}}{7}$

Answers and Explanations

1. E

Use the base of 5 as a factor four times: $5^4 = 5 \times 5 \times 5 \times 5 = 625$.

2. D

Evaluate the exponents first and then subtract. Thus, $13^0 = 1$, and $(-2)^3 = (-2)(-2)(-2) = -8$. The expression becomes $1 - (-8) = 1 + 8 = 9$.

3. E

Substitute the given value of e into the formula $SA = 6e^2$: $SA = 6 \times 5^2$. Evaluate the exponents first, then multiply by 6: $SA = 6 \times 25 = 150$ square inches.

4. E

Evaluate the exponents first: $3^2 = 9$ and $2^3 = 8$. Then multiply: $9 \times 8 = 72$.

5. C

Since you are raising a power to another power, multiply the exponents to get 5^6.

6. E

Since you are raising a product to a power, raise each part of the base expression to the power of 5: $2^5 \times y^{3 \times 5} = 32y^{15}$.

7. C

First simplify the term in the second set of parentheses by multiplying the exponents to get 6^8. Since you are now multiplying like bases, add the exponents: $6^2 \times 6^8 = 6^{2+8} = 6^{10}$.

8. A

First raise the entire fraction to the power of 5 by multiplying the exponents. The expression becomes $\dfrac{4^{40}}{4^{35}}$. Then simplify the expression by subtracting the exponents to get 4^5. In this problem, you could also evaluate within the parentheses first by subtracting the exponents. The expression would become $(4^1)^5$, which also equals 4^5.

9. A

Because each of the bases has a negative exponent, take the reciprocal of each base and write each base with a positive exponent. The expression becomes $\dfrac{2^3}{3^2} = \dfrac{2 \times 2 \times 2}{3 \times 3} = \dfrac{8}{9}$.

10. B

Write the expression with positive exponents by taking the reciprocal of any bases with negative exponents. The expression becomes $\dfrac{5^2 \times 5^2}{2^2}$. Now simplify by multiplying out the numerator and denominator: $\dfrac{5^{2+2}}{2^2} = \dfrac{5^4}{2^2} = \dfrac{5 \times 5 \times 5 \times 5}{2 \times 2} = \dfrac{625}{4}$.

11. C

Because $3^3 = 27$, then $3^{-3} = \dfrac{1}{27}$. Therefore, $x = 3$.

12. C

First write the nonzero digits as a number between 1 and 10, or 7.5. Then multiply by a factor of 10 to a power that represents the number of places the decimal moved to get between the 7 and 5, which is eight places. The expression in scientific notation is 7.5×10^8.

13. D

Start by writing the first factor in the expression, which is 6.02. Then move the decimal point six places to the left because of the exponent −6. The standard notation is 0.00000602.

14. D

The exponent of $\dfrac{3}{2}$ indicates the cube of the square root of the base. In other words, the 3 in the numerator is a power, and the 2 in the denominator is the root. First find the square root of the base, which is 5. Then raise 5 to the third power: $5^3 = 5 \times 5 \times 5 = 125$.

15. B

The largest perfect square factor of 48 is 16. Therefore, the radical can be expressed as $\sqrt{16} \times \sqrt{3} = 4\sqrt{3}$.

16. E

Because 81 is a perfect square, simplify inside the parentheses first to get $(9 \times 9)^2 = 81^2 = 6{,}561$.

17. E

First simplify to see if there is a common radicand. Since $\sqrt{28} = \sqrt{4} \times \sqrt{7} = 2\sqrt{7}$, now combine the terms by adding the coefficients and keeping the common radicand: $2\sqrt{7} + 3\sqrt{7} = 5\sqrt{7}$.

18. D

Multiply the coefficients by coefficients and radicals by radicals. The expression becomes $8 \times 4 \times \sqrt{3} \times \sqrt{2} = 32\sqrt{6}$.

19. C

To rationalize the denominator, multiply the numerator and denominator by $\sqrt{7}$:
$\dfrac{11}{\sqrt{7}} \times \dfrac{\sqrt{7}}{\sqrt{7}} = \dfrac{11\sqrt{7}}{\sqrt{49}} = \dfrac{11\sqrt{7}}{7}$.

20. E

Write the numerator and denominator as separate radicals and then simplify by multiplying by $\sqrt{7}$: $\sqrt{\dfrac{12}{7}} = \dfrac{\sqrt{12}}{\sqrt{7}} \times \dfrac{\sqrt{7}}{\sqrt{7}} = \dfrac{\sqrt{84}}{\sqrt{49}} = \dfrac{\sqrt{4} \times \sqrt{21}}{7} = \dfrac{2\sqrt{21}}{7}$.

SECTION II

Geometry

Lines, Angles, and Polygons

Geometry is the area of math that deals with the properties, measurement, and relationships of points, lines, angles, surfaces, and solids. This chapter will explore the geometry elements of lines, angles, and polygons (especially triangles and quadrilaterals). Chapter 9 will cover advanced shapes—circles, solids, and combinations of multiple figures.

BASIC GEOMETRY ELEMENTS

Start off your study of geometry by learning some basic terms and definitions:

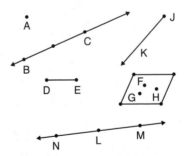

- **Point.** A point is a position in space. A point has no length or width. An example is point A in the figure above.

- **Line.** The shortest distance between two points determines a line. A line has no width and an infinite length. An example of a line is $\overleftrightarrow{BC}$.

- **Line segment.** A line segment is a piece of a line. A segment includes two points, called endpoints, and all the points in between. An example of a line segment is $\overline{DE}$.

- **Plane.** Any three noncollinear points (points that do not all lie on a single line) determine a plane. A plane has an infinite width and length. An example is plane *FGH*.

- **Ray.** A ray is one-half of a line. A ray includes an endpoint and all the collinear points on one side of this endpoint. An example of a ray is $\overrightarrow{JK}$ or $\overrightarrow{LM}$ (which is one-half of the line $\overleftrightarrow{NM}$).

When lines, line segments, or planes are named, the order of the points does not matter. In the above definitions, segment $\overline{DE}$ could also be named $\overline{ED}$, line $\overleftrightarrow{BC}$ could also be named $\overleftrightarrow{CB}$, and plane *FGH* could also be named *GFH* or other variations.

When a ray is named, however, the endpoint must be named first. In the previous figure, there is a ray $\overrightarrow{LM}$ and a different ray $\overrightarrow{LN}$. Both have the same starting point of *L*, but all their other points are different, as they extend on opposing sides of the line $\overleftrightarrow{NM}$.

By definition, line segments, lines, planes, and rays all have an infinite number of points.

Two geometric figures are **congruent** if each has the same measure. This relationship can apply to several geometric figures. The symbol for congruence is ≅.

A segment **bisector** is a line or line segment that divides the segment into two congruent segments.

The **midpoint** of a segment is the point where the bisector intersects the segment.

PRACTICE 1

Answer TRUE or FALSE for the following questions. Answers and explanations are located at the end of the chapter.

1. **T**　**F**　When a line segment is named, the order of the points named does not matter.

2. **T**　**F**　When a ray is named, the order of the points named does not matter.

3. **T**　**F**　A line segment has an infinite number of points.

4. **T**　**F**　If the length of segment $\overline{BC}$ is 14 cm and *B* is the midpoint of segment $\overline{AC}$, then the measure of segment $\overline{AC}$ is 7 cm.

Special Lines

There are two kinds of special lines:

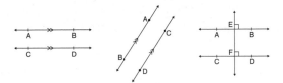

- **Parallel lines.** Lines in the same plane that do not intersect are parallel. There is a special symbol for parallel lines. In the figure above, lines $\overleftrightarrow{AB}$ and $\overleftrightarrow{CD}$ are parallel, as shown by $AB \parallel CD$. Line segments, rays, and planes can also be parallel.

- **Perpendicular lines.** Lines in the same plane that intersect at one point and form four 90° angles are perpendicular. In the figure above, line $\overleftrightarrow{EF}$ is perpendicular to both of the lines $\overleftrightarrow{AB}$ and $\overleftrightarrow{CD}$. This is shown by the symbols $\overleftrightarrow{EF} \perp \overleftrightarrow{AB}$ and $\overleftrightarrow{EF} \perp \overleftrightarrow{CD}$. Line segments, rays, and planes can also be perpendicular.

PRACTICE 2

Use the figure below to fill in each of the following blanks with either the word *parallel* or the word *perpendicular*. Answers and explanations are located at the end of the chapter.

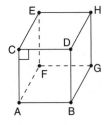

5. Segments $\overline{CD}$ and $\overline{EH}$ are _____.

6. Segments $\overline{CD}$ and $\overline{AC}$ are _____.

7. Segments $\overline{CD}$ and $\overline{FG}$ are _____.

ANGLES

An **angle** is defined by two distinct rays that have the same endpoint. The common endpoint the rays share is called the **vertex** of the angle. When an angle is named, you must use the symbol for an angle ($\angle$), and you must put the vertex of the angle in the middle of the three letters. The following figure has several angles, which are numbered for clarity.

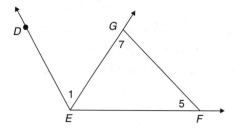

$\angle 1$ can be named $\angle DEG$ or $\angle GED$. $\angle 5$ can be named $\angle EFG$ or $\angle GFE$. $\angle 7$ can be named $\angle FGE$ or $\angle EGF$. Note that $\angle 5$ and $\angle 7$ use the same three points but name different angles, based on the vertex point.

An **angle bisector** is a ray in the interior of the angle that divides the angle into two congruent angles with the same measure. In the following figure, ray $\overline{BD}$ is an angle bisector: $\angle ABD \cong \angle DBC$. Note that congruent angles are indicated by tick marks in the figure.

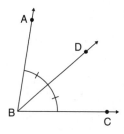

ANGLE CLASSIFICATION

Angles are classified according to their degree measure:

- **Acute angle.** An acute angle is one whose measure is greater than 0° and less than 90°.

- **Right angle.** A right angle is one that measures exactly 90°. As shown in the following figure, right angles are designated by a small box in the interior at the vertex.

- **Obtuse angle.** An obtuse angle is one whose measure is greater than 90° and less than 180°.

- **Straight angle.** A straight angle is one that measures exactly 180°.

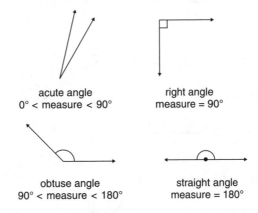

acute angle
0° < measure < 90°

right angle
measure = 90°

obtuse angle
90° < measure < 180°

straight angle
measure = 180°

SPECIAL ANGLE PAIR RELATIONSHIPS

- **Complementary angles.** Complementary angles are any two angles whose combined measures equal 90°. It is not necessary for these angles to share a side.

- **Supplementary angles.** Supplementary angles are any two angles whose combined measures equal 180°. It is not necessary for these angles to share a side.

- **Linear pair.** A linear pair consists of two supplementary angles that share a common side and no common interior points. They form a straight angle (a line).

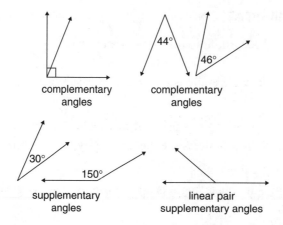

<table>
<tr><td>complementary
angles</td><td>complementary
angles</td></tr>
<tr><td>supplementary
angles</td><td>linear pair
supplementary angles</td></tr>
</table>

When a line cuts through two parallel lines, it is called a **transversal**, and eight angles are formed. These angles are numbered 1 through 8 in the following figures for clarity:

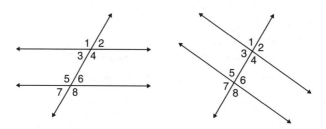

From this condition, several types of angles are defined:

- **Vertical angles.** Formed when two lines intersect, they are two angles that share a common vertex but share no common sides. In the figures above, $\angle 1$ and $\angle 4$, $\angle 2$ and $\angle 3$, $\angle 5$ and $\angle 8$, and $\angle 6$ and $\angle 7$ are all examples of vertical angle pairs.

- **Corresponding angles.** These are two angles on the same side of the transversal, but one is in the interior of the parallel lines and one is in the exterior of the parallel lines. In the figures above, $\angle 1$ and $\angle 5$, $\angle 2$ and $\angle 6$, $\angle 3$ and $\angle 7$, and $\angle 4$ and $\angle 8$ are all examples of corresponding angle pairs.

- **Alternate interior angles.** These are two angles on different sides of the transversal, both in the interior of the parallel lines. In the figures above, $\angle 3$ and $\angle 6$ and $\angle 4$ and $\angle 5$ are the alternate interior angle pairs.

- **Alternate exterior angles.** These are two angles on different sides of the transversal, both on the exterior of the parallel lines. In the figures above, $\angle 1$ and $\angle 8$ and $\angle 2$ and $\angle 7$ are the alternate exterior angle pairs.

Note that in the parallel line figures, there are also several examples of linear pairs: $\angle 1$ and $\angle 2$, $\angle 2$ and $\angle 4$, $\angle 7$ and $\angle 8$, and $\angle 5$ and $\angle 7$, among others.

REMEMBER THIS!

- When a line (called a **transversal**) cuts through two parallel lines,
- **vertical angles** are congruent.
- **corresponding angles** are congruent.
- **alternate interior angles** are congruent.
- **alternate exterior angles** are congruent.

In fact, if you study the first figure, you will realize that there are actually only two distinct angle measures in the figure. As long as the transversal is not perpendicular to the parallel lines, four acute angles and four obtuse angles are formed. All of the acute angles are congruent, and all of the obtuse angles are congruent. In addition, when any one of the acute angles is paired with any one of the obtuse angles, they form a supplementary pair. If the transversal is perpendicular to the parallel lines, then all eight angles are congruent and measure 90°.

PRACTICE 3

Using the figure and the word bank below, fill in the blanks with the names of the special pair of angles. Answers and explanations are located at the end of the chapter.

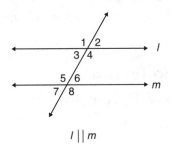

$l \parallel m$

complementary	supplementary	vertical
corresponding	alternate interior	alternate exterior

8. ∠5 and ∠8 are _____ angles.

9. ∠8 and ∠6 are _____ angles.

10. ∠7 and ∠3 are _____ angles.

11. ∠4 and ∠6 are _____ angles.

12. ∠4 and ∠5 are _____ angles.

13. ∠7 and ∠2 are _____ angles.

14. ∠1 and ∠2 are _____ angles.

Using the figure above, if the measure of ∠1 = 132°, give the following angle measures:

15. The measure of ∠5 is:

16. The measure of ∠6 is:

17. The measure of ∠7 is:

18. The measure of ∠8 is:

POLYGONS

Polygons are closed geometric figures composed of line segments and angles that are all in the same plane. Polygons have different names, based on the number of sides:

- A **triangle** is a three-sided polygon.
- A **quadrilateral** is a four-sided polygon.
- A **pentagon** is a five-sided polygon.
- A **hexagon** is a six-sided polygon.
- An **octagon** is an eight-sided polygon.

Perimeter

The **perimeter** is the distance around the outside of a polygon. Some real-world applications that require finding the perimeter of a polygon are fencing a yard or framing a picture. To find the perimeter of a polygon, add together the lengths of all its sides. For example, the perimeter of the following quadrilateral is $21 + 8 + 5 + 12 = 46$ cm.

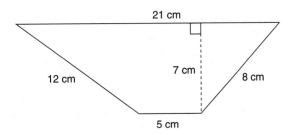

Notice that the height of the quadrilateral (7 cm) is indicated on the figure. However, this fact is *not* needed to calculate the perimeter.

REMEMBER THIS!

- **Squares** are quadrilaterals that have four congruent sides.
- **Parallelograms** are quadrilaterals that have two pairs of congruent sides.
- A **rectangle** is a parallelogram.
- The perimeter of a square with side s is given by the formula $P = 4s$.
- The perimeter of a parallelogram with sides y and z is given by the formula $P = 2y + 2z$.

PRACTICE 4

Repetition is the key to mastery! Try these questions concerning finding perimeters. Answers and explanations are located at the end of the chapter.

19. Find the perimeter of the following triangle:

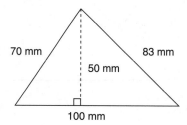

20. What is the perimeter of a square with a side length of 16 m?

21. Find the perimeter of the following parallelogram:

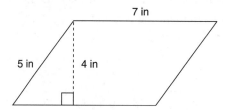

Area

The **area** of a polygon is the number of square units needed to cover the polygon. Some real-world applications that require finding the area of a polygon include carpeting or tiling a floor and painting or wallpapering walls. Area is calculated by multiplying two quantities, so an area is always given in square units. To use the formulas to calculate area, you need to know how to recognize and find the height of a polygon.

The **height** of a polygon is the length of the segment that is perpendicular to a side of the polygon called the **base**. Study the following figures to recognize the height of different polygons.

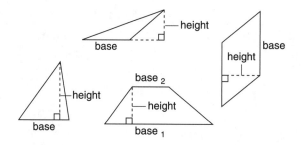

To distinguish the height from a side of the polygon, the figure usually shows the height as a dotted line. Sometimes, as in rectangles and squares, the height is also one of the sides.

Below are the formulas used to find the area of common polygons. Each polygon will also be discussed at greater length later in this chapter.

Area of Common Polygons

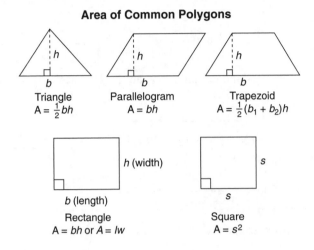

Triangle
$A = \frac{1}{2}bh$

Parallelogram
$A = bh$

Trapezoid
$A = \frac{1}{2}(b_1 + b_2)h$

Rectangle
$A = bh$ or $A = lw$

Square
$A = s^2$

To find the area of a polygon, substitute the given lengths into the formula and simplify. The units for area are always square units.

Use the following figure of a triangle and a parallelogram to find the respective areas.

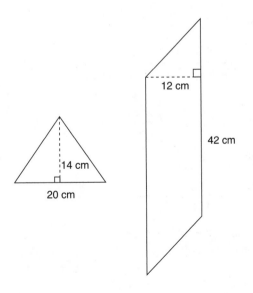

To find the area of the triangle shown above, substitute 14 cm for the height (the length of the segment perpendicular to the base) and substitute 20 cm for the base. Use the formula for the area of a triangle, that is $A = \frac{1}{2}bh$. The area is $\frac{1}{2} \times 20$ cm $\times$ 14 cm = 140 cm^2.

To find the area of the parallelogram, use the formula $A = bh$: that is $A = 42$ cm $\times$ 12 cm = 504 cm^2.

PRACTICE 5

Fill in the blanks. Answers and explanations are located at the end of the chapter.

22. Area is measured in _____ units.

23. The area is the number of square units it takes to _____ a polygon.

24. The area of a triangle is _____ times _____ times _____.

Use the bank of answers to list the areas for the figures below.

510 yd²   450 yd²   48 cm²   96 cm²

18 in²   81 m²   80 in²   160 in²

25.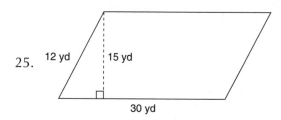

26.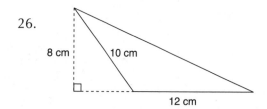

27.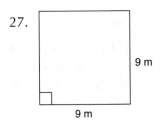

28.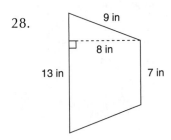

Angle Measure

The sum of the interior angles of a polygon is $180(n - 2)$, where n is the number of sides in the polygon. For example, how do you find the sum of the interior angles of a pentagon? Since a pentagon has five sides, $n = 5$. So the angles in a pentagon add up to $180(5 - 2) = 180(3) = 540°$.

PRACTICE 6

Try solving these two quick problems to solidify your understanding of angle measures of polygons. Answers and explanations are located at the end of the chapter.

29. What is the sum of the interior angles of an octagon?

30. Three angles of a quadrilateral are 48°, 144°, and 96°. What is the measure of the fourth angle?

Triangles

The triangle is the most common geometric figure used on the GMAT. A triangle is a closed geometric figure that has three sides and three angles. Triangles are classified according to their angles and their side lengths. Triangles are classified according to their angles as follows:

- An **acute** triangle has three acute angles.
- An **obtuse** triangle has exactly one obtuse angle and two acute angles.
- A **right** triangle has exactly one right angle and two acute angles.

Triangles are classified according to their sides as follows:

- A **scalene** triangle has three sides of different length.
- An **isosceles** triangle has two sides of the same length. This triangle also has two angles with the same measure—the angles opposite the two equal sides.
- An **equilateral** triangle has all three sides of the same length. This triangle also has three congruent angles, each with a measure of 60°.

Thus, every triangle can be classified in two ways, either by angles or by sides. Below are some examples of triangles and their classifications.

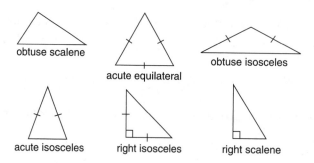

obtuse scalene

acute equilateral

obtuse isosceles

acute isosceles

right isosceles

right scalene

THE ANGLES OF A TRIANGLE

Some significant facts about triangles are important to understand when you perform operations with angles.

REMEMBER THIS!

- The sum of the measures of the angles in a triangle is 180°.

- The measure of an exterior angle to a triangle is equal to the sum of the two remote interior angles of the triangle.

- In a right triangle, the two acute angles are complementary; that is, the sum of the measures of these angles is equal to 90°.

In the following figure, $\triangle ABC$ is a right triangle. Therefore, $\angle BAC$ and $\angle ACB$ are complementary. The measure of $\angle ACB = 90 - 44 = 46°$. In addition, the measure of $\angle ACD$, which is an exterior angle to $\triangle ABC$, is equal to the sum of $\angle CAB$ and $\angle ABC$, the two remote interior angles. The measure of $\angle ACD = 90 + 44 = 134°$. You may also notice that $\angle ACD$ and $\angle BCA$ form a linear pair; therefore, the sum of their angle measures is 180°.

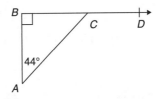

THE SIDES OF A TRIANGLE

The sum of the lengths of any two sides of a triangle must be greater than the length of the third side.

You may be given three side lengths and then asked whether it is possible for these side lengths to form a triangle. Test the sum of each possible pair to be sure that this sum exceeds the length of the other side. For example, to determine whether 4, 7, and 12 can be the sides of a triangle, check the sum of each pair of side lengths: 4 + 7 = 11, which is not greater than 12. Thus this set of lengths cannot represent the sides of a triangle. However, 4, 4, and 7 can be the sides of a triangle. Test the sides: 4 + 4 = 8, which is greater than 7; the other two tests would both be 7 + 4 = 11, which is greater than 4.

Likewise, if you are given two side lengths of a triangle, the length of the third side must be less than the sum of the two given side lengths and larger than the difference of the two side lengths. For example, if two sides of a triangle are given as 14 and 21, the other side must be between (21 − 14) and (14 + 21). Using x to represent the length of the third side, $7 < x < 35$.

REMEMBER THIS!

The length of a side of a triangle is always proportional to the measure of the angle opposite it. For example, in a triangle with angle measurements of 100°, 50°, and 30°, the side opposite the 100° angle will be the longest, the side opposite the 30° angle will be the shortest, and the side opposite the 50° angle will be in between.

PRACTICE 7

Repetition is the key to mastery! Try these problems concerning triangles. Answers and explanations are located at the end of the chapter.

31. A triangle has angles that measure 85°, 50°, and 45°. What is the classification of this triangle?

32. The measures of two of the angles in a triangle are 35° and 35°. What is the measure of the third angle?

33. Given the triangle below with angle measures as shown, what is the measure of $\angle BCD$?

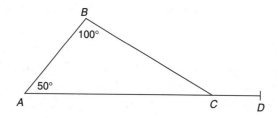

34. Two sides of a triangle measure 3 cm and 7 cm. What are the possible measures of the third side?

THE PYTHAGOREAN THEOREM

Right triangles are particularly common on the GMAT, and one of the most widely used theorems in mathematics—the **Pythagorean theorem**—is based upon right triangles.

- The **hypotenuse** of a right triangle is the side that is opposite the right angle.

- The **legs** of a right triangle are the sides that make up the right angle.

The Pythagorean theorem states that in every right triangle, the sum of the squares of the legs is equal to the square of the hypotenuse. This theorem is commonly written as follows, where a and b are the lengths of the legs of the right triangle and c is the length of the hypotenuse:

$$a^2 + b^2 = c^2$$

The converse of the Pythagorean theorem is also true: if a triangle has sides whose lengths follow the relationship $a^2 + b^2 = c^2$, then the triangle is a right triangle.

The Pythagorean theorem can be used to find the missing length of a side of a triangle when any two of the lengths are known. For example, given that a right triangle has legs with a length of 12 mm and 5 mm, you can find the length of the hypotenuse, c, by using the theorem $a^2 + b^2 = c^2$. Substitute 12 and 5 for a and b to get $144 + 25 = c^2$, or $169 = c^2$. The length of the hypotenuse is the square root of 169, or 13 mm.

FLASHBACK

Square roots were covered in chapter 7: Powers and Roots.

The converse of the theorem provides a convenient way to test whether a triangle is a right triangle. For example, if you are given that a triangle has sides of 5 in, 8 in, and 13 in, you can be assured that the triangle is *not* a right triangle because $5^2 + 8^2 \neq 13^2$—that is, $25 + 64 = 89$, not 169. However, a triangle with sides of 3 cm, 4 cm, and 5 cm *is* a right triangle because $3^2 + 4^2 = 5^2$—that is, $9 + 16 = 25$.

PRACTICE 8

Try these problems based on the Pythagorean theorem. To master mathematics, practice is the only route to success! Answer TRUE or FALSE to the following statements. Answers and explanations are located at the end of the chapter.

35. **T F** A triangle with sides of 7, 10, and 17 is a right triangle.

36. **T F** A triangle with sides of 9, 12, and 15 is a right triangle.

37. **T F** If the two legs of a right triangle are 10 and 24, then the hypotenuse is 26.

38. **T F** If one leg of a right triangle is 3 and the hypotenuse of the right triangle is 5, then the other leg is $\sqrt{34}$, or 5.83.

SPECIAL RIGHT TRIANGLES

The Pythagorean theorem is useful but can be time-consuming, especially without a calculator. To save time and reduce the risk of arithmetic errors, it's handy to memorize a few common right triangles. Memorize the following ratios (also known as "Pythagorean triples") before taking the GMAT:

- 3:4:5
- 5:12:13
- 8:15:17
- 7:24:25
- 9:40:41

Multiplying each side of any of these right triangles by a constant produces another right triangle. For example, multiplying each side of a 7:24:25 right triangle by 2 produces a 14:48:50 triangle, which is also a right triangle. This property of right triangles frequently allows you solve right triangle questions quickly and avoid the Pythagorean theorem altogether.

For example, if the hypotenuse of a right triangle is 39 and one of the legs is 15, what is the length of the other leg? You could solve for the second leg by using the Pythagorean theorem:

$$15^2 + x^2 = 39^2$$
$$x^2 = 1{,}521 - 225$$
$$x^2 = 1{,}296$$
$$x = \sqrt{1{,}296}$$
$$x = 36$$

But since the Quantitative section of the GMAT doesn't allow the use of a calculator, working with those exponents and radicals would take a lot of time. Much faster is to notice that a 5:12:13 triangle multiplied by 3 produces a 15:36:39 triangle. Therefore, in a right triangle with a hypotenuse of length 39 and one leg of length 15, the length of the other leg must be 36.

The GMAT often features two other types of right triangles with special angle measurements: 30-60-90 triangles and 45-45-90 triangles. In these triangles, the relationships of the side lengths are as follows:

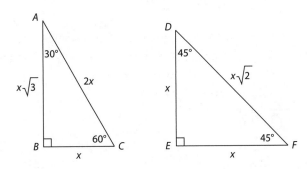

Knowing these two special triangles will allow you to solve for missing measurements quickly. For example, in a 30-60-90 triangle whose hypotenuse equals 4, what is the length of the other two sides? In this case, $2x = 4$, so $x = 2$. The leg opposite the 30 degree angle has a length of 2. The leg opposite the 60 degree angle has a length of $x\sqrt{3} = 2\sqrt{3}$.

PRACTICE 9

Mastering special right triangles will save you lots of time on the GMAT. Increase your fluency now by solving for the side length shown with a question mark in each of the figures below. Answers and explanations are located at the end of the chapter.

39.

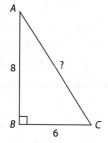

40.

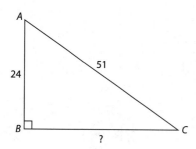

41.

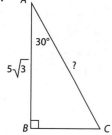

42.

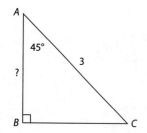

REMEMBER THIS!

- The Pythagorean theorem applies only to right triangles.

- The Pythagorean theorem is $a^2 + b^2 = c^2$, where c is the length of the hypotenuse and a and b are the lengths of the legs.

- On the GMAT, you can often bypass the Pythagorean theorem by knowing the common Pythagorean triples and the side-length ratios of 30-60-90 and 45-45-90 triangles.

Quadrilaterals

Quadrilaterals are four-sided polygons. There are two major classifications of common quadrilaterals:

- **Trapezoid.** A trapezoid is a quadrilateral with exactly one pair of parallel sides. Examples below are trapezoid *ABCD* and trapezoid *EFGH*.

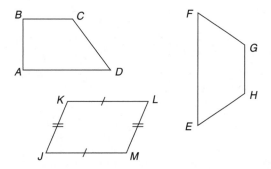

- **Parallelogram.** A parallelogram is a quadrilateral with two pairs of parallel sides. An example above is parallelogram *JKLM*.

For every quadrilateral, the sum of the measures of the angles is 360°. In a parallelogram, both pairs of opposite sides are parallel and congruent. Opposite angles are also congruent.

Trapezoids and parallelograms can be further classified into subcategories.

An **isosceles trapezoid** is a trapezoid with nonparallel sides that are equal in length. Examples are trapezoids *PQRS* and *WXYZ*, as shown in the following figure.

Because the nonparallel sides are congruent, there are two pairs of congruent angles in an isosceles trapezoid. In addition, an isosceles trapezoid has *congruent* diagonals.

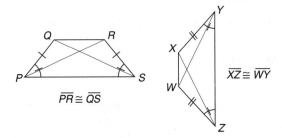

A **rectangle** is a parallelogram with four right angles, as shown in rectangles *LMNO* and *STUV* in the following figure. Like all parallelograms, rectangles have opposite sides and opposite angles that are congruent. In addition, the diagonals are *congruent*.

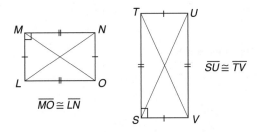

A **rhombus** is a parallelogram with four congruent sides, as shown in rhombuses *ABCD* and *WXYZ* in the following figure. Like all parallelograms, rhombuses have opposite sides and opposite angles that are congruent. In addition, the diagonals are *perpendicular*.

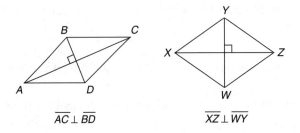

A **square** is both a rhombus and a rectangle. Therefore, it is a parallelogram with four 90° angles, and all sides are congruent. In addition, the diagonals of a square are both *congruent* and *perpendicular*. Square *JKLM* is shown below.

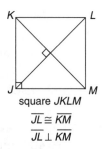

square *JKLM*

$\overline{JL} \cong \overline{KM}$

$\overline{JL} \perp \overline{KM}$

The following tree summarizes the relationships among the different classifications of special quadrilaterals. The characteristics are listed under each heading. All polygons lower in the tree share the characteristics of the polygons above them.

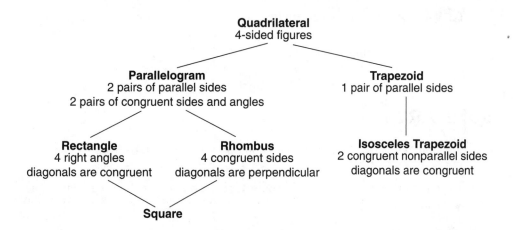

PRACTICE 10

For the following problems, match the description with the most specific classification from the word bank. Answers and explanations are located at the end of the chapter.

parallelogram   trapezoid   rectangle   square   rhombus

43. This quadrilateral has four right angles, four congruent sides, and diagonals that are both perpendicular and congruent.

44. This quadrilateral has two pairs of parallel sides.

45. This quadrilateral has four right angles and congruent diagonals.

46. This quadrilateral has two pairs of parallel sides, four congruent sides, and perpendicular diagonals.

47. This quadrilateral has four sides with exactly one pair of parallel sides.

Answer TRUE or FALSE for the following statements about quadrilaterals:

48. **T   F**   If one of the angles in a parallelogram measures 60°, the measures of the other angles are 60°, 40°, and 40°.

49. **T   F**   The four angles in all rhombuses measure 90°.

50. **T   F**   All rectangles are rhombuses.

51. **T   F**   All squares are rectangles.

52. **T   F**   All rhombuses are squares.

SUMMARY

In conclusion, here are 20 things about geometry you should take from this chapter:

1. The basic elements of geometric figures are the point, line, line segment, plane, ray, and angle.

2. Angles are classified as acute, obtuse, right, or straight.

3. Complementary angles sum to 90°; supplementary angles sum to 180°.

4. Special congruent angle pairs are formed when a transversal line cuts two parallel lines.

5. The special congruent angle pairs are corresponding, vertical, alternate interior, and alternate exterior angles.

6. Polygons are named according to the number of sides.

7. The perimeter of a polygon is the sum of its sides.

8. The interior angles in a polygon add up to $180(n - 2)$, where n is the number of sides in the polygon.

9. Triangles are classified in two ways, by sides and by angles.

10. The sum of the degree measures of the angles in a triangle is 180°.

11. The sum of the measures of any two sides of a triangle must be larger than the measure of the third side.

12. In a triangle, longer sides are always opposite larger angles and vice versa.

13. The area of a triangle equals $\frac{1}{2} \times$ base $\times$ height.

14. The Pythagorean theorem is $a^2 + b^2 = c^2$, where c is the length of the hypotenuse and a and b are the lengths of the legs.

15. Some common right triangles have side lengths in the ratios 3:4:5, 5:12:13, 8:15:17, 7:24:25, and 9:40:41. Multiplying any of these "Pythagorean triples" by a constant produces another right triangle.

16. In a 30-60-90 triangle, the ratio of side lengths is $x{:}x\sqrt{3}{:}2x$.

17. In a 45-45-90 triangle, the ratio of side lengths is $x{:}x{:}x\sqrt{2}$.

18. Quadrilaterals are classified into two major groups: parallelograms and trapezoids.

19. Parallelograms are classified into rectangles and rhombuses; the square fits into both of these categories.

20. The sum of the measures of the interior angles in a quadrilateral is 360°.

Practice Answers and Explanations

1. True

2. False

When you name a ray, the endpoint must be named first.

3. True

Even though a line segment is of a finite length, it contains an infinite number of points, since a point by definition has no length or width.

4. False

You are given that B is the midpoint of segment $\overline{AC}$. This means that segment $\overline{AC}$ is twice the length of either segment $\overline{AB}$ or $\overline{BC}$. You are told that the measure of segment $\overline{BC} = 14$ cm, so the measure of $\overline{AC} = 2 \times 14 = 28$ cm.

5. Parallel

These segments are in the same plane (the top face) and do not intersect.

6. Perpendicular

These segments intersect to form a right angle.

7. Parallel

These line segments are parallel in the plane that cuts diagonally through the solid.

8. Vertical

Vertical angles are formed when two lines intersect. They share a common vertex but are nonadjacent.

9. Supplementary

Two angles whose combined measure is 180° are supplementary angles. These angles are also linear angles and are always supplementary because together they form a straight line whose measure is 180°.

10. Corresponding

These angles are congruent angles on the same side of the transversal; one is in the interior, and the other is in the exterior of the parallel lines. This, by definition, is a pair of corresponding angles.

11. Supplementary

When two parallel lines are cut by a transversal line, any one of the acute angles and any one of the obtuse angles form a supplementary pair. In the figure, $\angle 4$ is an obtuse angle, and $\angle 6$ is an acute angle.

12. Alternate interior

These angles are both in the interior of the parallel lines and are on opposite sides of the transversal line. This pair of congruent angles is, by definition, alternate interior angles. These angles are therefore congruent.

13. Alternate exterior

These angles are both in the exterior of the parallel lines, and they are on opposite sides of the transversal line. This pair of congruent angles is, by definition, alternate exterior angles. These angles are therefore congruent.

14. Supplementary

Supplementary angles are a pair of angles whose combined measure is $180°$. These angles are also linear angles and are always supplementary because together they form a straight line whose measure is $180°$.

15. 132°

$\angle 5$ and $\angle 1$ are corresponding angles. They are congruent; thus, their measures are equal.

16. 48°

$\angle 6$ and $\angle 5$ are supplementary; they form a linear pair. Thus, $180 - 132 = 48°$.

17. 48°

$\angle 1$ and $\angle 8$ are alternate exterior angles and, therefore, congruent. $\angle 8$ and $\angle 7$ are supplementary.

18. 132°

One relationship you can use is that $\angle 5$ and $\angle 8$ are vertical angles. They are congruent and thus have the same measure. $\angle 1$ and $\angle 8$ are also alternate exterior angles and are therefore congruent.

19. 253 mm

The perimeter of a polygon equals the sum of its sides. $70 + 83 + 100 = 153 + 100 = 253$.

20. 64 m

The sides of a square are all equal. Hence, the perimeter is $16 \times 4 = 64$.

21. 24 in

In a parallelogram, the opposite sides are equal. Hence, the perimeter is $(2 \times 5) + (2 \times 7) = 10 + 14 = 24$.

22. Square

23. Cover

24. One-half × base × height

The formula for the area of a triangle is $A = \dfrac{1}{2}bh$.

25. 450 yd^2

The formula for the area of a parallelogram is base times height. Here, 15 is the height with a base of 30, and $30 \times 15 = 450$.

26. 48 cm^2

In this triangle, the height is 8 and the base is 12. The area is $\dfrac{1}{2} \times 12 \times 8 = 6 \times 8 = 48$.

27. 81 m^2

The area of a square is equal to the square of the side length. Here, $9^2 = 81$.

28. 80 in^2

The area formula for a trapezoid is $A = \dfrac{1}{2}(b_1 + b_2)h$. Plugging in the values from the figure yields $A = \dfrac{1}{2}(13 + 7)(8) = 4 \times 20 = 80$.

29. 1,080°

The sum of the angles of an n-sided polygon is $180(n - 2)$. An octagon has 8 sides, so its angles add up to $180(8 - 2) = 180(6) = 1,080°$.

30. 72°

The angles of a quadrilateral add up to $360°$. Thus, $360 - 48 - 144 - 96 = 360 - 240 - 48 = 120 - 48 = 72$.

31. Acute scalene

All of the angles in this triangle measure less than 90°, so it is an acute triangle. None of the angles have equal measure; therefore, none of the sides are of equal length, so the triangle is scalene. The classification is acute scalene.

32. 110°

The sum of the angles in a triangle is equal to 180°. Thus, $180 - 35 - 35 = 110°$.

33. 150°

The measure of the exterior angle $\angle BCD$ is equal to the sum of the two remote interior angles: $100 + 50 = 150°$.

34. Greater than 4 cm and less than 10 cm

The third side is between the sum and the difference of the two given side measures. If x represents the third side length, then $(7 - 3) < x < (7 + 3)$, or $4 < x < 10$.

35. False

$$7^2 + 10^2 \neq 17^2$$

36. True

$$9^2 + 12^2 = 15^2.$$

37. True

$$10^2 + 24^2 = 26^2.$$

38. False

$$3^2 + b^2 = 5^2$$

$$9 + b^2 = 25$$

$$b^2 = 16$$

$$b = 4$$

39. 10

This is a 3:4:5 triangle multiplied by 2: $3 \times 2 = 6$, $4 \times 2 = 8$, and $5 \times 2 = 10$.

40. 45

This is an 8:15:17 triangle multiplied by 3: $8 \times 3 = 24$, $17 \times 3 = 51$, and so the final side is $15 \times 3 = 45$.

41. 10

This is a 30-60-90 triangle. Since the side opposite the 60° angle is $5\sqrt{3}$, the side opposite the 30° angle must be 5, and the hypotenuse is $2 \times 5 = 10$.

42. $\dfrac{3\sqrt{2}}{2}$

This is a 45-45-90 triangle. Since the ratios of the side lengths are $x{:}x{:}x\sqrt{2}$ and the hypotenuse is 3, it must be the case that $3 = x\sqrt{2}$ and $x = \dfrac{3}{\sqrt{2}}$. Since the simplest form of a fraction can never have a radical in the denominator, we simplify it to $\dfrac{3\sqrt{2}}{2}$, as shown in chapter 7.

43. Square

44. Parallelogram

45. Rectangle

46. Rhombus

47. Trapezoid

48. False

In a parallelogram, there are two pairs of congruent angles. Therefore, if one of the angles measures 60°, then another angle measures 60°. The sum of all the angles is 360°, so subtract to find the measure of the other pair: $360 - 60 - 60 = 240°$. Thus, the measure of each of the other two congruent angles is 120°.

49. False

The only type of rhombus with 90° angles is the square.

50. False

The only rectangle that is a rhombus is the square.

51. True

52. False

Some, but not all, rhombuses are squares.

CHAPTER 8 TEST

You have now reviewed the key concepts of geometry and have tried various types of problems. Repetition is the key to mastery of any math concept! Use the chapter material, including the practice questions throughout, to assist you in solving these problems. The answer explanations that follow will provide additional help.

1. Which of the following is *TRUE* of the figure below?

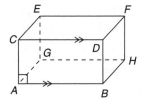

    (A) $\overline{AB} || \overline{GH}$
    (B) $\overline{AB} \perp \overline{AC}$
    (C) $\overline{AB} || \overline{EF}$
    (D) All of the above
    (E) None of the above

2. If an angle measures 85°, then it is

    (A) acute.
    (B) obtuse.
    (C) straight.
    (D) right.
    (E) isosceles.

3. In the figure below, $\overleftrightarrow{AB}$ is the bisector of $\overline{CD}$. If $\overline{CE} = 14$ cm, which of the following is *TRUE*?

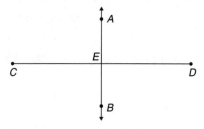

(A) $\overline{AE} = 14$ cm
(B) $\overline{AE} \cong \overline{EB}$
(C) $\overline{ED} = 14$ cm
(D) $\overline{CD} = 30$ cm
(E) All of the above

4. Which of the following is *TRUE* of the figure below?

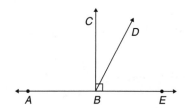

(A) $\angle CBA$ and $\angle CBE$ are complementary.
(B) $\angle CBD$ and $\angle DBE$ are supplementary.
(C) $\angle ABD$ and $\angle DBE$ form a linear pair.
(D) All of the above are true.
(E) None of the above are true.

5. Which of the following angle measures is supplementary to an angle of 19°?

   (A) 19°
   (B) 81°
   (C) 71°
   (D) 31°
   (E) 161°

Use the following figure for questions 6, 7, 8, and 9.

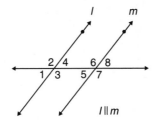

6. What type of angles are ∠1 and ∠8?

   (A) Corresponding
   (B) Supplementary
   (C) Alternate interior
   (D) Alternate exterior
   (E) Vertical

7. If the measure of ∠2 = 132°, then the measure of ∠6 =

   (A) 68°
   (B) 132°
   (C) 48°
   (D) 32°
   (E) None of the above

8. Which of the following is *NOT* true?

    (A) ∠2 and ∠3 are vertical angles.

    (B) ∠4 and ∠7 are supplementary angles.

    (C) ∠5 and ∠1 are congruent angles.

    (D) ∠3 and ∠5 are corresponding angles.

    (E) ∠4 and ∠5 are alternate interior angles.

9. Which angle is supplementary to ∠1?

    (A) ∠7

    (B) ∠5

    (C) ∠8

    (D) ∠4

    (E) None of the above

10. Classify the triangle below.

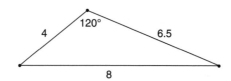

    (A) Acute isosceles

    (B) Obtuse isosceles

    (C) Obtuse scalene

    (D) Acute scalene

    (E) Acute obtuse

11. If two angles of a triangle measure 68° and 110°, what is the measure of the third angle?

    (A) 12°

    (B) 2°

    (C) 22°

    (D) 92°

    (E) 192°

12. Given the following figure, what is the measure of ∠CDF ?

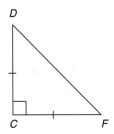

   (A) 100°
   (B) 45°
   (C) 75°
   (D) 65°
   (E) 125°

13. One acute angle of a right triangle measures 37°. What is the measure of the other acute angle?

   (A) 143°
   (B) 37°
   (C) 63°
   (D) 53°
   (E) 43°

14. If two sides of a triangle have measures of 2 cm and 7 cm, what is the possible range of values for the third side, denoted by x, in cm?

   (A) $7 < x < 2$
   (B) $2 < x < 7$
   (C) $1 < x < 8$
   (D) $5 < x < 9$
   (E) $9 < x < 5$

15. Which of the following is *ALWAYS* true?

   (A) The diagonals of a rectangle are perpendicular.
   (B) The diagonals of an isosceles trapezoid are perpendicular.
   (C) The diagonals of a square are perpendicular.
   (D) All of the above are true.
   (E) None of the above are true.

16. Which of the following is *TRUE?*

    (A) All rectangles are squares.

    (B) All squares are parallelograms.

    (C) All rhombuses are trapezoids.

    (D) All rhombuses have four congruent angles.

    (E) All parallelograms are rectangles.

17. Given the figure below, what is the measure of ∠*CDF?*

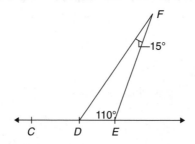

    (A) 135°

    (B) 45°

    (C) 125°

    (D) 65°

    (E) Cannot be determined from the information given

18. In parallelogram *JKLM* below, what is the measure of ∠*KLM* ?

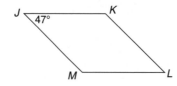

    (A) 53°

    (B) 133°

    (C) 147°

    (D) 47°

    (E) Cannot be determined from the information given

19. Given the rectangle *ABCD* below, what is the measure of $\overline{BD}$?

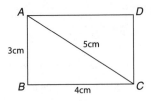

(A) 3 cm

(B) 4 cm

(C) 5 cm

(D) 7 cm

(E) Cannot be determined from the information given

20. What is the perimeter of a square with sides of 57 mm?

(A) 114 mm

(B) 324.9 mm

(C) 228 mm

(D) 61 mm

(E) 59 mm

21. Gracie wants to build a fence around a rectangular swimming pool area. The area has dimensions of 20 ft by 14 ft. How much fencing is needed?

(A) 280 ft

(B) 68 ft

(C) 80 ft

(D) 34 ft

(E) 596 ft

22. Find the area of the following polygon.

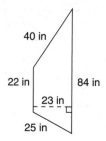

(A) 194 in²

(B) 2,438 in²

(C) 171 in²

(D) 1,219 in²

(E) 1,932 in²

23. Find the area of the triangle.

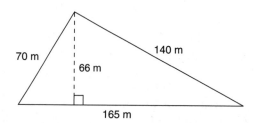

(A) 11,550 m²

(B) 10,890 m²

(C) 5,445 m²

(D) 5,775 m²

(E) 375 m²

24. Find the length of segment $\overline{BC}$ to the nearest tenth.

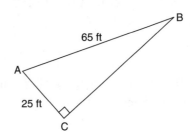

(A) 69.6 ft

(B) 40 ft

(C) 8.9 ft

(D) 60 ft

(E) 42 ft

Answers and Explanations

1. D

All of the statements are true. Segments $\overline{AB}$ and $\overline{GH}$ are parallel; they are opposite sides of the rectangular base. Segments $\overline{AB}$ and $\overline{AC}$ are perpendicular, as shown by the right angle designation. Segments $\overline{AB}$ and $\overline{EF}$ are parallel; they are in a plane that runs diagonally through the solid.

2. A

An angle whose measure is between 0° and 90° is an acute angle.

3. C

It is given that line $\overleftrightarrow{AB}$ is the bisector of segment $\overline{CD}$; thus, it divides segment $\overline{CD}$ into two congruent segments. The given statement tells nothing about the segments $\overline{AE}$ or $\overline{EB}$; choices (A) and (B) are thus not necessarily true. Segment $\overline{CD}$ is 28 cm long, not 30 cm long, as stated in choice (D).

4. C

The only true statement is choice (C), that $\angle ABD$ and $\angle DBE$ form a linear pair; these two angles are adjacent and together form a straight angle of 180°. $\angle CBA$ and $\angle CBE$ are supplementary, not complementary as stated in choice (A). $\angle CBD$ and $\angle DBE$ are complementary, not supplementary as stated in choice (B).

5. E

The measures of an angle and its supplement sum to 180°. Thus, the measure of the supplement to a 19° angle is $180° - 19° = 161°$.

6. D

These angles are alternate exterior angles. They are both on the exterior of the parallel lines on opposite sides of the transversal line.

7. B

$\angle 2$ and $\angle 6$ are corresponding angles. Therefore, their angle measures are the same.

8. D

All statements are true except choice (D), which states that $\angle 3$ and $\angle 5$ are corresponding angles. $\angle 3$ and $\angle 5$ are not corresponding because they are both in the interior of the parallel lines. $\angle 2$ and $\angle 3$ are vertical because they share a vertex but no common sides. $\angle 4$ and $\angle 7$ are supplementary because $\angle 4$ and $\angle 3$ are a linear pair, and $\angle 3$ is congruent to $\angle 7$ because they are corresponding angles. $\angle 5$ and $\angle 1$ are congruent because they are corresponding angles. Finally, $\angle 4$ and $\angle 5$ are alternate interior angles because they are on different sides of the transversal but are both in the interior of the parallel lines.

9. A

The angles that are supplementary to $\angle 1$, or add up to 180°, are angles $\angle 2$, $\angle 3$, $\angle 6$, and $\angle 7$. All of the other angles are congruent to $\angle 1$.

10. C

One angle measures more than 90°; therefore, the triangle is obtuse. All of the sides have different measures, so the triangle is scalene. The classification is thus obtuse scalene. An acute isosceles would have three angles less than 90° and two congruent sides. A triangle classified as obtuse isosceles has two congruent sides. In an acute scalene triangle, all three angles must have measures less than 90°, which is not true of this triangle. Choice (E) is also incorrect because it gives two different classifications based on the angles of a triangle, which is logically impossible. The given triangle is an obtuse, not an acute, triangle.

11. B

The sum of the measures of the angles in a triangle is 180°. Therefore, the third angle measure must be $180° - 110° - 68° = 2°$.

12. B

Since $\triangle CDF$ is a right triangle, $\angle CDF + \angle CFD = 90°$. Also, because it is an isosceles triangle, $\angle CDF$ and $\angle CFD$ are equal. Therefore, since $90 \div 2 = 45$, $\angle CDF$ measures $45°$.

13. D

The two acute angles in a right triangle are complementary; their measures have a sum of $90°$. Thus, the measure of the other acute angle is $90° - 37° = 53°$.

14. D

The possible values for the third side are between the difference $(7 - 2 = 5)$ and the sum $(7 + 2 = 9)$. So the length of the third side, or x, is between 5 and 9.

15. C

In choice (A), the diagonals of a rectangle are not always perpendicular; this is true only for a square. In choice (B), the diagonals of an isosceles trapezoid are always congruent but not necessarily perpendicular. All squares are rhombuses. Therefore, the diagonals of a square are always perpendicular.

16. B

The only true statement is that all squares are parallelograms; they have two sets of parallel and congruent sides. Choice (A) is not true. Only some rectangles are squares. Choice (C) is never true. No rhombuses are trapezoids. Choice (D) is true only when the rhombus is a square. Choice (E) is only sometimes true.

17. C

Since the two given angles in $\triangle DEF$ measure $15°$ and $110°$, then the third angle, $\angle FDE$, equals $180° - 15° - 110° = 55°$. Since $\angle FDE$ and $\angle CDF$ are supplementary, the degree measure of $\angle CDF$ must be $180° - 55° = 125°$. Therefore, the answer is $125°$. You could also solve this by knowing that the measure of an exterior angle of a triangle is equal to the sum of the measures of the two remote interior angles. Here, $15° + 110° = 125°$.

18. D

In parallelogram $JKLM$, by definition, there are two pairs of parallel sides. So if $\angle KJM$ equals $47°$, then supplementary $\angle JML$ must equal $133°$. In the same manner, $\angle JML$ is supplementary to $\angle KLM$. Therefore, $\angle KLM$ must equal $180° - 133° = 47°$.

19. C

In every rectangle, the diagonals are congruent. Since the diagonal segment $\overline{AC} =$ 5 cm, the other diagonal segment $\overline{BD}$ is also 5 cm.

20. C

Because all sides of a square are equal, the perimeter of a square is four times the length of one side: $4 \times 57 = 228$ mm.

21. B

The perimeter of a rectangle is two times the length plus two times the width: $P = (2 \times 20) + (2 \times 14) = 40 + 28 = 68$ ft.

22. D

The formula for the area of a trapezoid is $A = \frac{1}{2}(b_1 + b_2)\,h$. The bases are the lengths of the parallel sides, or 22 in and 84 in. The height (the dotted line perpendicular to the base) is 23 in. Therefore, $A = \frac{1}{2}(22 + 84)(23) = 1{,}219$ in^2.

23. C

The area of a triangle is found by the formula $A = \frac{1}{2}bh$. For this triangle, the base is 165 m, and the height (the dotted line perpendicular to the base) is 66 m. The area is $\frac{1}{2} \times 165 \times 66 = 5{,}445$ m^2.

24. D

This is a 5:12:13 right triangle multiplied by 5: $25 = 5 \times 5$ and $65 = 13 \times 5$. Thus, the remaining side, segment $\overline{BC}$, must be $12 \times 5 = 60$ ft.

Circles, Irregular Figures, and Solids

In chapter 8 we showed you how to work with basic geometric figures. In this chapter we'll explore more complicated shapes: circles, unusual figures, and three-dimensional figures.

CIRCLES

A **circle** is defined as the set of all points in a plane that are a given distance from a certain point called the **center**. The **radius**, r, of a circle is the segment whose endpoints are the center of the circle and any point on the circle. The **diameter**, d, of a circle is a segment that passes through the center of the circle and whose endpoints are both on the circle. The length of the diameter is twice the length of the radius.

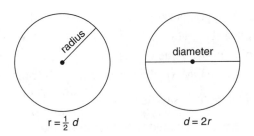

$r = \frac{1}{2}d$ $d = 2r$

A **central angle** is an angle formed by two radii. In circle O below, $\angle AOC$ is a central angle. $\angle COB$ and $\angle BOA$ are also central angles. The total degree measure of a circle is 360°.

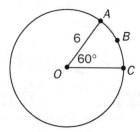

A **chord** is a line segment that joins two points on the circle. The longest chord of a circle is its diameter. In the diagram below, $\overline{AT}$ is a chord of circle P.

A **tangent** is a line that touches only one point on the circle. A line drawn tangent to a circle is perpendicular to the radius at the point of tangency. In the diagram below, line l is tangent to circle P at point T.

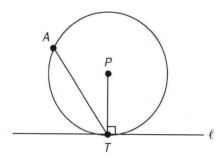

Circumference and Area

The distance around a polygon is called its perimeter; the distance around a circle is called its **circumference**. The ratio of the circumference of any circle to its diameter is a constant called **pi** (π). The value of π is roughly 3.14, but you will almost never need to use this value on the GMAT. Because π equals the ratio of the circumference (C) to the diameter (d), we can say that $\pi = \dfrac{\text{circumference}}{\text{diameter}} = \dfrac{C}{d}$. Therefore, the circumference of a circle is calculated with this formula:

$$C = \pi d$$

The formula to find the circumference can also be stated in terms of the radius (r), because the diameter is twice the length of the radius:

$$C = 2\pi r$$

The area of a circle is calculated with the following formula:

$$A = \pi r^2$$

For example, say you want to find the circumference and the area of a circle with a diameter of 34 inches. To find the circumference, use the formula for the circumference and calculate: $C = \pi d = \pi \times 34 = 34\pi$ inches. To find the area, you must first calculate the radius, which is one-half of the diameter, or 17 inches. Then use the formula for the area: $A = \pi r^2 = \pi \times 17 \times 17 = 289\pi$ in^2.

PRACTICE 1

Answer TRUE or FALSE to the following statements. Answers and explanations are located at the end of the chapter.

1. **T** **F** The diameter of a circle with a radius of 32 cm is 16 cm.

2. **T** **F** The circumference of a circle with a radius of 10 inches is 20π inches.

3. **T** **F** The area of a circle with a radius of 8 cm is twice the area of a circle with radius of 4 cm.

Arcs and Sectors

An **arc** is a section of the circumference of a circle. For example, in circle Q below, arc ABC is the portion of the circle's circumference that is defined by central angle AQC.

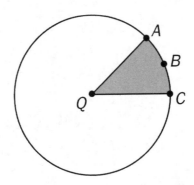

An arc that is exactly half the circumference of its circle is called a **semicircle**.

A **sector** is a section of the area of a circle. Think of the circle as a pizza: a sector is a slice of that pizza, and an arc is the length of the outside edge of the crust of that slice. For example, in the previous diagram, the shaded region is a sector of circle Q defined by central angle AQC.

What happens as you make a central angle bigger? You end up with a bigger slice of pizza (sector) and a longer outside edge of the crust (arc). Not surprisingly, making a central angle smaller also makes the corresponding arc and sector smaller. These measurements are all proportional to one another: the central angle as a fraction of 360° (the degree measure of a whole circle) is equal to the arc length as a fraction of the whole circumference, and both of these are equal to the sector's area as a fraction of the whole circle's area. This relationship is best remembered using the following formula:

$$\frac{\text{Central angle}}{360°} = \frac{\text{Arc length}}{2\pi r} = \frac{\text{Area of sector}}{\pi r^2}$$

For example, what is the length of arc ABC of circle O below?

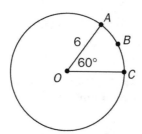

Since we're not interested in the area of the sector, we can use just the first two components of the above formula:

$$\frac{60°}{360°} = \frac{\text{arc } ABC}{2\pi r}$$

$$\frac{1}{6} = \frac{\text{arc } ABC}{2\pi(6)}$$

$$\text{arc } ABC = \frac{2\pi(6)}{6} = 2\pi$$

You can also think through this problem intuitively. Since 60° is one-sixth of the circle, arc ABC must be one-sixth of the circumference: $\frac{1}{6}(2\pi r) = \frac{1}{6}(12\pi) = 2\pi$.

PRACTICE 2

Repetition is critical to mastery. Try your hand at the following questions involving arcs and sectors. Answers and explanations are located at the end of the chapter.

4. A central angle cuts an arc of length 3π. If the diameter of the circle is 15, what is the measure of the central angle?

5. A central angle has a measure of 90°. If the radius of the circle is 8, what is the area of the resultant sector?

FINDING OTHER AREAS

Area of Irregular Figures

Perhaps you have used the concept of area with home improvement projects. If you ever wanted to wallpaper the walls of a room, for example, you needed to calculate the area of the walls in the room. Unless the room was a perfect rectangle, you needed to calculate the area of an irregularly shaped polygon. To accomplish this kind of task, break up the shapes into recognizable polygons and then calculate the area of each section. Add these areas together to find the total area. For example, look at the irregular figures below and identify the recognizable shapes.

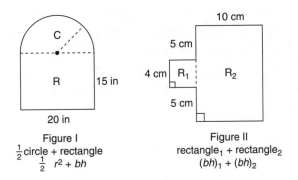

Figure I
$\frac{1}{2}$ circle + rectangle
$\frac{1}{2}$ r^2 + bh

Figure II
rectangle₁ + rectangle₂
$(bh)_1 + (bh)_2$

To find the area of figure I above, calculate $\frac{1}{2}$ of the area of a circle and add it to the area of a rectangle. So the area of figure I is $\frac{1}{2}\pi r^2 + lw = \left(\frac{1}{2}\pi \times 10 \times 10\right) + (20 \times 15) = 50\pi + 300$ in².

To find the area of figure II, add together the area of the two rectangles. The smaller rectangle has an area of $4 \times 5 = 20$, and the larger rectangle has an area of $10 \times (5 + 4 + 5) = 10 \times 14 = 140$. In total, the area is $20 + 140 = 160$ cm^2.

Area of Shaded Regions

At times, questions on the GMAT will ask you to find the area of shaded regions, such as those shown below.

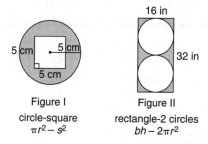

Figure I
circle-square
$\pi r^2 - s^2$

Figure II
rectangle-2 circles
$bh - 2\pi r^2$

In these examples, the shaded region is part of the outer portion of a recognizable figure, and the unshaded area is a second recognizable figure in the interior. One way to calculate the shaded area is to find the area of the entire outer shape and then subtract the area of the unshaded inner shape. For example, in figure I above, the outer figure is a circle with a radius of 5 cm, and the inner polygon is a square with side length of 5 cm. The area of the shaded region is therefore (area of circle) – (area of square). Expressed algebraically, the area is $\pi r^2 - s^2 = (\pi \times 5 \times 5) - (5 \times 5)$. This simplifies to $25\pi - 25$ cm^2.

In figure II above, the outer figure is a rectangle with dimensions of 16 inches and 32 inches, and the inner figures are two congruent circles, each with a radius of 8 inches. (Because the circles touch both sides of the rectangle, their diameters are 16 inches; therefore, their radii are 8 inches.) The area of the shaded region is (area of the rectangle) – (2 × area of one circle). Expressed algebraically, the area is $lw - 2\pi r^2 = (16 \times 32) - (2 \times \pi \times 8 \times 8) = 512 - 128\pi$ in^2.

PRACTICE 3

Repetition is the key to mastery. Calculate the area for each of the following figures. Answers and explanations are located at the end of the chapter.

6. Find the area of the following irregular figure.

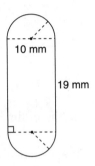

10 mm

19 mm

7. Find the area of the following irregular figure.

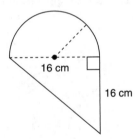

16 cm

16 cm

8. Find the area of the shaded region.

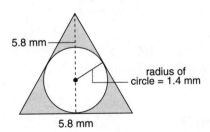

5.8 mm

radius of circle = 1.4 mm

5.8 mm

9. Find the area of the shaded region.

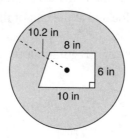

Surface Area

The measure of surface area applies to three-dimensional solids.

- **Prism.** The prism is a three-dimensional solid with two congruent bases and any number of other faces that are all rectangles. Examples include the rectangular prism and triangular prism shown below.

- **Cylinder.** This solid has two congruent circular bases, with one rectangular face wrapped around the bases.

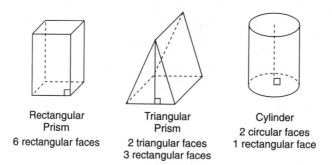

Rectangular Prism
6 rectangular faces

Triangular Prism
2 triangular faces
3 rectangular faces

Cylinder
2 circular faces
1 rectangular face

The faces of these solids are common polygons; therefore, you can solve for their surface area using the formulas for the areas of polygons that you already know.

REMEMBER THIS!

The surface area of any three-dimensional solid is the sum of the areas of all its faces.

To find the surface area of any solid, calculate the area of each of its faces and then add them all together. The units for surface area, as for any area, are square units.

The most common solid is the rectangular prism, which has six rectangular faces. For this solid, all of the opposite faces are congruent, so the surface area can be calculated as follows:

$$(2 \times \text{front face}) + (2 \times \text{left face}) + (2 \times \text{top face})$$

The formula for each of these faces is *length times width*. To find the surface area of the following rectangular prism, substitute the given dimensions into the formula.

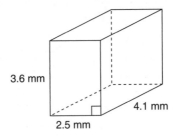

The surface area is $(2 \times 2.5 \times 3.6) + (2 \times 3.6 \times 4.1) + (2 \times 2.5 \times 4.1) = 18 + 29.52 + 20.5 = 68.02$ mm^2.

To find the surface area of a cylinder, use the formula $SA = 2\pi r^2 + 2\pi rh$, where r is the radius and h is the height of the cylinder.

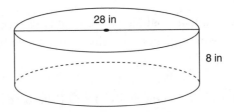

To find the surface area of this cylinder, first recognize that the diameter is given in the figure. Calculate the radius by taking one-half of the diameter, or 14 in. Then substitute this radius and the height of 8 in into the formula. The surface area is $(2 \times \pi \times 14 \times 14) + (2 \times \pi \times 14 \times 8) = 392\pi + 224\pi = 616\pi$ in^2.

PRACTICE 4

Find the surface area of each of the solids below. Answers and explanations are located at the end of the chapter.

10.

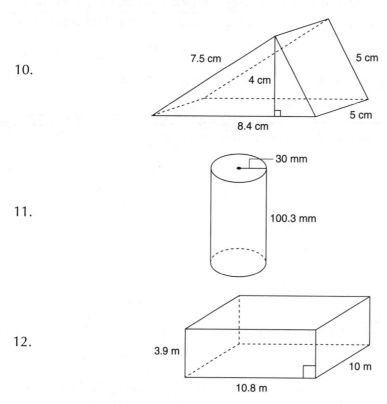

11.

12.

VOLUME

The **volume** of a three-dimensional solid is the number of cubic units needed to fill the solid. The volume of a prism or a cylinder is the area of one of the bases, B, multiplied by the height, h.

For a prism, the formula for volume is the area of the base, B, multiplied by the height, h. So for a triangular prism, the volume is the area of the triangular base, $\frac{1}{2}bh$, multiplied by the height of the prism. The two most common solids for which you will need to find the volume are the rectangular prism and the cylinder.

▨ REMEMBER THIS! ▨

- The volume of a rectangular solid is $V = Bh$, or $V = lwh$, where B is the area of the base (that is, $l \times w$) and h is the height.

- The volume of a cylinder is $V = \pi r^2 h$, where r is the radius and h is the height of the cylinder.

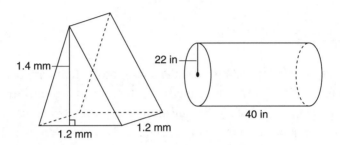

The figure on the left above is a triangular prism. The volume is thus the area of the base, a triangle, times the height, shown as 1.2 mm: $V = \left(\dfrac{1}{2}bh\right) \times h = \left(\dfrac{1}{2} \times 1.2 \times 1.4\right) \times 1.2 = 1.008 \text{ mm}^3$. The figure on the right above is a cylinder. The volume is the area of the base, a circle, times the height, shown as 40 in: $V = \pi r^2 h = \pi \times 22^2 \times 40 = 19{,}360\pi \text{ in}^3$.

PRACTICE 5

Find the volumes of the following three-dimensional solids. Answers and explanations are located at the end of the chapter.

13.

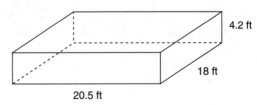

14.

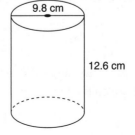

15.

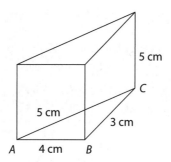

SIMILARITY

When figures have corresponding sides that are in proportion with one another and corresponding angles with the same measure, the figures are **similar**. Proportions can be used to determine that figures are similar and can also be used to calculate the missing part or parts of known similar figures. Take, for example, the following diagram of similar triangles. Each set of corresponding angles is congruent, or has the same measure, and each of the known corresponding sides is in proportion to one another.

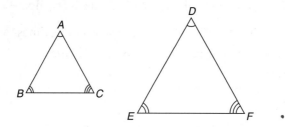

In the above diagram, $\angle A$ corresponds with $\angle D$, $\angle B$ corresponds with $\angle E$, and $\angle C$ corresponds with $\angle F$. In the same manner, side $\overline{AB}$ corresponds with side $\overline{DE}$, side $\overline{BC}$ corresponds with side $\overline{EF}$, and side $\overline{AC}$ corresponds with side $\overline{DF}$.

▨ FLASHBACK ▨

Proportions were covered in chapter 4: Ratios and Proportions.

Having established that triangles *ABC* and *DEF* are similar, you can now use a proportion to find the value of *x*, given the measurements shown in the following figure.

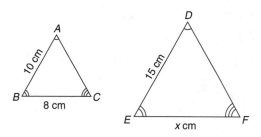

Set up the proportion as follows:

$$\frac{\text{side of } \triangle ABC}{\text{corresponding side of } \triangle DEF} = \frac{\text{side of } \triangle ABC}{\text{corresponding side of } \triangle DEF}$$

Because the side of triangle ABC that measures 10 cm corresponds with the side of triangle DEF that measures 15 cm and the side of triangle ABC that measures 8 cm likewise corresponds with the side of triangle DEF labeled x cm, the proportion becomes $\frac{10}{15} = \frac{8}{x}$. Cross multiply to get $10x = 120$. Divide each side of the equation by 10 to get $x = 12$.

There is another way to look at this problem. Because two corresponding sides were 10 cm and 15 cm and $\frac{15}{10} = 1.5$, then each side of triangle DEF is 1.5 times the length of the corresponding side of triangle ABC. In other words, the side lengths of these two triangles are in the ratio 1:1.5. Multiply 8 cm by 1.5 to get the corresponding measurement of 12 cm.

REMEMBER THIS!

The ratio of the sides of two similar figures will be the same as the ratio of the perimeters of the same two similar figures. For example, if the sides of two similar triangles are in the ratio 1:3, then the perimeters of the triangles will also be in the ratio 1:3.

An additional place where similarity and scale are often used is in shadow problems. In this type of problem, you use indirect measurement to find the height of something that may be too tall or too large to measure yourself. Take, for example, the following scenario. Justin, who is 5.5 feet tall, is standing next to a building that casts a shadow of 12 feet. If, at the same time, Justin casts a shadow that is 3 feet long, what is the height of the building?

Drawing diagrams is a great way to visualize scenarios. A picture of the scenario could look like this:

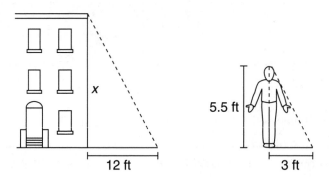

Notice the similar triangles that appear once the diagram is drawn; the corresponding angles are congruent, and the corresponding sides are in proportion. To solve this problem, set up a proportion like the ones used for similar triangles. Line up the corresponding parts and labels as in the proportion $\dfrac{\text{height of person}}{\text{shadow of person}} = \dfrac{\text{height of building}}{\text{shadow of building}}$. The proportion then becomes $\dfrac{5.5}{3} = \dfrac{x}{12}$. Cross multiply to get the equation $66 = 3x$; divide each side of the equation by 3 to get $x = 22$. The building is 22 feet tall.

PRACTICE 6

The following TRUE or FALSE questions ask you to use the skills just presented on similar figures. Remember, repetition is the key to mastery. Answer and explanations are located at the end of the chapter.

16. **T F**   If the triangles in the figure below are similar, then the length of side $\overline{AB}$ is equal to 11 cm.

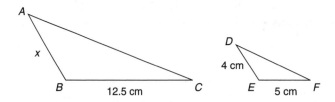

17. **T F**   If the perimeters of two similar triangles are 33 inches and 42 inches, respectively, and the measure of the shortest side of the smaller triangle is 11 inches, then the shortest side of the larger triangle measures 14 inches.

18. **T F**   A 24-foot flagpole casts a shadow that is 16 feet long. At the same time, a person 6 feet tall will cast a shadow that is 4 feet long.

SUMMARY

In conclusion, here are six things about advanced shapes you should take from this chapter:

1.   The circumference of a circle is πd or $2\pi r$.
2.   The area of a circle is πr^2.
3.   Central angle measure, arc length, and sector area are all related by the proportion $\dfrac{\text{Central angle}}{360°} = \dfrac{\text{Arc length}}{2\pi r} = \dfrac{\text{Area of sector}}{\pi r^2}$.
4.   The surface area of a three-dimensional geometric solid is the sum of the areas of all its faces.
5.   Volume is the number of cubic units needed to fill a geometric solid. For prisms and cylinders, it is found by multiplying the area of the base times the height.
6.   When two figures are similar, their corresponding sides are all in the same proportion to one another.

Practice Answers and Explanations

1. False

$D = 2r$, so the diameter would be 2×32, or 64.

2. True

$$C = 2\pi r$$
$$= 2 \times \pi \times 10$$
$$= 20\pi \text{ inches}$$

3. False

Since the radius is squared in the area formula, the area of the larger circle is four times the area of the smaller circle.

4.   72°

Since the diameter of the circle is 15, the circumference is $\pi d = 15\pi$. To find the central angle, set up a proportion as follows:

$$\frac{\text{Central angle}}{360} = \frac{\text{Arc length}}{\text{Circumference}}$$

$$\frac{\text{Central angle}}{360} = \frac{3\pi}{15\pi}$$

$$\frac{\text{Central angle}}{360} = \frac{1}{5}$$

Now multiply both sides of the equation by 360; the central angle is $360° \div 5 = 72°$.

5.   16π

Since the radius of the circle is 8, the area is $\pi r^2 = 64\pi$. The area of the sector is a quarter of the total area, since 90° is a quarter of 360°. Divide the total area by 4 to find the sector area: $64\pi \div 4 = 16\pi$.

6.   25π + 190 mm²

The figure contains two congruent halves of a circle, so it is the area of a circle, plus the area of a rectangle: $A = \pi r^2 + lw$. The radius is one-half of the diameter. The diameter is the same as a side of the rectangle.

$$A = \pi(5^2) + (10)(19)$$
$$= 25\pi + 190 \text{ mm}^2$$

7.   32π + 128 cm²

The figure is one-half of a circle plus a triangle.

$$A = \frac{1}{2}\pi r^2 + \frac{1}{2}bh$$
$$= \frac{1}{2}\pi(8)^2 + \frac{1}{2}(16)(16)$$
$$= 32\pi + 128 \text{ cm}^2$$

8.   16.82 – 1.96π mm²

The area of the shaded region of the figure is the area of the triangle minus the area of the unshaded circle.

$$A = \frac{1}{2}bh - \pi r^2$$

$$= \frac{1}{2}(5.8)(5.8) - \pi(1.4)^2$$

$$= 16.82 - 1.96\pi \text{ mm}^2$$

9. $104.04\pi - 54 \text{ in}^2$

The area of the shaded region of the figure is the area of the circle minus the area of the unshaded trapezoid.

$$A = \pi r^2 - \frac{1}{2}(b_1 + b_2)h$$

$$= \pi(10.2)^2 - \frac{1}{2}(8 + 10)(6)$$

$$= 104.04\pi - 54 \text{ in}^2$$

10. 138.1 cm^2

This is a triangular prism with two congruent triangular faces and three rectangular faces. Find each of these areas and add them together.

$$SA = (2 \times \frac{1}{2} \times 4 \times 8.4) + (5 \times 5) + (7.5 \times 5) + (5 \times 8.4)$$

$$= 33.6 + 25 + 37.5 + 42$$

$$= 138.1 \text{ cm}^2$$

11. $7{,}818\pi \text{ mm}^2$

This is a cylinder, so the surface area is $2\pi r^2 + 2\pi rh$.

$$SA = (2 \times \pi \times 30^2) + (2 \times \pi \times 30 \times 100.3)$$
$$= 1{,}800\pi + 6{,}018\pi$$
$$= 7{,}818\pi \text{ mm}^2$$

12. 378.24 m^2

This is a rectangular prism. There are three pairs of congruent rectangular faces.

$$SA = (2 \times 3.9 \times 10.8) + (2 \times 3.9 \times 10) + (2 \times 10 \times 10.8)$$
$$= 84.24 + 78 + 216$$
$$= 378.24 \text{ m}^2$$

13.   1,549.8 ft³

The volume of a rectangular solid is $V = lwh$. $V = 20.5 \times 18 \times 4.2 = 1{,}549.8$ ft³.

14.   302.526π cm³

The volume of a cylinder is $V = \pi r^2 h$. $V = \pi \times (4.9)^2 \times 12.6 = 302.526\pi$ cm³.

15.   30 cm³

The formula for the volume of a triangular prism is the area of its base times its height. To find the area of the base, use the formula for the area of a triangle: $A = \dfrac{1}{2}\,bh$. Because the side lengths of the base are in the ratio 3:4:5, this is a right triangle (a special right triangle known as a Pythagorean triple, discussed in chapter 8), so its legs can be used as the base and height in the area formula. Therefore, the area of the triangular base is $\dfrac{1}{2} \times 3 \times 4 = 6$ cm². Finally, multiply the area of the base by the triangular prism's height to find the volume: $V = 6 \times 5 = 30$ cm³.

16.   False

$12.5 \div 5 = 2.5$. Therefore the similar triangles are in the ratio of 2.5:1. Thus side $\overline{AB}$, or x, equals $4 \times 2.5 = 10$ cm, not 11 cm as stated, so the statement is false.

17.   True

The perimeters of similar figures are proportional, just as the sides are. Because $42 \div 33 = 1.\overline{27}$, the smallest side of the larger triangle should be equal to $11 \times 1.\overline{27}$, which is indeed 14 inches.

18.   True

The person is a quarter of the height of the flagpole ($24 \div 6 = 4$). Thus, the person's shadow would be one quarter of the flagpole's shadow: $16 \div 4 = 4$ feet.

CHAPTER 9 TEST

Now that you have studied and practiced with advanced shapes, try the following questions to test your skills and knowledge. The answers and explanations that follow will help to clarify new concepts.

1. Every time its wheel turns, a bicycle travels a distance equal to the circumference of the wheel. If a bicycle wheel's diameter is 0.5 m, approximately how many turns will the wheel have to make for the bike to travel 100 meters?

   (A) 200 turns

   (B) 20 turns

   (C) 64 turns

   (D) 50 turns

   (E) 500 turns

2. What is the area of a circle with a diameter of 58 mm?

   (A) 29π mm^2

   (B) $3,364\pi$ mm^2

   (C) 58π mm^2

   (D) 116π mm^2

   (E) 841π mm^2

3. Find the surface area.

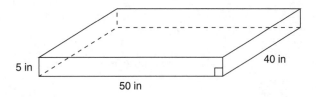

   (A) 10,000 in^2

   (B) 2,450 in^2

   (C) 95 in^2

   (D) 2,000 in^2

   (E) 4,900 in^2

4. Find the surface area.

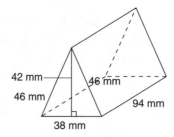

(A) 150,024 mm²

(B) 75,012 mm²

(C) 13,018 mm²

(D) 13,816 mm²

(E) 15,412 mm²

5. What is the surface area of a box with dimensions of 2 feet by 1.5 feet by 3 feet?

(A) 27 ft²

(B) 9 ft²

(C) 6.5 ft²

(D) 13.5 ft²

(E) 13 ft²

6. The school district wants to install sod in the interior of the track field. How much sod is needed if the dimensions and shape are as shown below?

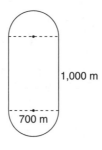

(A) 1,400π + 350,000 m²

(B) 1,400π + 700,000 m²

(C) 700,000 m²

(D) 61,250π + 700,000 m²

(E) 122,500π + 700,000 m²

7. Find the area.

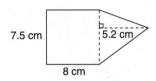

(A) 79.5 cm²

(B) 99 cm²

(C) 101.6 cm²

(D) 80.8 cm²

(E) 36.2 cm²

8. Find the area.

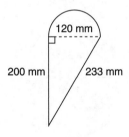

(A) 3,600π + 6,000 mm²

(B) 3,600π + 12,000 mm²

(C) 1,800π + 12,000 mm²

(D) 1,800π + 24,000 mm²

(E) 3,600π + 24,000 mm²

9. Find the area of the shaded region.

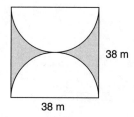

38 m

38 m

(A) $1,444 - 180.5\pi$ m^2

(B) $1,444 - 361\pi$ m^2

(C) $1,444 - 38\pi$ m^2

(D) $1,444 - 19\pi$ m^2

(E) $722 - 38\pi$ m^2

10. Find the area of the shaded region.

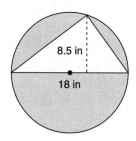

8.5 in

18 in

(A) $324\pi - 153$ in^2

(B) $324\pi - 76.5$ in^2

(C) $81\pi - 153$ in^2

(D) $81\pi - 76.5$ in^2

(E) $18\pi - 76.5$ in^2

11. What is the volume of the following cylinder?

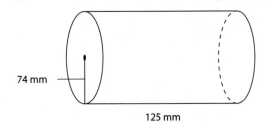

74 mm

125 mm

(A) 684,500π mm³

(B) 18,500π mm³

(C) 29,452π mm³

(D) 1,369,000π mm³

(E) 217,994π mm³

12. What is the volume of the triangular prism?

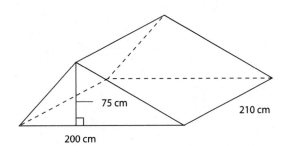

75 cm

210 cm

200 cm

(A) 49,500 cm³

(B) 1,575,000 cm³

(C) 3,150,000 cm³

(D) 72,750 cm³

(E) 81,000 cm³

13. Dave wants to put an ice rink in his backyard. The rink will be 30 feet by 20 feet with ice 6 inches deep. How much ice will the rink contain?

    (A) 3,600 ft³

    (B) 300 ft³

    (C) 7,200 ft³

    (D) 600 ft³

    (E) 1,250 ft³

14. In the diagram below, triangle *JKL* is similar to triangle *MNO*. What is the measure of side $\overline{MO}$?

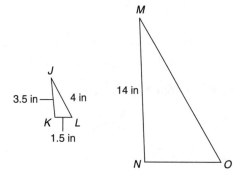

    (A) 7 in

    (B) 10.5 in

    (C) 14.5 in

    (D) 16 in

    (E) 9 in

Answers and Explanations

1. C

The circumference of the wheel is the distance the bicycle will travel with each turn of the wheel. The circumference of a circle is πd, so the distance traveled with one turn is 0.5π m. Divide this into the total distance of 100 m: $\dfrac{100}{0.5\pi} = \dfrac{200}{\pi}$, or roughly 64 turns.

2. E

The area of a circle is found using the formula πr^2. The radius is one-half of the diameter, or 29 mm. The area is thus $\pi \times 29 \times 29 = 841\pi$ mm^2.

3. E

The surface area of a solid is the sum of the areas of its faces. There are three pairs of congruent rectangular faces on a rectangular solid, and the area of each face is given by the formula length times width. The surface area is $(2 \times 50 \times 5) + (2 \times 5 \times 40) + (2 \times 40 \times 50) = 4,900$ in^2.

4. D

A triangular prism has five faces: two congruent triangular bases and three rectangular faces. The surface area is $2 \times \left(\dfrac{1}{2} \times 38 \times 42\right) + (94 \times 46) + (94 \times 46) + (94 \times 38) = 13,816$ mm^2.

5. A

This is a surface area problem. There are three pairs of congruent rectangular faces on a rectangular solid. The surface area is thus $(2 \times 2 \times 1.5) + (2 \times 2 \times 3) + (2 \times 1.5 \times 3) = 27$ ft^2.

6. E

The track field is an irregularly shaped figure featuring two congruent halves of a circle with a radius of 350 m (or one complete circle) and one rectangle with dimensions of 700 m by 1,000 m. Find the area of the rectangle and the circle and add them together: $A = \pi r^2 + bh = (\pi \times 350 \times 350) + (700 \times 1,000) = 122,500\pi + 700,000$ m^2.

7. A

The polygon is a triangle and a rectangle. Find the area of each shape and add them together: $A = \dfrac{1}{2}bh + lw = \dfrac{1}{2}(7.5 \times 5.2) + (7.5 \times 8) = 79.5$ cm^2.

8. C

The irregularly shaped figure is one-half of a circle plus a triangle. Thus, $A = \frac{1}{2} \pi r^2 + \frac{1}{2} bh$. The radius of the circle is one-half the diameter shown (the base of the triangle), or 60 mm. $A = \left(\frac{1}{2} \times \pi \times 60 \times 60 \right) + \frac{1}{2} (120 \times 200) = 1,800\pi + 12,000$ mm^2.

9. B

The area of the shaded region is the area of the outer figure (a square) minus the area of the unshaded inner region (two congruent halves of a circle, or one complete circle). The area of the shaded region is thus $s^2 - \pi r^2$. $A = (38 \times 38) \times (\pi \times 19 \times 19) = 1,444 - 361\pi$ m^2.

10. D

The area of the shaded region is the area of the outer figure (a circle) minus the area of the unshaded inner region (a triangle). $A = \pi r^2 - \frac{1}{2} bh = (\pi \times 9 \times 9) - \left(\frac{1}{2} \times 18 \times 8.5 \right) = 81\pi - 76.5$ in^2.

11. A

The volume of a cylinder is $\pi r^2 h$. The volume is thus $\pi \times 74 \times 74 \times 125 = 684,500\pi$ mm^3.

12. B

The volume of a triangular prism is the area of the base (a triangle) times the height. The area of a triangle is given by the formula $A = \frac{1}{2} bh$. Here that is $A = \frac{1}{2} bh = \frac{1}{2} \times 200 \times 75 = 750$ cm^2. The height of the prism is 210 cm, so the volume of the prism is $V = 750 \times 210 = 1,575,000$ cm^3.

13. B

This is a rectangular solid whose height is 0.5 feet (6 inches is one-half of a foot). $V = 30 \times 20 \times 0.5 = 300$ ft^3.

14. D

Side $\overline{MN}$ is proportional to side $\overline{JK}$, so each side of MNO is $14 \div 3.5 = 4$ times the length of the corresponding side of JKL. Hence, side $\overline{MO}$ is 4 times the length of side $\overline{JL}$, and $4 \times 4 = 16$ in.

Coordinate Geometry

Have you ever tried to locate a city on a map using a key or used a grid to help you calculate an area? Coordinate geometry is a way to use a rectangular grid to locate particular places and determine measurements, such as area or distance. In this chapter, you will learn about the coordinate plane, along with various applications such as the midpoint formula, distance formula, slope, linear equations and inequalities, and systems of equations. In addition, you will be introduced to transformational geometry.

THE COORDINATE PLANE

The **coordinate plane** is formed by the intersection of two perpendicular number lines. The horizontal number line is known as the x-axis, and the vertical number line is known as the y-axis. When the lines intersect, four regions, called **quadrants**, are formed. They are numbered I, II, III, and IV in counterclockwise fashion, starting from the upper right-hand quadrant. The point where the two number lines intersect is called the **origin** and has the coordinates $(0, 0)$. The number lines are labeled with positive numbers to the right of the origin on the x-axis and above the origin on the y-axis, with negative numbers to the left of the origin on the x-axis and below the origin on the y-axis.

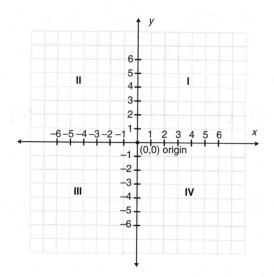

Each point in the coordinate system has a location determined by the number of spaces the point lies to the right or left of the origin and the number of spaces it lies above or below the origin. Therefore, each point in the system is named with two numbers: an *x*-coordinate and a *y*-coordinate. These coordinates are always written in *x, y* order and placed in parentheses.

Take, for example, the point named by the coordinates (4, 5). The first number in the pair is 4, so this point is 4 spaces to the right of the origin on the *x*-axis. The second number is 5, so the point is 5 spaces above the origin on the *y*-axis. Therefore, to find the location of this point, start at the origin, move four spaces to the right and five spaces up from there. Note the location in quadrant I of the point (4, 5) in the figure below.

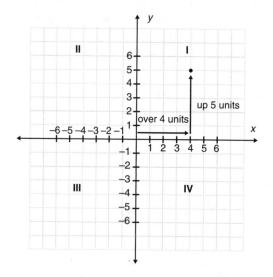

Here are some additional examples of how to find the locations of points in the coordinate plane. The location of each is noted in the following figure.

- **Point A.** To find the location of point A, start at the origin, move two spaces to the left on the *x*-axis, and then move six spaces up. This is the point (–2, 6), located in quadrant II.

- **Point B.** To find the location of point B, start at the origin, move three spaces to the left on the *x*-axis, and then move four spaces down. This is the point (–3, –4), located in quadrant III.

- **Point C.** To find the location of point C, start at the origin, move five spaces to the right on the *x*-axis, and then move six spaces down. This is the point (5, –6), located in quadrant IV.

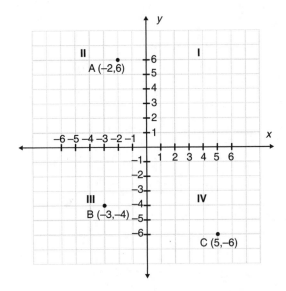

Notice the following pattern when graphing points in the four quadrants:

- In quadrant I, both the *x*- and *y*-coordinates are positive.

- In quadrant II, all *x*-values are negative, while the *y*-values are positive.

- In quadrant III, both the *x*- and *y*-coordinates are negative.

- In quadrant IV, all *x*-values are positive, while the *y*-values are negative.

Repetition is important if you want to master plotting points in the coordinate plane. Try the next set of practice questions to help develop proficiency in identifying coordinates.

PRACTICE 1

Use the graph below to match each point with the correct coordinates. Answers and explanations are located at the end of the chapter.

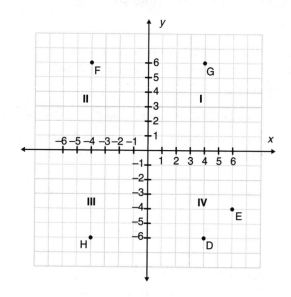

1. Point D   A. $(-4, 6)$

2. Point E   B. $(4, -6)$

3. Point F   C. $(-4, -6)$

4. Point G   D. $(6, -4)$

5. Point H   E. $(4, 6)$

FORMULAS

The Midpoint Formula

It is often helpful to know the halfway point, or **midpoint**, between two endpoints of a line segment. You can find this location by using the following formula, where (x_1, y_1) and (x_2, y_2) represent the two endpoints:

$$\left(\frac{x_1 + x_2}{2}, \frac{y_1 + y_2}{2} \right)$$

To find the midpoint between the points (2, 5) and (4, –3), for example, first plug in the values of x and y from each point, and then evaluate the formula. $\left(\dfrac{x_1+x_2}{2},\dfrac{y_1+y_2}{2}\right)=\left(\dfrac{2+4}{2},\dfrac{5+(-3)}{2}\right)=\left(\dfrac{6}{2},\dfrac{2}{2}\right)=(3,1)$. The midpoint between the points (2, 5) and (4, –3) is (3, 1).

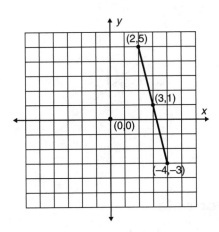

To help you remember the midpoint formula, notice that you are actually finding the sum of the two x-values and dividing it by 2, and then you are doing the same for the y-values. In other words, you are finding the average (mean) x-value and the average (mean) y-value when you are finding the midpoint between two points.

You can also use this formula to find an endpoint when given the value of the other endpoint and the midpoint. Take the segment $\overline{AB}$ with point A at (4, –7) and the midpoint of $\overline{AB}$ at (–1, –3). To find the location of point B, substitute the known values into the formula and set it equal to the midpoint: $\left(\dfrac{x_1+x_2}{2},\dfrac{y_1+y_2}{2}\right)=\left(\dfrac{4+x_2}{2},\dfrac{-7+y_2}{2}\right)=(-1,-3)$. Now set each expression in the formula equal to its coordinate at the midpoint: $\dfrac{4+x_2}{2}=-1$ and $\dfrac{-7+y_2}{2}=-3$. Cross multiply in the first equation: $4+x_2=-2$, so $x_2=-6$. Cross multiply in the second equation: $-7+y_2=-6$, so $y_2=1$. Therefore, the coordinates of point B are (–6, 1).

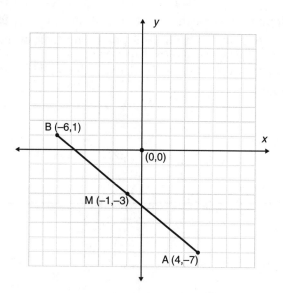

The Distance Formula

Another formula frequently used in the coordinate plane is the **distance formula**. This formula will help you calculate the distance between any two points in the coordinate plane. To find the distance between any two points (x_1, y_1) and (x_2, y_2), use the following formula, which is based on the Pythagorean theorem:

$$d = \sqrt{(x_1 - x_2)^2 + (y_1 - y_2)^2}$$

For example, to find the distance between the points $(0, -2)$ and $(5, -2)$, substitute the values for x and y from each point into the formula:

$$\sqrt{(x_1 - x_2)^2 + (y_1 - y_2)^2} = \sqrt{(0 - 5)^2 + (-2 - (-2))^2}$$
$$= \sqrt{(-5)^2 + (0)^2}$$
$$= \sqrt{25 + 0}$$
$$= \sqrt{25}$$
$$= 5$$

The distance between the points $(0, -2)$ and $(5, -2)$ is 5 units. Note that the distance between two points can be an irrational number.

FLASHBACK

Review information regarding **irrational numbers** from chapter 1 and **simplifying square roots** from chapter 7.

Here's another example. Take the points (4, 2) and (–3, 6). To find the distance between them, substitute into the distance formula:

$$\sqrt{(x_1 - x_2)^2 + (y_1 - y_2)^2} = \sqrt{(4 - (-3))^2 + (2 - 6)^2}$$
$$= \sqrt{(7)^2 + (-4)^2}$$
$$= \sqrt{49 + 16}$$
$$= \sqrt{65}$$

Notice that in this case, the number under the radical sign is not a perfect square. Since the square root of 65 is approximately equal to 8, the distance can be rounded to 8 units using a calculator, but the exact answer is $\sqrt{65}$ units.

REMEMBER THIS!

- The **midpoint** between two points can be found using the formula $\left(\dfrac{x_1 + x_2}{2}, \dfrac{y_1 + y_2}{2} \right)$.

- The **distance** between two points can be found using the formula $d = \sqrt{(x_1 - x_2)^2 + (y_1 - y_2)^2}$.

PRACTICE 2

Use the following bank of answers to fill in each blank below. Answers and explanations are located at the end of the chapter.

(–11, –12)   (–2, –5)   (–1, –5)   (11, –12) $\sqrt{13}$ 13 $3\sqrt{3}$ $\sqrt{29}$ 29

6. The midpoint between (2, –3) and (–4, –7) is _____.

7. If point C is (5, 4) and the midpoint of segment $\overline{CD}$ is (–3, –4), then point D is located at _____.

8. The distance between (–2, –3) and (–7, –15) is _____.

9. The distance between the points (1, 4) and (6, 2) is _____.

Slope and Its Applications

Slope is an important concept to master when studying coordinate geometry. It helps you draw conclusions about the pattern of a graph and tells you the **rate of change** of a situation.

The slope (m) of the line between two points (x_1, y_1) and (x_2, y_2) can be found by using this formula:

$$m = \frac{\text{change in } y}{\text{change in } x} = \frac{y_1 - y_2}{x_1 - x_2}$$

Slope is commonly known as "the rise over the run." In other words, the number in the numerator of the fraction tells how many units to move up or down, and the number in the denominator tells how many units to move to the right or left. If the slope is written as a whole number, write that value over the number 1. For example, a slope of 3 is written as $\frac{3}{1}$ because the rise is 3 and the run is 1.

Read the following example to see the slope formula in action. Find the slope of the line between the points (4, 8) and (–1, 6). Use the following formula: $m = \frac{\text{change in } y}{\text{change in } x} = \frac{y_1 - y_2}{x_1 - x_2} = \frac{8 - 6}{4 - (-1)} = \frac{2}{5}$. The slope of the line between these points is $\frac{2}{5}$. The rate of change between the points on this line is up two units and to the right five units.

Another type of slope problem is one where the slope of the line is given but one or more of the coordinates of a point on the line is unknown.

For example, find the value of t if the slope of the line between the points (1, t) and (2, 1) is 2. Use the slope formula with the given coordinates and set it equal to the slope of 2, or $\frac{2}{1}$. We get $\frac{y_1 - y_2}{x_1 - x_2} = \frac{t - 1}{1 - 2} = \frac{2}{1}$. Simplify the left side of the proportion: $\frac{t - 1}{-1} = \frac{2}{1}$. Cross multiply to get $t - 1 = -2$. Add 1 to both sides of the equation to get $t = -1$. The missing y-coordinate is –1.

SPECIAL CASES OF SLOPE

The slope of a line can fall into four major categories: positive slope, negative slope, slope of 0, or no slope.

Positive slopes are lines that go up as you move from left to right. When using the slope, count up and over to the right when plotting the graph. These lines appear to be "uphill," as shown in the figure below.

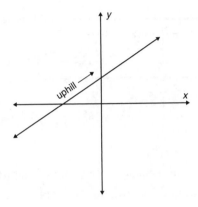

Negative slopes are lines that go down as you move from left to right. The figure below shows a line with negative slope.

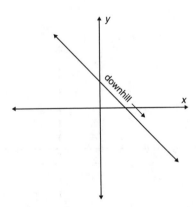

Two additional special cases of slope are horizontal and vertical lines.

When the rate of change in the y-values is equal to 0, the line formed will be a **horizontal line**. In this case, the slope would have a rise of 0 and a run of any real number. This would cause the graph to travel horizontally across but not have any steepness. Each horizontal line is in the form $y = k$, where k represents a constant value. All horizontal lines have a slope of 0. A few examples are shown in the figure below.

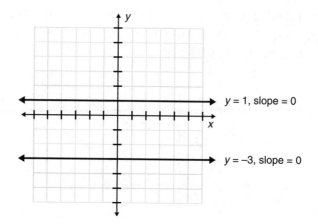

When the rate of change of the x-values is 0, then the line formed is a **vertical line**. Because the 0 is at the bottom of the fraction, no real number slope can exist. Each vertical line is in the form $x = k$, where k represents a constant value. All vertical lines have an undefined slope. A few examples of vertical lines and their equations are shown in the figure below.

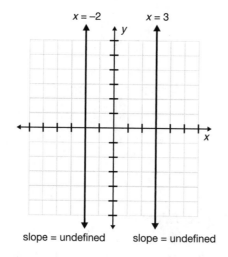

INTERCEPTS

Two intercepts are commonly used when graphing lines in the coordinate plane.

The first is the **x-intercept**. The x-intercept is the location at which a line intersects, or crosses, the x-axis. This point is written in the form $(x, 0)$. Notice that the y-value at the x-intercept is always 0.

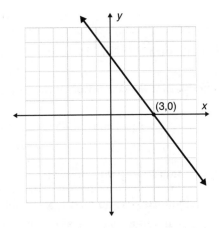

The **y-intercept** is the location at which a line intersects the y-axis. This point is written in the form $(0, y)$. Notice that in this case, the x-value at the y-intercept is always 0.

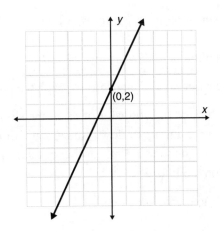

PRACTICE 3

Answer TRUE or FALSE for each of the following questions.

10. **T F** The slope of a line can be found by calculating the change in x over the change in y.

11. **T F** The slope of the line between (6, –1) and (–1, 3) is $-\dfrac{4}{7}$.

12. **T F** The line in the form $y = 5$ is a horizontal line.

13. **T F** The line in the form $x = -3$ is a horizontal line.

14. **T F** The x-intercept of a line could be at the point (0, –2).

15. **T F** The y-intercept of a line could be at the point (0, –10).

GRAPHING IN SLOPE-INTERCEPT FORM

Now that you have learned about slopes and intercepts in detail, you will have a better understanding of how to graph lines and use slope-intercept form.

The **slope-intercept form** of a linear equation is as follows, where m is the slope of the line and b is the y-intercept:

$$y = mx + b$$

To graph a line written in slope-intercept form, follow these four steps:

1. Make sure the equation is in the form $y = mx + b$.

2. Use b from the equation (the y-intercept) to graph the point (0, b) on the y-axis.

3. Using the numerator and denominator of m, or the slope of the equation, start at the y-intercept and count up or down (the amount of the rise) and then right or left (the amount of the run) to find another point. Repeat the process to find additional points on the line.

4. Connect the points to create your line.

Practice this procedure with the linear equation $y = 3x + 1$.

1. Since the equation is in the form $y = mx + b$, first identify that $m = 3$ and $b = 1$.

2. Place a point at the y-intercept of (0, 1).

3. Since the slope is 3, or $\dfrac{3}{1}$, count up 3 units and to the right 1 unit to find another point on the line. This is the point (1, 4). Note that since the slope is positive, you count up and over to the right. Repeat the process of counting up 3 and over 1 to the right to find additional points.

4. Connect the points to form the graph of the line.

This equation is graphed in the figure below.

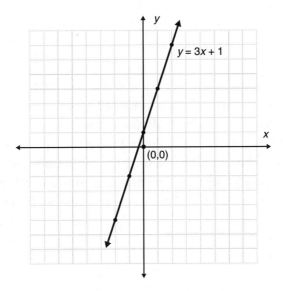

Try another practice example using the equation $2y + x = 4$.

1. Since the equation is not in the form $y = mx + b$, first subtract x from both sides of the equation, and then divide each term by 2 to get $y = -\dfrac{1}{2}x + 2$. Now identify that $m = -\dfrac{1}{2}$ and $b = 2$.

2. Place a point at the y-intercept of (0, 2).

3. Since the slope is $-\dfrac{1}{2}$, count up 1 unit and to the left 2 units to find another point on the line. This is the point (–2, 3). Note that since the slope is negative, you are counting up and to the left. Repeat the process of counting up 1 and 2 to the left to find additional points.

4. Connect the points to form the graph of the line.

This equation is graphed in the figure below.

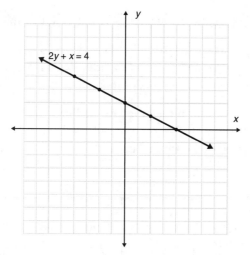

You can use linear equations to represent real-world situations. For example, say a health club charges an initial $50 to register and then $25 per month. This can be modeled with the equation $y = 25x + 50$, where x is the number of months and y is the total cost of the membership. The slope of the equation is the rate of change—in other words, the monthly fee. The y-intercept of the equation is the initial, or one-time, cost. Using this equation, you can determine the cost of joining this club for one year. Since there are 12 months in a year, substitute $x = 12$ into the equation.

$$y = 25(12) + 50$$
$$y = 300 + 50$$
$$y = 350$$

The membership would cost $350 for one year.

PRACTICE 4

Fill in the blank to make each statement TRUE.

16. If a video at Video Valley costs $2.50 to rent and the initial membership fee is $4, this can be represented by the linear equation _____.

17. If the cost of a cab ride can be represented by the linear equation $y = 2x + 3$, where x represents the number of miles and y is the total cost, the cost per mile is _____ dollars.

SOLVING SYSTEMS OF EQUATIONS

When more than one equation is graphed on the same set of axes, a **system of equations** is created. To solve a system of equations, look for the intersection of the lines. These point(s) of intersection, if they exist, are the solution(s) to the system.

Here is an example of how to solve a system of equations. Take the following system:

$$y = -2x + 3$$
$$y = x - 3$$

First, graph each equation on the same set of axes. In the first equation, the slope is equal to -2 and the y-intercept is 3. In the second equation, the slope is 1 and the y-intercept is -3. The figure below shows these two equations graphed on the same set of axes.

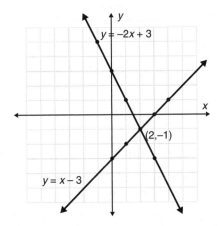

Since the two lines intersect at the point $(2, -1)$, this point is the solution to the system of equations. To check this solution, substitute the coordinates $x = 2$ and $y = -1$ into each of the original equations and check to make sure they are equal.

$$
\begin{array}{ll}
y = -2x + 3 & \qquad y = x - 3 \\
-1 = -2(2) + 3 & \qquad -1 = 2 - 3 \\
-1 = -4 + 3 & \qquad -1 = -1 \\
-1 = -1 &
\end{array}
$$

Here is another example of a system of equations:

$$y + x = 4$$
$$y = x - 2$$

Again, first graph each equation on the same set of axes using the slope-intercept form. Since the first equation is not in slope-intercept form, subtract x from each side of the equation to get $y = -x + 4$. The slope of this line is -1 and the y-intercept is 4. In the second equation, the slope is 1, and the y-intercept is -2. The figure below shows these two lines graphed on the same set of axes, intersecting at the point (3, 1).

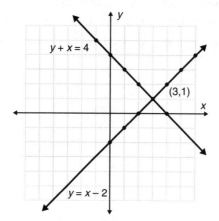

What is special about the two lines in this system is that they meet to form 90° angles, or right angles. In other words, these two lines are perpendicular. Notice that the slope of the first line is -1 and the slope of the second line is 1. If the slopes of two lines are **negative reciprocals**, like -1 and 1 or -2 and $\dfrac{1}{2}$, then the lines are perpendicular.

To review different types of lines, including **perpendicular lines**, refer to the geometry concepts in chapter 8.

Special Systems of Equations

There are three different cases of solutions to systems of linear equations: one solution, infinite solutions, or no solution.

The first case, **one solution**, was discussed previously when one solution was found for the system—the two lines intersect at a single point.

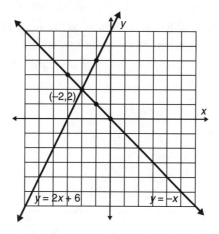

The second case, **infinite solutions**, is when the lines appear to have different equations but end up being the same line after the equations are transformed to $y = mx + b$ form. These lines are called **coincident lines** and actually share all the same points. Therefore, there are infinite solutions to a system of coincident lines.

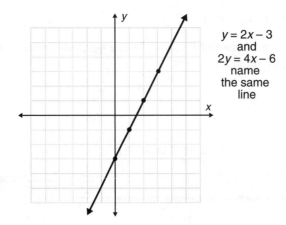

$y = 2x - 3$
and
$2y = 4x - 6$
name
the same
line

The third case, **no solution**, is when the lines do not intersect at all. The only way this can happen in a plane is if the lines are parallel. Parallel lines in the same plane slant at the same rate, running next to each other but never touching. Therefore, parallel lines have the same slope. If two lines on the same set of axes have the same slope, then there is no solution to this system of parallel lines. In the figure below, each line has a slope of -1; therefore, the lines are parallel and do not intersect.

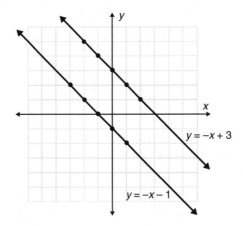

$y = -x + 3$

$y = -x - 1$

REMEMBER THIS!

- **Parallel lines** have the same slope.

- **Perpendicular lines** have slopes that are negative reciprocals of one another.

PRACTICE 5

Fill in each blank with the best possible answer. Answers and explanations are located at the end of the chapter.

18. The solution to the system $y = 2x - 1$ and $y = -x + 5$ is _____.

19. The system of equations $y = 2x - 5$ and $-4x + 2y = -10$ has _____ solution(s).

20. In the system $6y = 3x + 6$ and $y = \frac{1}{2}x - 1$, there is (are) _____ solution(s).

21. _____ lines have the same slope.

22. _____ lines have slopes that are negative reciprocals.

23. A line that is perpendicular to the line $4x = 3y - 15$ has a slope of _____.

SUMMARY

Coordinate geometry is an important application in mathematics that involves both algebraic and geometric concepts. In conclusion, remember these four things about working in the coordinate plane:

1. When plotting points, move left or right the number of units of the x-coordinate and move up or down the number of units of the y-coordinate.

2. Use the midpoint, distance, and slope formulas for calculating these measures. Use the slope-intercept form ($y = mx + b$) to graph linear equations.

3. To solve a system of equations, look for the point of intersection of the lines. A linear system of equations will have one solution, infinite solutions, or no solution.

4. Parallel lines have the same slope, and perpendicular lines have slopes that are negative reciprocals of one another.

Practice Answers and Explanations

1. B

This point is located in quadrant IV, 4 units to the right and 6 units below the origin.

2. D

This point is located in quadrant IV, 6 units to the right and 4 units below the origin.

3. A

This point is located in quadrant II, 4 units to the left and 6 units above the origin.

4. E

This point is located in quadrant I, 4 units to the right and 6 units above the origin.

5. C

This point is located in quadrant III, 4 units to the left and 6 units below the origin.

6. (–1, –5)

The midpoint can be found by substituting the points into the formula

$$\left(\frac{x_1+x_2}{2}, \frac{y_1+y_2}{2}\right) = \left(\frac{2+-4}{2}, \frac{-3+-7}{2}\right) = \left(\frac{-2}{2}, \frac{-10}{2}\right) = (-1, -5).$$

7. (–11, –12)

The point can be found by substituting into the midpoint formula and setting it equal to the known midpoint: $\left(\frac{x_1+x_2}{2}, \frac{y_1+y_2}{2}\right) = \left(\frac{5+x_2}{2}, \frac{4+y_2}{2}\right) = (-3, -4).$ Now set each expression in the formula equal to its coordinate at the midpoint: $\frac{5+x_2}{2} = -3$ and $\frac{4+y_2}{2} = -4$. Cross multiply in the first equation to get $5 + x_2 = -6$, so $x_2 = -11$. Cross multiply in the second equation to get $4 + y_2 = -8$, so $y_2 = -12$. Therefore, the coordinates of point B are $(-11, -12)$.

8. 13

Substitute the coordinates of each point into the distance formula.

$$\sqrt{(x_1-x_2)^2 + (y_1-y_2)^2} = \sqrt{((-2)-(-7))^2 + ((-3)-(-15))^2}$$

$$= \sqrt{(5)^2 + (12)^2}$$

$$= \sqrt{25+144}$$

$$= \sqrt{169}$$

$$= 13$$

9. $\sqrt{29}$

Substitute the coordinates of each point into the distance formula.

$$\sqrt{(x_1 - x_2)^2 + (y_1 - y_2)^2} = \sqrt{(1-6)^2 + (4-2)^2}$$
$$= \sqrt{(-5)^2 + (2)^2}$$
$$= \sqrt{25+4}$$
$$= \sqrt{29}$$

10.   False

The slope of a line is the change in y over the change in x.

11.   True

Use the slope formula: $m = \dfrac{\text{change in } y}{\text{change in } x} = \dfrac{y_1 - y_2}{x_1 - x_2} = \dfrac{-1-3}{6-(-1)} = \dfrac{-4}{7}$.

12.   True

Any line with the equation $y = k$ is a horizontal line.

13.   False

Any line with the equation $x = k$ is a vertical line.

14.   False

The point $(0, -2)$ lies on the y-axis. This point could be a y-intercept, not an x-intercept.

15.   True

The point $(0, -10)$ lies on the y-axis and could be the y-intercept of an equation.

16. $y = 2.5x + 4$

Since each video costs \$2.50 to rent, $m = 2.50$, or 2.5. The initial cost of the membership is \$4, so this is the y-intercept, or b.

17.   \$2 per mile

The cost per mile will be the value of m in the linear equation, which is 2.

18.   (2, 3)

When the two lines are graphed on the same set of axes, they cross at the point (2, 3). This is shown in the figure below.

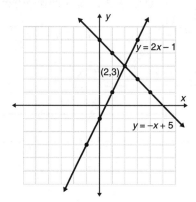

19.   Infinite

When the equation $-4x + 2y = -10$ is converted to $y = mx + b$ form, it becomes $y = 2x - 5$. Since the equations are the same, the lines coincide, and every point on the line is in the solution set. Therefore, there are infinite solutions.

20.   No

When the equations are in $y = mx + b$ form, they each have a slope of $\frac{1}{2}$. Since they have the same slope and are not the same line, the lines are parallel and will never intersect. Therefore, there is no solution to this system of equations.

21.   Parallel

Parallel lines have the same slope and never intersect.

22.   Perpendicular

Perpendicular lines meet to form right angles, and their slopes are negative reciprocals.

23. $\boxtimes \dfrac{3}{4}$

When the equation $4x = 3y - 15$ is converted to $y = mx + b$ form, it becomes $y = \frac{4}{3}x + 5$. Its slope is therefore $\frac{4}{3}$. Perpendicular lines have slopes that are negative reciprocals of one another. The negative reciprocal of $\frac{4}{3}$ is $\boxtimes \frac{3}{4}$.

CHAPTER 10 TEST

Try the following questions to test your knowledge of coordinate geometry.

1. In the figure below, what letter corresponds with the coordinates (4, –2)?

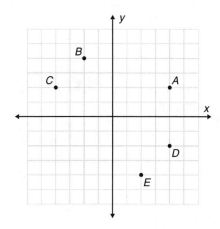

(A) A

(B) B

(C) C

(D) D

(E) E

2. In which quadrant is the point (–2, 3) located?

(A) I

(B) II

(C) III

(D) IV

(E) None of these

3. If the endpoints of segment $\overline{AB}$ are $A(3, 8)$ and $B(-1, 2)$, what is the midpoint of segment $\overline{AB}$?

   (A) $(-2, 5)$

   (B) $(2, 5)$

   (C) $(1, 2)$

   (D) $(5, 1)$

   (E) $(1, 5)$

4. If the midpoint M of line segment $\overline{CD}$ has coordinates $(6, -2)$ and C is $(3, 4)$, what are the coordinates of point D?

   (A) $(-8, -9)$

   (B) $(9, 2)$

   (C) $(9, -8)$

   (D) $(3, 1)$

   (E) $(-3, -1)$

5. Which of the following represents the distance between the points $(-2, 5)$ and $(3, 0)$?

   (A) 5

   (B) 25

   (C) 50

   (D) $10\sqrt{2}$

   (E) $5\sqrt{2}$

6. If a line containing the two points $(7, 3)$ and $(t, 5)$ has a slope of $\frac{2}{3}$, what is the value of t?

   (A) -10

   (B) 6

   (C) 20

   (D) 10

   (E) -6

7. What is the slope of the line $2x - y = 5$?

   (A) −2

   (B) 2

   (C) 5

   (D) −5

   (E) $\dfrac{5}{2}$

8. Which of the following lines has a slope equal to 0?

   (A) $y = 3x + 1$

   (B) $y = x$

   (C) $y = 4$

   (D) $x = 0$

   (E) $x = -3$

9. Which of the following equations could represent the line in the figure below?

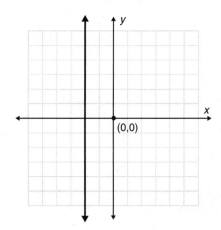

   (A) $x = 2$

   (B) $x = -2$

   (C) $x = 0$

   (D) $y = 2$

   (E) $y = -2$

10. Based on the graph below, which of the following is the solution to the system of equations?

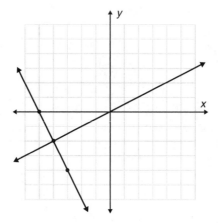

(A) $(-2, 4)$

(B) $(-4, 2)$

(C) $(-6, 0)$

(D) $(-4, -2)$

(E) $(0, -6)$

11. What is the solution to the following system of equations?

$$y = 3x - 1$$
$$-3x + y = 5$$

(A) $(1, 5)$

(B) $(0, -1)$

(C) $(-3, 1)$

(D) $(-3, 5)$

(E) There is no solution.

12. Which of the following equations would *NOT* intersect with the line $2y + 4 = x$?

(A) $y = 2x + 4$

(B) $y = -2x + 2$

(C) $y = \dfrac{1}{2}x - 4$

(D) $y = -\dfrac{1}{2}x + 4$

(E) $y = -2x - 2$

13. Which of the following statements *BEST* describes the system of equations below?

$$3y = 3x + 9$$
$$y - x = 3$$

(A) The lines are skew.

(B) The lines are perpendicular.

(C) The lines intersect at two points.

(D) The lines do not intersect.

(E) The lines are coincident.

14. The cost of parking at a city lot is $5.50 for the first hour and $4.00 for each additional hour. If y represents the total cost and x is the number of additional hours parked, which of the following linear equations could represent this situation?

(A) $y = 4x + 5.50$

(B) $y = -4x + 5.50$

(C) $y = 4x - 5.50$

(D) $y = 5.5x + 4$

(E) $y = 5.5x - 4$

15. Using the situation in question 14, how much will it cost to park at this garage for eight hours?

(A) $9.50

(B) $32.00

(C) $33.50

(D) $37.50

(E) $76.00

Answers and Explanations

1. D

To graph the point (4, –2), start at the origin and move four units to the right. From there, move two units down. The letter at this placement is *D*.

2. B

To graph the point (–2, 3), start at the origin and move two units to the left. From there, move three units up. This location is in the second quadrant, or quadrant II.

3. E

The midpoint can be found by substituting the coordinates for *A* and *B* into the midpoint formula: $\left(\dfrac{x_1+x_2}{2}, \dfrac{y_1+y_2}{2}\right) = \left(\dfrac{3+-1}{2}, \dfrac{8+2}{2}\right) = \left(\dfrac{2}{2}, \dfrac{10}{2}\right) = (1, 5)$.

4. C

Point *D* can be found by substituting into the midpoint formula and setting it equal to the known midpoint: $\left(\dfrac{x_1+x_2}{2}, \dfrac{y_1+y_2}{2}\right) = \left(\dfrac{3+x_2}{2}, \dfrac{4+y_2}{2}\right) = (6, -2)$.
Now set each expression in the formula equal to its coordinate at the midpoint: $\dfrac{3+x_2}{2} = 6$ and $\dfrac{4+y_2}{2} = -2$. Cross multiply in the first equation to get $3 + x_2 = 12$, so $x_2 = 9$. Cross multiply in the second equation to get $4 + y_2 = -4$, so $y_2 = -8$. Therefore, the coordinates of point *D* are (9, –8).

5. E

Substitute the coordinates of each point into the distance formula:

$$\sqrt{(x_1-x_2)^2 + (y_1-y_2)^2} = \sqrt{((-2)-(3))^2 + (5-0)^2}$$

$$= \sqrt{(-5)^2 + (5)^2}$$

$$= \sqrt{25+25}$$

$$= \sqrt{50}$$

$$= \sqrt{25}\sqrt{2}$$

$$= 5\sqrt{2}$$

6. D

Use the slope formula with the given coordinates and set it equal to the slope of $\frac{2}{3}$:
$\frac{y_1 - y_2}{x_1 - x_2} = \frac{3-5}{7-t} = \frac{2}{3}$. Simplify the left side of the proportion: $\frac{-2}{7-t} = \frac{2}{3}$. Cross multiply to get $14 - 2t = -6$. Subtract 14 from both sides of the equation and then divide by -2 to get $t = 10$. The missing x-coordinate is 10.

7. B

Convert the equation to $y = mx + b$ form. First subtract $2x$ from each side of the equation to get $-y = -2x + 5$. Then divide each side of the equation by -1 to get $y = 2x - 5$. The value of m, which is the slope, is 2.

8. C

Any line of the form $y = k$ is a horizontal line and has a slope of 0. The only line in this form is choice (C). Choice (A) has a slope of 3, choice (B) has a slope of 1, and choices (D) and (E) are vertical lines that have undefined slope.

9. B

Since the line in the figure is a vertical line, it is in the form $x = k$. The line crosses the x-axis at -2, so the equation of the line is $x = -2$.

10. D

Since the two lines in the system of equations intersect at the point $(-4, -2)$, this is the solution to the system.

11. E

First change each equation to $y = mx + b$ form. Since the first equation is already in this form, add $3x$ to each side of the second equation to get $y = 3x + 5$. Each equation has a slope of 3 and different y-intercepts. Therefore, the lines are parallel, and there is no solution to this system of equations.

12. C

To find the equation of the line that would not intersect with the given line, find the equation of the line that has the same slope. Since the equation $2y + 4 = x$ is equal to $y = \frac{1}{2}x - 2$ in slope-intercept form, the slope of this line is $\frac{1}{2}$. Since choice (C) also has a slope of $\frac{1}{2}$, it is parallel to the given line and does not intersect it.

13. E

When the first line is written in slope-intercept form, it is equivalent to $y = x + 3$. When the second line is written in slope-intercept form, it is also equal to $y = x + 3$. Since the equations are the same, the lines are coincident and represent the same line when graphed.

14. A

The initial cost is \$5.50, so this is the y-intercept, or b, of the equation. Parking costs \$4.00 per additional hour, so this number needs to be multiplied by the number of additional hours parked (x). This makes 4 the slope, or m. Thus, the equation becomes $y = 4x + 5.50$.

15. C

The cost for eight hours can be calculated by using the formula $y = 4x + 5.50$. Keep in mind that the number of additional hours, or x, is equal to 7 because the first hour is paid for by the initial cost of \$5.50. $y = 4(7) + 5.50 = 28 + 5.50 = \$33.50$.

SECTION III

Algebra

CHAPTER 11

Algebra

In this chapter, you will embark on a study of the concepts of algebra, including such topics as translating statements into expressions and equations, defined operations, polynomials and factoring, rational expressions, and simplifying complex fractions.

TRANSLATING ALGEBRAIC EXPRESSIONS

Algebra is a mathematical language that uses numbers and symbols to create statements and solve problems. The variables, or unknown quantities, for which you are solving are commonly represented by letters such as x or n. Before starting your study of algebraic concepts, it is important to be able to translate word sentences and word problems into algebraic expressions and equations. When translating word phrases into symbols, look for key words that represent certain operations and symbols. The following chart contains the basic operations and some of the common key words and phrases used with each one.

Add (+)	Subtract (−)	Multiply (×)	Divide (÷)	Equal (=)
sum, increased by, more than, plus, exceeds	difference, decreased by, less than, minus, reduced	product, multiplied by, of, times	quotient, divided by, into	is, result, total, equal to

It is important to understand the difference between an algebraic expression and an equation.

An **algebraic expression** contains numbers, variables, and operations to state a relationship. An **equation** is two algebraic expressions set equal to each other. Therefore, an equation contains an equal sign, whereas an expression does not.

To convert a statement into an expression or equation, identify the key words for the operations mentioned above and translate the statement. This process is similar to translating from one language to another.

For example, to translate the statement "6 times a number n, added to 4," focus on the key word *times*, which represents multiplication, and the phrase *added to*, which indicates addition. Note that n represents the unknown number in the statement. Using the numbers in the statement, translate in order from left to right. Therefore, the expression would read $6 \times n + 4$, or $6n + 4$.

Let's try another example. Translate the sentence "Twice the difference of a number n and 4 is 20." The word *twice* tells you to multiply the remaining part of the statement by 2. Since *difference* is a key word for subtraction, the difference of a number and 4 is written as $n - 4$. The end of the statement "*is* 20" indicates that the expression should be set equal to 20. Therefore, the equation becomes $2(n - 4) = 20$. In this case, the parentheses are important in indicating the correct order of operations.

Most cases of translating expressions are literal; the order of the words/numbers/variables in the sentence is the same as the order in the algebraic expression. However, the exceptions to this rule are the key words *more than* and *less than*. In each case, these phrases change the order of the elements in the statement. For instance, the statement "6 less than x" would be translated as $x - 6$, not $6 - x$. Keep this in mind as you continue your study of translating expressions.

DEFINED OPERATIONS

A **defined operation** is an operation in which symbols (sometimes strange symbols such as @ or #) are used to represent algebraic expressions. Defined operations often use a combination of common operations like addition, subtraction, multiplication, and division. For example, say you are told that the operation a & b, where a and b

represent integers, is defined as $ab + 4a$. Therefore, to evaluate 2 & 3, substitute 2 for a and 3 for b. The operation becomes as follows:

$$2 \& 3$$
$$= 2 \times 3 + 4 \times 2$$
$$= 6 + 8$$
$$= 14$$

Don't forget to use the correct order of operations when evaluating defined expressions.

FLASHBACK

Refer to chapter 1 to review the correct **order of operations**.

As another example of a defined operation, say the operation # a # is defined as $a^2 - 1$. To evaluate # 4 #, substitute 4 for a:

$$\# 4 \#$$
$$= 4^2 - 1$$
$$= 16 - 1$$
$$= 15$$

PRACTICE 1

Match the phrase in the first column with the correct translation in the second column. Answers and explanations are located at the end of the chapter.

1. Three more than twice a number
   A. $2n - 3$

2. Three times the sum of a number and 2
   B. $2n + 3$

3. Two less than three times a number is 5
   C. $3(n + 2)$

4. The product of two and a number, decreased by 3
   D. $3n - 2 = 5$

Fill in the blank with the correct solution.

5. If $a \# b$ is defined as $2a^2 - b$, then the value of $1 \# 2$ is _____.

6. If $\&c\&$ is defined as $(3c)^2$, then the value of $\&4\&$ is _____.

MONOMIALS AND POLYNOMIALS

When learning the basic elements of algebra, it is important to know the different parts of algebraic expressions.

Numbers, in algebra, are called **constants**. Letters used to represent unknown quantities are **variables**. A number that appears in front of a variable (that is connected by multiplication) is called a **coefficient**. Together, a coefficient and a variable, like $6x$, is called a **term**.

Algebraic expressions containing more than one term are called **polynomials**, in which the prefix *poly-* means "many." A single term is called a **monomial**, in which the prefix *mono-* means "one." Some examples of monomials are 3, $4x$, $-6ab$, and $24x^2y$.

Algebraic terms are separated by addition and subtraction. Expressions such as $a + b$ or $3x - 4yz$ are called **binomials**, because they contain two terms that do not have exactly the same variables and exponents. Binomials are polynomials with two terms; the prefix *bi-* means "two."

As you might have guessed, a **trinomial** is a polynomial with three distinct terms, such as $x^2 + 3x - 4$. The prefix *tri-* means "three."

Adding and Subtracting Polynomials

There are special rules for performing the basic operations with polynomials. The first, which involves adding and subtracting polynomials, is called **combining like terms**.

The phrase *like terms* refers to polynomial terms that contain exactly the same variable(s) and exponent(s).

Some examples of like terms are $3x$ and $4x$, $5ab$ and $-10ab$, and $8r^2t$ and $-9r^2t$. Notice that in like terms, the variables and exponents must be the same, but the coefficients do not have to be the same. When adding and subtracting polynomials, only like terms can be combined. Take the following examples.

In $6c + 3c = 9c$, the variables are the same, so the terms can be combined. To combine the terms, add the coefficients of 6 and 3 and keep the variable the same.

The equation $14x^2 - 5x^2 = 9x^2$ also contains terms that have the same variables with the same exponents. To simplify the expression, subtract the coefficients of 14 and 5 to get 9. The simplified answer is $9x^2$.

In the expression $7x + 8y$, the variables are not the same. Therefore, these terms cannot be combined. The simplified answer is still $7x + 8y$.

Problems that contain grouping symbols sometimes take an additional step to simplify. You must eliminate the grouping symbols before any like terms can be combined.

Take, for example, the expression $(9x - 3y) - (5x - 8y)$. The first step is to use the distributive property to eliminate the parentheses. The expression becomes $9x - 3y - 5x + 8y$. Notice that because $8y$ is a negative term, it becomes positive when the subtraction is distributed. Now combine like terms to get $9x - 5x - 3y + 8y = 4x + 5y$. This expression cannot be simplified any further, since the variable in each term is different.

PRACTICE 2

Using each term no more than once, fill in each blank with the choice from the word bank below that best completes the statement. Answers and explanations are located at the end of the chapter.

binomial	constant	trinomial	monomial	like
coefficient	variable	unlike	distributive	property

7. The expression $3x^2 + 5x$ can be described as a _____.

8. In the expression $5x + 6$, the 6 is the _____ term.

9. The polynomial $4c^3 + 8c^3$ contains _____ terms.

10. After the like terms are combined, the polynomial $7x - 4x + 8x$ becomes a _____.

11. In the expression $25p^5q$, p represents a _____.

12. In the expression $10b^4$, the number 10 is the _____.

Multiplying Polynomials

When multiplying polynomials, coefficients are multiplied separately from variables. It is important to note the rules for multiplying the exponents of like bases.

FLASHBACK

To review the **laws of exponents**, refer to chapter 7: Powers and Roots.

FLASHBACK

Refer to chapter 1: Properties of Numbers to review the **distributive property**.

Here are four situations that occur when multiplying polynomials.

MULTIPLYING A MONOMIAL BY A MONOMIAL

When multiplying a monomial by a monomial, multiply the coefficients and then follow the rules for multiplying the exponents of like bases.

In the example $3x^2 \times 4x^3$, multiply the coefficients and add the exponents of the like bases. Thus, the result is $3x^2 \times 4x^3 = 12x^5$.

MULTIPLYING A MONOMIAL BY A POLYNOMIAL

To multiply a monomial by a polynomial, use the distributive property.

For the expression $6y^3(2y + 3)$, multiply the factor of $6y^3$ by both terms inside the parentheses. The expression becomes $6y^3 \times 2y + 6y^3 \times 3$. Now simplify each term by multiplying the coefficients and adding the exponents of the like bases. The result is $12y^4 + 18y^3$.

MULTIPLYING A BINOMIAL BY A BINOMIAL

To multiply a binomial by a binomial, use a special form of the distributive property known by the following acronym:

F   O   I   L

FOIL can be used when multiplying two binomials together.

For example, to multiply $(x + a)(x + b)$:

First: Multiply the first term in each binomial, $x \times x = x^2$.

Outer: Multiply the outer terms in each binomial, $b \times x = bx$.

Inner: Multiply the inner terms in each binomial, $a \times x = ax$.

Last: Multiply the last term in each binomial, $a \times b = ab$.

The final result is $x^2 + bx + ax + ab = x^2 + (a + b)x + ab$.

Let's practice this process. Using FOIL, simplify $(x + 5)(x - 4)$. To begin, multiply the first terms $x \times x = x^2$. Then multiply the outer terms to get $x \times -4 = -4x$. Multiply the inner terms to get $5 \times x = 5x$. Then multiply the last terms to get $5 \times -4 = -20$. The expression becomes $x^2 - 4x + 5x - 20$. Combine like terms for a final answer of $x^2 + x - 20$.

Try another example with the expression $(2x - 3)(3x - 1)$. The product of the first terms is $6x^2$, the product of the outer terms is $-2x$, the product of the inner terms is $-9x$, and the product of the last terms is 3. Combine each of these products to get $6x^2 - 2x - 9x + 3$. Combine like terms to get a final result of $6x^2 - 11x + 3$.

MULTIPLYING A POLYNOMIAL BY ANOTHER POLYNOMIAL

To multiply any polynomial by another polynomial, you can use the distributive property.

In the example $(3x^2 + 4x - 1)(2x^2 - 3x + 3)$, there are two trinomials. Multiply each term from the first trinomial by each term in the second trinomial, as follows: $(3x^2 \times 2x^2) - (3x^2 \times 3x) + (3x^2 \times 3) + (4x \times 2x^2) - (4x \times 3x) + (4x \times 3) - (1 \times 2x^2) + (1 \times 3x) - (1 \times 3)$.

Perform all of the multiplication first, according to the order of operations. The expression becomes $6x^4 - 9x^3 + 9x^2 + 8x^3 - 12x^2 + 12x - 2x^2 + 3x - 3$.

Combine like terms to get $6x^4 - x^3 - 5x^2 + 15x - 3$.

When simplifying, some expressions contain a combination of operations. Take the expression $4(x - 5) + 3(2x + 1)$. The first step in simplifying an expression like this is to multiply using the distributive property to eliminate the parentheses. The expression becomes $4x - 20 + 6x + 3$. The next step is to combine like terms to get a result of $10x - 17$.

PRACTICE 3

Simplify each of the following expressions. Answers and explanations are located at the end of the chapter.

13. $7(x - 3) =$ _____

14. $3x(x^2 + 2x - 4) =$ _____

15. $(x - 3)(x + 4) =$ _____

16. $(x - 2)(3x + 2) =$ _____

17. $(3x - 2) + 5(x + 1) =$ _____

18. $(2x - 1)(3x^2 - 5x + 2) =$ _____

FACTORING

To simplify algebraic expressions, it is necessary to know how to factor them. The **factors** of a number or expression are the pieces of the number or expression that multiply together to form the expression. When you are finding the factors of an expression, you are breaking it down into smaller parts.

REMEMBER THIS!

Finding the **factors** of a number or expression is the opposite of finding its multiples.

For example, to find factors of the number 6, think of all of the pairs of numbers that can be multiplied together to get 6. In other words, think of any number that would divide evenly into 6 without a remainder. The factors of 6 are 1, 2, 3, and 6.

To find the factors of an algebraic expression, such as $2x^2y$, break down the expression into smaller pieces. The expression $2x^2y$ can be expressed as the product of $2 \times x \times x \times y$. These are all factors of $2x^2y$.

Listed below are various types of expressions and the techniques used to factor these particular expressions.

Using a Greatest Common Factor

When an expression contains more than one term, it is often helpful to find the greatest common factor (GFC) of the terms to simplify. To find the GFC of any polynomial, look for common factors in the coefficients and common variables in each term. For example, in the trinomial $3x^3 - 6x^2 + 9x$, each term has a coefficient multiple of 3 and variable multiple of x. Factor out $3x$ from each term: $3x^3 - 6x^2 + 9x = 3x(x^2 - 2x + 3)$.

The Difference between Two Squares

There are some special cases of factoring polynomials. One of these cases is finding the difference between two perfect squares, like $x^2 - 25$, $y^2 - 49$, or $4c^2 - 9$. To factor the difference between two perfect squares, take the square root of each term. For example, in the binomial $x^2 - a^2$, x is the square root of x^2 and a is the square root of a^2. Then write the factors in the form $(x - a)(x + a)$. Following this model, the factors of the expressions above are as follows:

$$x^2 - 25 = (x - 5)(x + 5)$$
$$y^2 - 49 = (y - 7)(y + 7)$$
$$4c^2 - 9 = (2c - 3)(2c + 3)$$

REMEMBER THIS!

When factoring the **difference between two perfect squares**, the factors are in the form $x^2 - a^2 = (x - a)(x + a)$.

How to Factor Trinomials

When factoring certain trinomials, the result is often two binomials. To factor a trinomial in the form $ax^2 + bx + c$, where a, b, and c represent real numbers, take a look at the values of a, b, and c. If the value of a is 1, then the second terms in each binomial factor must have a sum of b and a product of c.

For example, take the expression $x^2 + 5x + 6$. The value of $a = 1$, $b = 5$, and $c = 6$. To find the factors of this expression, first list factors of 6 (c): 1 and 6, −1 and −6, 2 and 3, and −2 and −3. The only pair of factors that has a sum of 5 (b) is 2 and 3. So now use the 2 and 3 as the second terms in the binomial factors. This makes the factors of the expression equal to $(x + 2)(x + 3)$.

To check to see if these binomials are the correct factors, use FOIL to multiply them together: $(x + 2)(x + 3) = x^2 + 3x + 2x + 6 = x^2 + 5x + 6$, which is the original trinomial.

Practice this procedure again with the trinomial $x^2 - 5x - 14$. The value of $a = 1$, $b = -5$, and $c = -14$. Again, first list the factors of −14: 1 and −14, −1 and 14, 2 and −7, and −2 and 7. The only pair of factors in this list that has a sum of −5 is 2 and −7. So use the 2 and −7 as the second terms in the binomial factors. This makes the factors of the expression equal to $(x + 2)(x - 7)$.

Not all instances contain a trinomial where the value of a is 1. Take, for example, the expression $3x^2 + 13x + 4$. Since the values are $a = 3$, $b = 13$, and $c = 4$, you will need to do some trial and error with the factors of 4 to find the binomial factors. Once again, first list the factors of 4: 1 and 4, −1 and −4, 2 and 2, and −2 and −2. Since the value of a is no longer 1 and the first terms need to be factors of $3x^2$, you know the binomials will be in the form $(3x + \_)(x + \_)$. Now you need to experiment with different placements of the pairs of factors of 4. Start with the factors $(3x + 2)(x + 2)$ and use FOIL to multiply them together. The expression becomes $3x^2$ (F) + $6x$ (O) + $2x$ (I) + 4(L). Combine like terms to get $3x^2 + 8x + 4$. Since this is not the original expression, try again.

This time, try 1 and 4 for the factors of 4. The factors become $(3x + 1)(x + 4)$. Use FOIL to multiply them together. The expression becomes $3x^2$ (F) + $12x$ (O) + $1x$ (I) + 4(L). Combine like terms to get $3x^2 + 13x + 4$. Since this is the original expression, these are the correct factors.

When factoring any factorable polynomial in the form $ax^2 + bx + c$, where $a = 1$, the constant terms of the factors have a sum of b and a product of c. If the value of $a \neq 1$, use trial and error with the factors of c to find the factors.

One thing to keep in mind is that not all trinomials are factorable. An example of a nonfactorable trinomial is $x^2 + 3x - 1$. No factors of -1 also have a sum of 3.

Perfect Square Trinomials

A **perfect square trinomial** is another special case that is the product of two equal binomials. These trinomials are factored in the same way as mentioned above, looking for the sum of b and the product of c.

An example of a perfect square trinomial is $x^2 + 10x + 25$. Factors of 25 that have a sum of 10 are 5 and 5. The factors then become $(x + 5)(x + 5)$, or $(x + 5)^2$. Another example of a perfect square trinomial is $n^2 - 6n + 9$. Since the factors of 9 that have a sum of -6 are -3 and -3, the factors of the trinomial are $(n - 3)(n - 3)$, or $(n - 3)^2$.

A **perfect square trinomial** has two equal binomial factors. They have two forms and are factored as follows: $x^2 + 2ax + a^2 = (x + a)^2$, and $x^2 - 2ax + a^2 = (x - a)^2$.

Factoring Completely

For polynomials to be factored completely, the expression must be broken down into its smallest possible factors. This means that two or more steps may be involved to factor the expression.

Take the expression $2x^2 - 128$. First look for any common factors between the terms, or the GCF. Each term contains a factor of 2, so the expression becomes $2(x^2 - 64)$. Since the binomial within the parentheses is the difference between two squares, you can break it down even more: the factors become $2(x - 8)(x + 8)$. The expression is now factored completely.

Another example is the trinomial $3x^3 + 12x^2 - 36x$. First look for a common factor among the three terms. Each contains a factor of $3x$, so the expression becomes $3x(x^2 + 4x - 12)$ when $3x$ is factored out. Now see if the trinomial inside the parentheses can be factored. Since the factors of -12 that also combine to a sum of 4 are -2 and 6, the factors are $3x(x - 2)(x + 6)$. Now the expression is factored completely.

REMEMBER THIS!

Use these steps to make sure that the expression is factored completely:

1. Factor out the GCF, if it exists.

2. Factor the difference between two squares.

3. Factor the trinomial into two binomials (FOIL).

PRACTICE 4

Answer TRUE or FALSE to each of the following. Answers and explanations are located at the end of the chapter.

19. **T F**   The greatest common factor of $4x^4$ and $12x^3$ is $4x^2$.

20. **T F**   The factored form of $x^2 - 16$ is $x(x - 16)$.

21. **T F**   When factored completely, $4x^2 - 24x$ is equal to $4x(x - 6)$.

22. **T F**   The two binomial factors of $a^2 - 81$ are $(a - 9)$ and $(a - 9)$.

23. **T F**   The trinomial $c^2 - 2c - 35$ is equivalent to the factors $(c - 5)$ and $(c + 7)$.

24. **T F**   The expression $x^2 + 6x + 9$ is equivalent to $(x + 3)^2$.

25. **T F**   When factored completely, the expression $5x^3 + 15x^2 - 10x$ is equivalent to $5x(x - 1)(x - 2)$.

RATIONAL EXPRESSIONS

Simplifying

A **rational expression** is an expression that may involve constants and/or variables in the form $\frac{a}{b}$, where b cannot equal 0. When a fraction contains any common factors between the numerator and denominator, it can be reduced or simplified. Take the fraction $\frac{4}{6}$. Since each number has a factor of 2, divide each number by 2 to reduce the fraction: $\frac{4 \div 2}{6 \div 2} = \frac{2}{3}$. This is the simplified form of the fraction.

FLASHBACK

For more review and practice **simplifying rational numbers**, refer to chapter 3: Fractions and Decimals.

This section will concentrate on rational expressions that contain variables as well as constants. To simplify them, you will continue to look for common factors. Let's look at a few examples.

Take the rational expression $\frac{3x}{6x^2}$. When examining the numerator and denominator, each has a factor of $3x$. Divide each by this common factor to simplify the expression: $\frac{3x \div 3x}{6x^2 \div 3x} = \frac{1}{2x}$.

In the expression $\frac{4x - 16}{2x - 8}$, both the numerator and denominator need to be factored first to see how you can simplify: $\frac{4x - 16}{2x - 8} = \frac{4(x - 4)}{2(x - 4)}$. Each has a common factor of $x - 4$. When this factor is divided out of the numerator and denominator, or canceled, the result is $\frac{4}{2} = \frac{2}{1}$, which is equal to 2.

In the expression $\frac{x^2 - x - 6}{x^2 - 9}$, both the numerator and denominator can be factored into two binomials. The numerator is a factorable trinomial, and the denominator is the difference between two perfect squares: $\frac{x^2 - x - 6}{x^2 - 9} = \frac{(x - 3)(x + 2)}{(x - 3)(x + 3)}$. Notice that the common factor of $x - 3$ can be canceled out. The expression becomes

$\dfrac{\cancel{(x-3)}(x+2)}{\cancel{(x-3)}(x+3)} = \dfrac{x+2}{x+3}$. It is important to note at this point that you are allowed to divide out, or cancel, only common factors. Notice in the last example that the xs could not be canceled out because they are not factors; in other words, they are connected to other terms by addition, not multiplication.

REMEMBER THIS!

When simplifying rational expressions, it is important to factor first and be sure to cancel *only* factors.

Adding and Subtracting

When adding and subtracting rational expressions in the form of fractions, it is necessary to have a common denominator. To find the least common denominator (LCD), find the smallest expression that each denominator will divide into without a remainder. When this denominator is found, multiply both the numerator and denominator of the rational expressions by the missing factor needed to make the LCD. Then combine the expressions and keep the common denominator.

For example, to add the expressions $\dfrac{2}{x^2} + \dfrac{5}{x}$, find the least common denominator of the terms. The LCD of x^2 and x is x^2. Now multiply each term by the necessary factor to make each denominator equal to x^2. Since the first fraction already has this denominator, keep it as is. In the second fraction, the denominator of x needs to be multiplied by another factor of x to make it x^2. Therefore, both the numerator and denominator of the second term need to be multiplied by x: $\dfrac{2}{x^2} + \dfrac{5}{x} = \dfrac{2}{x^2} + \dfrac{5 \times x}{x \times x} = \dfrac{2}{x^2} + \dfrac{5x}{x^2}$. Now that there is a common denominator, add the numerators and keep the common denominator to get $\dfrac{2+5x}{x^2}$. Since there are no common factors between the numerator and denominator, the fraction is simplified.

Here are a few more examples of adding and subtracting rational expressions. Take $\dfrac{8}{x^2 - x} - \dfrac{3}{x-1}$. Factor each expression first to get $\dfrac{8}{x(x-1)} - \dfrac{3}{x-1}$. The LCD is $x(x-1)$.

Since the first fraction already has this as a denominator, keep it as is. Multiply the numerator and denominator of the second fraction by x to get the common denominator: $\dfrac{8}{x(x-1)} - \dfrac{3}{x-1} = \dfrac{8}{x(x-1)} - \dfrac{3 \times x}{x(x-1)} = \dfrac{8-3x}{x(x-1)}$. Since there are no common factors between the numerator and denominator, the fraction is simplified.

Now let's work with $\dfrac{x-4}{x^2+3x+2} + \dfrac{x+1}{x^2-x-2}$. Factor each expression first to get $\dfrac{x-4}{(x+2)(x+1)} + \dfrac{x+1}{(x-2)(x+1)}$. The LCD is $(x+2)(x+1)(x-2)$. Therefore, to create two fractions with this common denominator, multiply the numerator and denominator in the first expression by $(x-2)$ and the numerator and denominator in the second expression by $(x+2)$: $\dfrac{(x-2)(x-4)}{(x-2)(x+2)(x+1)} + \dfrac{(x+2)(x+1)}{(x-2)(x+1)(x+2)}$. Use FOIL when multiplying in each numerator. The expression becomes $\dfrac{x^2-6x+8}{(x-2)(x+2)(x+1)} + \dfrac{x^2+3x+2}{(x-2)(x+1)(x+2)}$. Combine like terms in the numerator to get $\dfrac{2x^2-3x+10}{(x-2)(x+2)(x+1)}$.

PRACTICE 5

Repetition is the key to math success. Try these questions to help refine your skills with simplifying and combining rational expressions.

26. When simplified completely, the expression $\dfrac{9x}{x^3}$ is equal to _____.

27. When simplified completely, the expression $\dfrac{6x-2}{3x^2+5x-2}$ is equal to _____.

28. If finding the sum of $\dfrac{7x}{2x^2} + \dfrac{4}{x^2}$, the common denominator is _____.

29. To convert to a common denominator in the difference $\dfrac{5}{x^2-49} - \dfrac{6x+1}{x-7}$, the numerator and denominator of the second fraction must be multiplied by _____.

30. After subtracting and simplifying, the expression $\dfrac{1}{x+2} - \dfrac{2}{x+1}$ is equivalent to _____.

Multiplying and Dividing

When performing multiplication and division with rational expressions, a common denominator is not necessary. For these problems, first factor each fraction in the numerator and denominator when possible. Then cancel out any common factors between the numerators and denominators. Finally, multiply across any remaining factors.

Take the example $\frac{xy^2}{ab} \times \frac{b^2}{xv}$. Each part of the expression is the product of factors, so no factoring is necessary. Now cancel the common factors of xy and b from both fractions and multiply across the remaining factors. The expression becomes $\frac{xy^2}{ab} \times \frac{b^2}{xy} = \frac{yb}{a}$.

Another example is $\frac{x^2 - 25}{2x - 10} \times \frac{2x^2 + 4x}{x + 5}$. First factor each part of the fractions to get $\frac{(x-5)(x+5)}{2(x-5)} \times \frac{2x(x+2)}{x+5}$. Cancel the common factors: $\frac{(x-5)\ (x+5)}{2\ (x-5)} \times \frac{2x(x+2)}{x+5}$.
The expression simplifies to $x(x+2)$ or $x^2 + 2x$.

The difference between dividing and multiplying rational expressions which are fractions boils down to one step: dividing by a fraction is the same as multiplying by its reciprocal. Therefore, when the operation is division, simply take the reciprocal of the fraction you are dividing by and then multiply as explained above. Take, for example, the quotient $\frac{36 - x^2}{4ab} \div \frac{x - 6}{2a}$. The first step is to take the reciprocal of the second fraction and change the operation to multiplication, so the expression becomes $\frac{36 - x^2}{4ab} \times \frac{2a}{x - 6}$. Now factor to get $\frac{(6-x)(6+x)}{4ab} \times \frac{2a}{x-6}$. Cancel any common factors. Since two of the factors are $x - 6$ and $6 - x$, a little more work needs to be done before canceling. First, change $6 - x$ to $-x + 6$ and factor out a -1. This expression now becomes $-1(x - 6)$. Therefore, when you cancel $x - 6$ and $6 - x$, the result is -1, not $+1$. In addition, when the 2 from the numerator of the second fraction is canceled with the 4 from the denominator of the first fraction, a 2 remains where the 4 once was, since $4 \div 2 = 2$: $\frac{\overset{-1}{(6-x)}(6+x)}{\underset{2}{4}ab} \times \frac{\overset{}{2a}}{x-6}$. The product becomes $\frac{-1(6+x)}{2b} = \frac{-6-x}{2b}$.

REMEMBER THIS!

Any factors in the form $\dfrac{x-a}{a-x}$ will be equal to -1.

PRACTICE 6

For each question, perform the indicated operation. Answers and explanations are located at the end of the chapter.

31. $\dfrac{3x^2}{4y^3} \times \dfrac{12y^2}{9x^2} =$

32. $\dfrac{r^2-81}{2t} \times \dfrac{6t^2}{r+9} =$

33. $\dfrac{2x-4}{z} \div \dfrac{4-x^2}{3z} =$

SIMPLIFYING COMPLEX FRACTIONS

A complex fraction is a fraction that contains other fraction(s) in the numerator and/ or denominator. One way to simplify complex fractions is to find the least common denominator of each fraction within the complex fraction and multiply each term by this LCD.

In the example $\dfrac{\frac{1}{x}}{\frac{6}{x^2}}$, the LCD is x^2. By multiplying each term by x^2, the result is $\dfrac{\frac{1}{x} \times x^2}{\frac{6}{x^2} \times x^2} = \dfrac{x}{6}$ after the common factors are canceled out.

For another example, look at the complex fraction $\dfrac{\frac{x}{y}+x}{\frac{1}{y^2}+\frac{1}{y}}$. The LCD is y^2, so multiply each of the four terms by y^2: $\dfrac{\frac{x}{y} \times y^2 + x \times y^2}{\frac{1}{y^2} \times y^2 + \frac{1}{y} \times y^2}$. Simplify by canceling common factors to get $\dfrac{xy+xy^2}{1+y}$. Factor the numerator to get $\dfrac{xy(1+y)}{1+y}$, which reduces to just xy.

PRACTICE 7

Answer TRUE or FALSE to each statement below. Answers and explanations are located at the end of the chapter.

34. **T   F**   When simplifying the complex fraction $\dfrac{\frac{1}{x^2}}{\frac{2}{3x}}$, the least common denominator is $3x^2$.

35. **T   F**   When simplified, the complex fraction $\dfrac{\frac{1}{a}+\frac{1}{b}}{ab}$ becomes $a + b$.

SUMMARY

Algebra is a critical branch in the world of mathematics and a foundation of many mathematical concepts and procedures. In conclusion, remember these seven points about working with algebra and its related topics:

1. When translating statements into mathematical expressions and equations, use key words to determine the correct operations and symbols.

2. When evaluating defined operations, use substitution and evaluate using the correct order of operations.

3. When adding and subtracting polynomials, combine only like terms, or terms with exactly the same variables and exponents.

4. Use the distributive property (FOIL) when multiplying polynomials.

5. When factoring polynomials, always look for the greatest common factor (GCF) of the terms first, the difference between two squares second, and the two binomial factors of a trinomial last.

6. When simplifying or performing operations with rational expressions in the form of fractions, factor first and cancel only common factors.

7. To simplify complex fractions, multiply each term of the fraction by the least common denominator (LCD).

Practice Answers and Explanations

1.   B

Twice a number is represented by $2n$, and three more than the number is represented by $+3$ to get $2n + 3$.

2. C

The sum of a number and 2 is represented by $n + 2$, and three times this sum is represented by $3(n + 2)$.

3. D

Two less than three times a number is represented by $3n - 2$. Setting this expression equal to 5 results in the equation $3n - 2 = 5$.

4. A

The product of 2 and a number is represented by $2n$. When this amount is decreased by 3, the related expression is $2n - 3$.

5. 0

Substitute $a = 1$ and $b = 2$ into the defined operation: $2(1)^2 - 2 = 2(1) - 2 = 2 - 2 = 0$.

6. 144

Substitute $c = 4$ into the defined operation: $(3 \times 4)^2 = 12^2 = 144$.

7. Binomial

This expression contains two terms.

8. Constant

This term contains only the number 6, a constant or unchanging value.

9. Like

Each term in the polynomial contains exactly the same variables and exponents on those variables.

10. Monomial

Since all of the terms in the expression are like terms, they can be combined to form a single term, or a monomial.

11. Variable

Letters, in algebra, are used to represent unknown quantities, or variables.

12. Coefficient

A number that appears in front of a variable connected by multiplication is known as a coefficient.

13. $7x - 21$

Multiply using the distributive property: $7(x - 3) = 7x - 21$.

14. $3x^3 + 6x^2 - 12x$

Multiply using the distributive property. Be sure to add the exponents when multiplying like bases: $3x(x^2 + 2x - 4) = 3x^3 + 6x^2 - 12x$.

15. $x^2 + x - 12$

Multiply using FOIL: $(x - 3)(x + 4) = x^2 + 4x - 3x - 12$. Combine like terms to get $x^2 + x - 12$.

16. $3x^2 - 4x - 4$

Multiply using FOIL: $(x - 2)(3x + 2) = 3x^2 + 2x - 6x - 4$. Combine like terms to get $3x^2 - 4x - 4$.

17. $8x + 3$

First multiply the second term using the distributive property. The expression becomes $3x - 2 + 5x + 5$. Then combine like terms to get $8x + 3$.

18. $6x^3 - 13x^2 + 9x - 2$

Multiply using the distributive property: $(2x - 1)(3x^2 - 5x + 2) = 6x^3 - 10x^2 + 4x - 3x^2 + 5x - 2$. Combine like terms to get $6x^3 - 13x^2 + 9x - 2$.

19. **False**

The greatest common factor is $4x^3$.

20. **False**

This is an example of the difference between two perfect squares. The factored form is $(x - 4)(x + 4)$.

21. **True**

22. **False**

This is another example of the difference between two perfect squares. The factors are $(a - 9)$ and $(a + 9)$.

23. **False**

The two binomial factors of this trinomial are $(c + 5)(c - 7)$.

24. True

This is an example of a perfect square trinomial, since the two factors are equal.

25. False

The factors of this trinomial are $5x$ and $(x^2 + 3x - 2)$. This trinomial cannot be factored any further.

26. $\dfrac{9}{x^2}$

Cancel the common factor of x from the numerator and denominator: $\dfrac{9\cancel{x}}{x^{\cancel{3}^2}} = \dfrac{9}{x^2}$.

27. $\dfrac{2}{x+2}$

First factor the numerator and denominator, and then cancel out any common factors:
$\dfrac{6x-2}{3x^2+5x-2} = \dfrac{2\,(\cancel{3x-1})}{\cancel{(3x-1)}\,(x+2)} = \dfrac{2}{x+2}$.

28. $2x^2$

The least common denominator between $2x^2$ and x^2 is $2x^2$.

29. $x+7$

Since the factors of the denominator of the first fraction are $(x + 7)$ and $(x - 7)$ and the denominator of the second fraction is only $(x - 7)$, then the least common multiple is $(x + 7)(x - 7)$. The missing factor is $(x + 7)$, so this factor is multiplied by the numerator and denominator of the second fraction to convert to a common denominator.

30. $\dfrac{-x-3}{(x+2)(x+1)}$

Multiply the numerator and denominator of the first fraction by $(x + 1)$ and the numerator and denominator of the second fraction by $(x + 2)$ to convert to a common denominator: $\dfrac{1(x+1)}{(x+2)(x+1)} - \dfrac{2(x+2)}{(x+1)(x+2)}$. Use the distributive property to simplify the numerators: $\dfrac{x+1}{(x+2)(x+1)} - \dfrac{2x+4}{(x+1)(x+2)}$. Write the numerators over the common denominator; be sure to subtract both terms in the second fraction: $\dfrac{x+1-2x-4}{(x+1)(x+2)}$. Combine like terms in the numerator: $\dfrac{-x-3}{(x+2)(x+1)}$.

31. $\dfrac{1}{y}$

Cancel any common factors between the numerators and denominators:

$\dfrac{\cancel{3}\,\cancel{x^2}}{\cancel{4}\,y^{\cancel{3}\,1}} \times \dfrac{^3\cancel{12}\,\cancel{y^2}}{\cancel{9}_3\,\cancel{x^2}}$. Now multiply the remaining factors of the numerators and denominators to get $\dfrac{3}{3y} = \dfrac{1}{y}$.

32. $3t(r-9)$

First factor and then cancel any common factors between the numerators and denominators: $\dfrac{r^2-81}{2t} \times \dfrac{6t^2}{r+9} = \dfrac{(r-9)\,\cancel{(r+9)}}{\cancel{2}\,\cancel{t}} \times \dfrac{^3\cancel{6}\,t^{\cancel{2}}}{\cancel{r+9}}$. Multiply the remaining factors to get $\dfrac{3t(r-9)}{1}$, or $3t(r-9)$.

33. $\dfrac{-6}{2+x}$

First factor the expressions: $\dfrac{2x-4}{z} \div \dfrac{4-x^2}{3z} = \dfrac{2(x-2)}{z} \div \dfrac{(2-x)(2+x)}{3z}$. Now change the operation to multiplication and the second fraction to its reciprocal: $\dfrac{2(x-2)}{z} \times \dfrac{3z}{(2-x)(2+x)}$. Cancel any common factors between the numerators and denominators (recall that factors in the form $x - a$ and $a - x$ cancel to become -1): $\dfrac{2^{-1}\cancel{(x-2)}}{\cancel{z}} \times \dfrac{3\cancel{z}}{\cancel{(2-x)}(2+x)}$. Multiply the remaining factors of the numerators and denominators: $\dfrac{2(-1)(3)}{2+x} = \dfrac{-6}{2+x}$.

34. True

Since the denominators are x^2 and $3x$, the least common multiple is $3x^2$.

35. False

Multiply each term by the least common denominator of ab: $\dfrac{\dfrac{1}{a}\times ab + \dfrac{1}{b}\times ab}{ab \times ab}$. This simplifies to $\dfrac{b+a}{a^2b^2}$, which is in its most simplified form.

CHAPTER 11 TEST

Try the following questions to test your knowledge and understanding of basic algebraic concepts: translating, factoring, and rational expressions.

1. Which of the following is the correct translation of the statement "five less than six times a number"?

    (A) $5 - 6n$

    (B) $5 + 6n$

    (C) $6 - 5n$

    (D) $6n - 5$

    (E) $5n - 6$

2. If the operation $*a*$ is defined as $*a* = 2a + 1$, then what is the value of $*5*$?

    (A) 9

    (B) 10

    (C) 11

    (D) 25

    (E) 26

3. If the operation $b\% \ c$ is defined as $b\% \ c = 5b - c$, then what is the value of $3\% -2$?

    (A) −13

    (B) 10

    (C) 13

    (D) 15

    (E) 17

4. The algebraic expression $9x^2 + 3x - 2$ can be *BEST* described as which of the following?

    (A) Monomial

    (B) Binomial

    (C) Trinomial

    (D) Pentanomial

    (E) None of these

5. In the expression $4x^3y^6z^5$, which of the following numbers represents a coefficient?

   (A) 3
   (B) 4
   (C) 5
   (D) 6
   (E) All of the above

6. Perform the operation: $4z^2 \times 8z$

   (A) $12z^2$
   (B) $12z^3$
   (C) $32z^2$
   (D) $32z^3$
   (E) $32z$

7. What is the product of $7x^2$ and $2x - 5$?

   (A) $70x^3$
   (B) $14x^2 - 5$
   (C) $14x^2 - 35x$
   (D) $14x^3 - 35x^2$
   (E) $14x^2 - 35x^3$

8. Peter's rectangular living room has dimensions that can be expressed as $x - 3$ and $x + 4$. What is the area of his living room expressed as a polynomial?

   (A) $x^2 - 1$
   (B) $x^2 - 12$
   (C) $x^2 - x - 12$
   (D) $x^2 + x + 12$
   (E) $x^2 + x - 12$

9. What is the product of the factors $(x - 3)(x + 3)$?

   (A) $x^2 + 9$

   (B) $x^2 - 9$

   (C) $x^2 + 3x - 9$

   (D) $x^2 + 6x - 9$

   (E) $x^2 - 6x - 9$

10. Multiply: $(x + 2)(x^2 - 3x + 4)$

    (A) $x^3 - x^2 - 2x + 8$

    (B) $x^3 - x^2 + x + 8$

    (C) $x^3 + x^2 + 2x + 8$

    (D) $x^3 + 5x^2 - 10x + 8$

    (E) $x^3 - 5x^2 + 10x + 8$

11. What are the factors of the binomial $3x^2 + 9x$?

    (A) $3x^2$ and $9x$

    (B) 3 and $x^2 + 3x$

    (C) $3x$ and $x + 3$

    (D) $3x$ and $x + 9$

    (E) $3x^2$ and $x + 3$

12. Factor the expression: $b^2 - 121$

    (A) $b(b - 121)$

    (B) $(b - 11)(b - 11)$

    (C) $(b + 11)(b + 11)$

    (D) $(b - 11)(b + 11)$

    (E) $(11 - b)(b - 11)$

13. Factor the expression: $2x^2 + 5x + 2$

    (A) $(2x + 1)(x + 2)$

    (B) $(2x + 2)(x + 1)$

    (C) $(2x - 2)(x - 1)$

    (D) $2(x + 5)(x + 1)$

    (E) $2(x + 2)(x + 1)$

14. Factor completely: $3x^3 - 12x^2 - 15x$

    (A) $3(x + 1)(x - 5)$

    (B) $3(x - 1)(x - 5)$

    (C) $3x(x + 1)(x - 5)$

    (D) $3x(x - 1)(x + 5)$

    (E) $3x^2(x - 1)(x - 5)$

15. Find the sum: $\dfrac{3c}{4x} + \dfrac{5c}{3x}$

    (A) $\dfrac{15c}{7x^2}$

    (B) $\dfrac{15c^2}{12x^2}$

    (C) $\dfrac{11c}{12x}$

    (D) $\dfrac{29c}{12x^2}$

    (E) $\dfrac{29c}{12x}$

16. Find the difference: $\dfrac{4}{x-1} - \dfrac{10}{x}$

    (A) $\dfrac{-6x-10}{x(x-1)}$

    (B) $\dfrac{6x+10}{x(x-1)}$

    (C) $\dfrac{-6x+10}{x(x-1)}$

    (D) $\dfrac{6x-10}{x(x-1)}$

    (E) $\dfrac{-6}{x(x-1)}$

17. Find the quotient: $\dfrac{x^2-9x+20}{4x+8} \div \dfrac{x-4}{2x+4}$

    (A) $\dfrac{2}{x-5}$

    (B) $\dfrac{2(x-5)}{x+4}$

    (C) $\dfrac{x-5}{x+2}$

    (D) $\dfrac{x+5}{x+4}$

    (E) $\dfrac{x-5}{2}$

18. Simplify the expression: $\dfrac{\frac{x}{y}+\frac{1}{y^2}}{\frac{1}{y^2}+1}$

    (A) $\dfrac{x+1}{y^2}$

    (B) $\dfrac{x+y}{1+y}$

    (C) $\dfrac{y^2+1}{y^2}$

    (D) $\dfrac{xy+1}{1+y^2}$

    (E) $\dfrac{y+1}{y^2+1}$

Answers and Explanations

1. D

The key phrase "five less than" tells you to subtract 5 *from* a quantity, and "six times a number" can be written as $6n$. Therefore, the expression becomes $6n - 5$.

2. C

Substitute $a = 5$ into the defined operation and use the correct order of operations: *5* = $2(5) + 1 = 10 + 1 = 11$.

3. E

Substitute $b = 3$ and $c = -2$ into the defined operation and evaluate using the correct order of operations: $3\% -2 = 5(3) - (-2) = 15 + 2 = 17$.

4. C

This polynomial has three terms that cannot be combined. A polynomial with three terms is known as a trinomial; the prefix *tri-* means "three."

5. B

Since the number 4 is in front of the variables and is connected to them by multiplication, 4 is the coefficient of the term. The 3, 6, and 5 each represent the exponents of the variables used in the expression.

6. D

To find the product, multiply the coefficients and add the exponents of the like bases. The expression becomes $4 \times 8 \times z^{2+1} = 32z^3$.

7. D

To find the product, use the distributive property. The expression becomes $7x^2 \times 2x - 7x^2 \times 5 = 14x^3 - 35x^2$.

8. E

To find the area of the room, multiply the dimensions of the room together. To multiply the two binomials, use the acronym FOIL. Multiply the first terms in each binomial (F), multiply the outer terms (O), multiply the inner terms (I), and multiply the last terms in each (L). The product becomes $x^2 + 4x - 3x - 12$. Combine like terms to get $x^2 + x - 12$.

9. B

To multiply the two binomials, use the acronym FOIL. Multiply the first terms in each binomial (F), multiply the outer terms (O), multiply the inner terms (I), and multiply the last terms in each (L). The product becomes $x^2 + 3x - 3x - 9$. Combine like terms to get $x^2 - 9$.

10. A

To multiply the two polynomials, use the distributive property. Multiply each term from the first set of parentheses by the three terms in the second set. The product becomes $x^3 - 3x^2 + 4x + 2x^2 - 6x + 8$. Combine like terms to get $x^3 - x^2 - 2x + 8$.

11. C

Look for the greatest common factor of each term of the binomial, which is $3x$. If $3x$ is factored out of each term, the remaining binomial is $x + 3$. Therefore, the two factors are $3x$ and $x + 3$.

12. D

This is an example of the difference between two perfect squares. The factors are in the form $(x - a)(x + a)$, where x and a are the square roots of the perfect squares. Since the square root of b^2 is b and the square root of 121 is 11, the factors are $(b - 11)(b + 11)$.

13. A

Since the coefficient of x^2 is 2, the factors of this trinomial will be in the form $(2x + a)(x + b)$, where the product of a and b is also 2. Since the only positive factors of 2 are 1 and 2, try the factors $(2x + 1)(x + 2)$. Checking these factors using FOIL results in the expression $2x^2 + 5x + 2$, which is the original polynomial.

14. C

To factor completely, first look for any common factors among all three terms. Each has a factor of $3x$, so when this is factored out, the expression becomes $3x(x^2 - 4x - 5)$. The trinomial within the parentheses can also be factored to $(x + 1)(x - 5)$ because the sum of 1 and -5 is -4 and the product is -5. Therefore, the factors are $3x(x + 1)(x - 5)$.

15. E

Find your common denominator of $3x$ and $4x$, which is $12x$. Multiply the numerator and denominator of the first fraction by 3 and the numerator and denominator of the second fraction by 4 to convert to the common denominator: $\frac{3 \times 3c}{3 \times 4x} + \frac{4 \times 5c}{4 \times 3x} = \frac{9c}{12x} + \frac{20c}{12x}$. Write the numerators over the common denominator and combine like terms to simplify: $\frac{9c + 20c}{12x} = \frac{29c}{12x}$.

16. C

Multiply the numerator and denominator of the first fraction by x and the numerator and denominator of the second fraction by $(x - 1)$ to convert to a common denominator: $\frac{4x}{x(x-1)} - \frac{10(x-1)}{x(x-1)}$. Use the distributive property to simplify the numerator of the second fraction: $\frac{4x}{x(x-1)} - \frac{10x-10}{x(x-1)}$. Write the numerators over the common denominator; be sure to subtract both terms in the second fraction: $\frac{4x - 10x + 10}{x(x-1)}$. Combine like terms in the numerator: $\frac{-6x + 10}{x(x-1)}$.

17. E

First factor the expressions: $\frac{x^2 - 9x + 20}{4x + 8} \div \frac{x - 4}{2x + 4} = \frac{(x-4)(x-5)}{4(x+2)} \div \frac{x-4}{2(x+2)}$. Now change the operation to multiplication and the second fraction to its reciprocal: $\frac{(x-4)(x-5)}{4(x+2)} \times \frac{2(x+2)}{x-4}$. Cancel any common factors between the numerators and denominators: $\frac{\cancel{(x-4)}(x-5)}{\cancel{2}4\ \cancel{(x+2)}} \times \frac{\cancel{2}\ \cancel{(x+2)}}{\cancel{x-4}}$. Multiply the remaining factors of the numerators and denominators: $\frac{x-5}{2}$.

18. D

Multiply each term by the least common denominator of y^2: $\frac{\frac{x}{y} \times y^2 + \frac{1}{y^2} \times y^2}{\frac{1}{y^2} \times y^2 + 1 \times y^2}$. This simplifies to $\frac{xy + 1}{1 + y^2}$, which cannot be simplified further.

CHAPTER 12

Equations

In this final chapter, you will conclude your mathematics review by studying equations. You will notice several flashback sidebars in this chapter, because much of the material covered in previous chapters of this book is used to solve algebraic equations.

SOLVING LINEAR EQUATIONS

An **equation** is a mathematical sentence that states that two expressions are equal. A **linear** equation is one in which the variable is never raised to a power higher than 1. For example, $6x - 17 = \frac{x}{3}$ is a linear equation because every x is to the first power, but $3x^2 - 4 = -1$ is nonlinear because the x term is squared.

An algebraic equation contains at least one variable and an equal sign. The equal sign divides the equation into a left-hand side and a right-hand side. When you solve an equation, you simplify expressions and then perform other operations until the variable is alone on one side of the equation. This is called **isolating the variable**.

REMEMBER THIS!

The goal when solving an equation is to **isolate the variable**.

An equation is presented as an equivalence. Therefore, whenever you perform a mathematical operation on an equation (such as +, −, ×, or ÷), whatever you do to one side, you must do to the other side so that the equation stays in balance. Every action or operation you perform on an equation should change the equation into a simpler form, until the variable is isolated.

You might think that because there are so many different equations out there, learning how to solve them must be bewilderingly complicated. It's not. There's a simple chronological process that you can use to solve any linear equation that has only one variable. Here it is:

Step 1: Eliminate all the fractions.

Step 2: Gather all the terms with the variable on one side.

Step 3: Combine like terms.

Step 4: Factor out the variable.

Step 5: Divide to isolate the variable.

Not all equations require all five steps. In fact, most don't. Still, you should check each step in chronological order to see whether it's needed, and after Step 5, your equation will be solved!

For example, solve this equation for x: $\dfrac{4x}{5} - 4 = \dfrac{2x}{3}$. First, check Step 1: are there any fractions? Yes, there are, so eliminate them. To eliminate a fraction, multiply both sides of the equation by the denominator. First, multiply by 5 to get rid of the fraction on the left side:

$$5\left(\frac{4x}{5} - 4\right) = 5\left(\frac{2x}{3}\right)$$
$$4x - 20 = \frac{10x}{3}$$

Next, multiply by 3 to get rid of the fraction on the right side:

$$3(4x - 20) = 3\left(\frac{10x}{3}\right)$$
$$12x - 60 = 10x$$

There are now no more fractions, so advance to Step 2: are all the terms with x on the same side? They aren't. At this point, use addition or subtraction to "move" terms from one side of the equation to the other. Here, we can subtract $12x$ from both sides:

$$(12x - 60) - 12x = (10x) - 12x$$

$$-60 = 10x - 12x$$

Every term with an x is now on one side of the equation, and every term without an x is on the other. Now do Step 3: combine like terms.

$$-60 = 10x - 12x$$
$$-60 = -2x$$

FLASHBACK

The phrase **like term** was defined in chapter 11: Algebra.

Check Step 4: is it necessary to factor? Not this time. Go ahead to Step 5: divide to isolate the variable. Since the x has a coefficient of -2, that's what you'll divide by to get x by itself:

$$\frac{-60}{-2} = \frac{-2x}{-2}$$
$$30 = x$$

So, x equals 30. Notice that when we started solving this equation, we didn't need to "see everything through" to the end. We just "blindly" followed each step and at the end, the equation was solved. You can be assured that following these steps will solve a linear equation every time.

After you solve an equation, you can easily check your answer. Just substitute the answer value for the variable in the original equation and verify that you arrive at a true statement. For example, in the preceding equation, $\frac{4x}{5} - 4 = \frac{2x}{3}$, the resultant value for x is 30. Evaluate the original equation using this value:

$$\frac{4(30)}{5} - 4 = \frac{2(30)}{3}$$
$$4(6) - 4 = 2(10)$$
$$24 - 4 = 20$$
$$20 = 20$$

This is a true statement, so $x = 30$ must be correct.

REMEMBER THIS

To eliminate fractions, use multiplication. To undo addition, use subtraction—and vice versa. Division should be the last step you perform to isolate the variable.

Sometimes a problem will be presented in word format, and you must translate the words into an algebraic equation to solve the problem.

Take this example. When you multiply a number by 9 and then subtract 45, the result is 81. What is the number? First, translate the words into algebra: $9x - 45 = 81$. Then solve this equation. There aren't any fractions to eliminate, so move to Step 2. To get the x term by itself, add 45 to both sides of the equation, because addition is the inverse operation of subtraction. Thus, $9x - 45 + 45 = 81 + 45$ or, when simplified, $9x = 126$. There's nothing to factor here, so on to the last step: divide both sides of the equation by 9 to get the variable by itself: $\dfrac{9x}{9} = \dfrac{126}{9}$, or $x = 14$.

FLASHBACK

Translation of words into algebra was covered in chapter 11: Algebra.

PRACTICE 1

Remember, repetition is the key to mastery! Fill in the blanks. Answers and explanations are located at the end of the chapter.

1. When solving an equation, the goal is to _____ the variable.

2. To solve $x - 7 = 10$, you _____ to both sides of the equation.

3. To solve $3x + 9 = 25$, the first step is to _____ from both sides of the equation.

4. Solve for x: $x + 10 = -8$.

5. Solve for w: $-2w - 6 = 24$.

6. One-fourth of a number less 3 is 17. What is the number?

Applying the Distributive Property

If you are given an equation with parentheses on either side, you'll need to simplify them before you can get all the variable terms on one side (Step 2). Usually, you need to use the distributive property to simplify this type of expression. After applying the distributive property, continue following the five-step process to solve the equation. For example, to solve $-4(x+5) = -64$, first apply the distributive property to get rid of the parentheses: $(-4 \times x) + (-4 \times 5) = -64$, or $-4x - 20 = -64$. Now add 20 to both sides to get $-4x - 20 + 20 = -64 + 20$, or $-4x = -44$. Finally, divide both sides of the equation by -4: $\dfrac{-4x}{-4} = \dfrac{-44}{-4}$, or $x = 11$.

FLASHBACK

The distributive property was covered in chapter 1: Properties of Numbers and in chapter 11: Algebra.

Check your result by substituting the value of 11 for x in the original equation: $-4(11+5) = -64$, which simplifies to $-4 \times 16 = -64$, or $-64 = -64$, a true statement.

FLASHBACK

The order of operations was explained in chapter 1: Properties of Numbers.

Here's another example. To solve the equation $12x - 5(x-2) = 66$, first distribute the -5 to the terms in parentheses: $12x + -5x - (-10) = 66$. Then combine like terms: $7x + 10 = 66$. Now subtract 10 from both sides: $7x + 10 - 10 = 66 - 10$, or $7x = 56$. Divide both sides of this simpler equation by 7 to isolate the variable: $\dfrac{7x}{7} = \dfrac{56}{7}$, or $x = 8$.

In this example, you might have noticed that we combined like terms (Step 3) before getting all the x's on one side (Step 2). This is okay; the steps do not have to be performed in order. As you get more comfortable solving equations, you'll find that it's acceptable and convenient in some cases to do the steps out of order.

When solving an equation, follow these steps to ensure your success:

1. Eliminate all the fractions.

2. Gather all the terms with the variable on one side.

3. Combine like terms.

4. Factor out the variable.

5. Divide to isolate the variable.

A geometry problem can require you to solve an equation, as in this example. If the perimeter of the rectangle below is 112 cm, what are the dimensions of the rectangle?

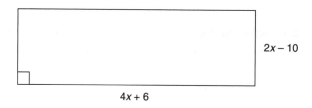

$2x - 10$

$4x + 6$

Perimeter is covered in chapter 8: Lines, Angles, and Polygons.

The perimeter of a polygon is the sum of its sides, or for this figure, $2(4x + 6) + 2(2x - 10) = 112$. Because there are no fractions to eliminate, apply the distributive property first: $8x + 12 + 4x - 20 = 112$. Now combine like terms to get $12x - 8 = 112$. Add 8 to both sides: $12x - 8 + 8 = 112 + 8$, or $12x = 120$. Finally, divide both sides by 12: $x = 10$. The value of x is 10 cm, so the base of the rectangle, $4x + 6$, is $(4 \times 10) + 6$, which equals 46. The height is $2x - 10$, or $(2 \times 10) - 10 = 10$. Verify that $(2 \times 46) + (2 \times 10) = 112$. Simplify to get $92 + 20 = 112$, or the true statement $112 = 112$.

PRACTICE 2

Use the number bank to find the solutions to the equations below. Answers and explanations are located at the end of the chapter.

−12	−24	18.4	−0.5	−11	−3
4	10	8	36.4	36.1	4.375

7. $-2(x + 8) = 32$

8. $-5(x + 3) = -12.5$

9. $4x - 6 - 7x = 27$

10. $10x - 2(x - 12) = 59$

11. Two times the sum of a number and 4 is 24. What is the number?

12. Given the following triangle, what is the value of the variable x, in degrees?

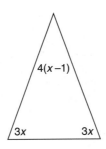

FACTORING

So far, we haven't had to use Step 4: factor out the variable. This step is sometimes relevant when there are multiple variables in an equation and you need to solve for one of them in terms of the other. For example, solve for x in terms of y: $4x - 3 = 5xy - 2y$. Because there are no fractions, start by getting all the x terms on one side and all the other terms on the other:

$$4x - 3 + (3 - 5xy) = 5xy - 2y + (3 - 5xy)$$

$$4x - 5xy = 3 - 2y$$

At this point, you can't combine like terms (Step 3), but you can't quite finish off the equation by dividing by x either, since there are two terms left that contain an x. Now you need to use Step 4: factoring. Pull out an x from each term on the left side of the equation to get $x(4 - 5y) = 3 - 2y$. Now you can do Step 5 and divide both sides of the equation by $(4 - 5y)$ to solve for x: $x = \dfrac{3 - 2y}{4 - 5y}$.

FLASHBACK

Factoring was discussed in chapter 11: Algebra.

PRACTICE 3

Solve for the variables indicated below. Answers and explanations are located at the end of the chapter.

13. In the diagram below, what is the value of the variable x?

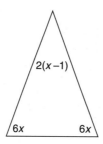

14. Solve for c in terms of b: $6(c - 4) = 4cb + 18$

15. Solve for y: $8y + 12 - 10y = 48$

16. Solve for y in terms of x: $5yx = 3y + 8$

17. Solve for x: $\dfrac{2}{3}x + \dfrac{1}{2} = 8$

18. Solve for x: $\dfrac{5x}{12} + \dfrac{5}{6} = 100$

19. Solve for x: $\dfrac{1}{2}x + \dfrac{1}{3}x = 1$

SOLVING SYSTEMS OF EQUATIONS

A **system of equations** is a set of equations containing more than one variable, typically labeled x and y. To solve a system of equations, you must find the values of x and y that will make every equation in the system true. There are two algebraic methods for solving a system: the substitution method and the combination method.

The Substitution Method

To use the **substitution method** for solving a system of equations, solve one of the equations for one of the variables, say y, and then substitute that expression for y in the second equation. The second equation then becomes an equation with one variable, in this case x, which you solve as described earlier in this chapter.

For example, solve the following system of equations:

$$3x + y = -2$$
$$7x - 3y = -26$$

Solve the first equation for y. First isolate the variable y by subtracting $3x$ from both sides of the equation to get $y = -3x - 2$. Then take $-3x - 2$ and substitute it into the second equation in place of y to get $7x - 3(-3x - 2) = -26$. The second equation now contains only one variable, so you can find a solution. Apply the distributive property: $7x + 9x + 6 = -26$. Combine like terms and subtract 6 from both sides: $16x + 6 - 6 = -26 - 6$. This simplifies to $16x = -32$. Divide both sides by 16 to get $x = -2$. This is the value for x in the system of equations.

Now use either of the equations above and substitute -2 for x to solve for y: the first equation, $3x + y = -2$, becomes $(3 \times -2) + y = -2$, or $-6 + y = -2$. Add 6 to both sides to get $y = 4$. The solution to the system is the ordered pair $(-2, 4)$. This means that in both equations, the solutions are $x = -2$ and $y = 4$. Keep in mind that although there is an infinite number of solutions to each of these equations separately, there is usually just one solution for a system of two or more equations.

Just as for all equations, you can check this solution. It is important to check the solution in both equations given in the system. To check the equation $3x + y = -2$, substitute: $(3 \times -2) + 4 = -2$, or $-6 + 4 = -2$, which is the true statement $-2 = -2$. To check the second equation, use the same procedure: $7x - 3y = -26$ becomes $(7 \times -2) + (-3 \times 4) = -26$. This simplifies to $-14 + (-12) = -26$ and then to $-26 = -26$.

The Combination Method

To use the **combination method** for solving a system of equations, multiply each term of one of the equations by some factor so that when you combine the two equations, one of the variables is eliminated. Let's go back and solve the previous system by the combination method:

$$3x + y = -2$$
$$7x - 3y = -26$$

Look at the variable terms. Since the y term in the first equation has a coefficient of 1 and the y term in the second equation has a coefficient of -3, multiply each of the terms in the first equation by positive 3:

$$9x + 3y = -6$$
$$7x - 3y = -26$$

Now combine the like terms of the two equations and notice that the y terms are eliminated: $(9x + 7x) + (3y + -3y) = -6 + -26$. This simplifies to $16x = -32$, and again, as in the other method above, $x = -2$. From this point, follow the procedures outlined in the substitution method to arrive at the value of 4 for y and perform the checks on both equations.

To solve the next system, look at the equations and find the most convenient variable to eliminate:

$$-4x + 2y = -6$$
$$-2x + 3y = 11$$

It is easy to find a common factor for the coefficients of -4 and -2. To turn the coefficient of x in the bottom equation to a $+4$, multiply each term of the second equation by -2 so that the x variable terms will be eliminated when the equations are combined:

$$-4x + 2y = -6$$
$$4x + (-6y) = -22$$

Combine the like terms in the two equations: $(-4x + 4x) + (2y + -6y) = -6 + -22$. This simplifies to $-4y = -28$. Divide both sides by -4 to get $y = 7$. Now use this value of 7 for y in the first equation to solve for x: $-4x + (2 \times 7) = -6$, or the simplified version $-4x + 14 = -6$. Subtract 14 from both sides, so that $-4x = -20$, and then divide both sides by −4 to get $x = 5$. The solution to the above system is (5, 7); that is, $x = 5$ and $y = 7$. You can check this system in the same manner as you checked the other systems of equations.

▮ REMEMBER THIS! ▮

When you check the ordered pair solution to a system of linear equations, be sure to check the solution in every equation in the system.

Some real-life situations can be solved using a system of equations. For example, consider the following problem: Reza bought six pounds of fruit, consisting of apples and bananas only. The total cost for the fruit was $6.94. If apples are $0.99 per pound and bananas are $1.49 per pound, how many pounds of each type of fruit did Reza buy?

Let the variable a represent the number of pounds of apples and the variable b represent the number of pounds of bananas. There is a total of six pounds of fruit, so the first equation is $a + b = 6$. The price per pound and total cost are given in the problem. Apples are $0.99 per pound, so the total cost of the apples equals $0.99a$; bananas are $1.49 per pound, so the total cost of the bananas equals $1.49b$. To find the total cost of both fruits, form the second equation: $0.99a + 1.49b = 6.94$. So the system of equations is as follows:

$$a + b = 6$$
$$0.99a + 1.49b = 6.94$$

Using the combination method, multiply each term of the first equation by -0.99 to eliminate the variable a:

$$a + b = 6$$
$$-0.99a + (-0.99b) = -5.94$$

Now look at the first and second equations together:

$$-0.99a + (-0.99b) = -5.94$$
$$0.99a + 1.49b = 6.94$$

Combine the like terms in the two equations to get $(-0.99a + 0.99a) + (-0.99b + 1.49b) = (-5.94 + 6.94)$. This simplifies to $0.5b = 1$. Divide both sides of the equation by 0.5 to get $b = 2$. Reza therefore bought two pounds of bananas. Substitute the value of 2 for b in the first equation: $a + 2 = 6$. Subtract 2 from both sides to get $a = 4$, which means Reza bought four pounds of apples.

DISTINCT EQUATIONS

In order to solve a system of equations, you need at least as many distinct equations as you have variables. "Distinct" means different: sometimes two equations look different but are actually the same.

For example, it's not possible to solve for x and y in the system of equations $x + y = 3$ and $2x + 2y = 6$. Dividing both sides of the second equation by 2 yields $x + y = 3$, which is the same as the first equation. Since the equations aren't distinct, there are infinitely many possible values for x and y.

PRACTICE 4

Repetition is the key to mastering solving equations! Try either the substitution or the combination method to solve the following systems of equations. Answers and explanations are located at the end of the chapter.

20. $6x + y = 16$

$-4x - 2y = -16$

21. $x + 3y = -1$

$3x + 2y = 11$

22. The booster club bought jerseys and pants for the basketball team. A total of 21 items were bought at a total cost of $214.50. If the price of one jersey is $8.50 and the price of one pair of pants is $12.50, how many of each item did the club purchase?

Answer TRUE or FALSE for the following questions.

23. **T   F**   The system of equations $2x + 5y = 10$ and $y = 2 - \dfrac{6x}{15}$ can be solved for x and y.

24. **T   F**   The system of equations $3x + y = 8$ and $12x - 4y = 32$ can be solved for x and y.

25. **T   F**   The system of equations $7x + 8y = 13$ and $-7x - 8y = -13$ can be solved for x and y.

SOLVING QUADRATIC EQUATIONS

A **quadratic equation** has the form $ax^2 + bx + c = 0$, where a, b, and c are constants and a does not equal zero.

Factoring

To solve a quadratic equation, get all terms of the equation on one side of the equation; the other side should equal zero. Then factor the trinomial into two binomials.

FLASHBACK

Factoring trinomials was covered in depth in chapter 11: Algebra.

For example, to solve the quadratic equation $x^2 + 12 = 7x$, first add $-7x$ to both sides of the equation to get all terms on the left side. The equation is now $x^2 - 7x + 12 = 0$.

If we factor this trinomial, we find that the factors are $(x - 3)(x - 4)$. Now write the equation using these factors: $(x - 3)(x - 4) = 0$. This equation says that the product of two factors is equal to 0. This means that if either the first factor $(x - 3)$ or the second factor $(x - 4)$ is zero, the equation will be true. Solve each of these simple equations to find the two solutions to the quadratic equation. When $x - 3 = 0$, $x = 3$, and when $x - 4 = 0$, $x = 4$. The two solutions to the quadratic are $x = \{3, 4\}$.

These solutions can be checked by substituting in the values for x into the original equation to ensure that the simplified statement is true. Use the original equation of $x^2 + 12 = 7x$. Check 3 as the value of x: $3^2 + 12 = 7 \times 3$; $9 + 12 = 21$; and $21 = 21$. Check 4 as the value of x: $4^2 + 12 = 7 \times 4$; $16 + 12 = 28$; and $28 = 28$.

Sometimes a quadratic equation has two identical solutions. Consider the following quadratic equation: $x^2 + 16x = -64$. Again, the first step is to get all of the terms on one side of the equation. Add 64 to both sides to get $x^2 + 16x + 64 = 0$. Now factor the trinomial. This trinomial is a perfect square, or $(x + 8)(x + 8) = 0$. If either of these binomials equals 0, the equation is true. In both cases, the equation is $x + 8 = 0$. When you subtract 8 from both sides, you get $x = -8$. Now check this solution in the original equation: $x^2 + 16x = -64$. $(-8)^2 + (16 \times -8) = -64$. This simplifies to $64 + (-128) = -64$, which results in the true statement $-64 = -64$.

A quadratic equation will have two solutions that are unequal, two solutions that are equal, or no real solution.

Sometimes when solving quadratics with real-world problems, you may have to reject one of your two solutions.

For example, if the area of the rectangle below is 12 m², what are the possible values of the base and height?

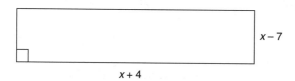

$x - 7$

$x + 4$

Area is base times height, so $(x + 4)(x - 7) = 12$. Use the distributive property (in this case, FOIL) to multiply the factors on the left-hand side: $x^2 - 3x - 28 = 12$. Subtract 12 from both sides to get $x^2 - 3x - 28 - 12 = 0$, or $x^2 - 3x - 40 = 0$. Factor the trinomial to get $(x - 8)(x + 5) = 0$. Solve each of these equations to get that either $x = 8$ or $x = -5$. Now substitute in these values for the base and height to find the possible dimensions. When $x = 8$, the base is $8 + 4$, or 12 m, and the height is $8 - 7$, or 1 m. When $x = -5$, the base would be $-5 + 4$, or -1 m. But there is a problem with this measure—it is not possible to have a negative value for a measurement. Therefore, this solution must be rejected for this geometric problem.

The Quadratic Formula

If you cannot factor the resultant trinomial after transforming a quadratic to be equal to 0, then either the quadratic has no real solution, or the solutions are not rational numbers. The formula used to solve a quadratic equation is called the **quadratic formula**. This formula will find solutions to any quadratic equation, whether or not the trinomial could have been factored.

The following is the quadratic formula:

$$x = \frac{-b \pm \sqrt{b^2 - 4ac}}{2a}$$

Notice the plus-minus symbol (±) in the formula. This yields the two solutions to the quadratic equation.

Take as an example the equation $2x^2 + 8x + 3 = 0$. You cannot factor the trinomial, so you must use the quadratic formula, where $a = 2$, $b = 8$, and $c = 3$. Substitute these values into the formula to get $x = \dfrac{-8 \pm \sqrt{8^2 - (4 \times 2 \times 3)}}{2 \times 2}$, or $x = \dfrac{-8 \pm \sqrt{40}}{4}$.

Simplify the radical to get $x = \dfrac{-8 \pm 2\sqrt{10}}{4}$. Divide out a common factor of 2, and the solutions are thus $x = -2 \pm \dfrac{\sqrt{10}}{2}$. In other words, the solutions for x are $-2 + \dfrac{\sqrt{10}}{2}$ and $-2 - \dfrac{\sqrt{10}}{2}$.

FLASHBACK

Simplifying radicals was covered in chapter 7: Powers and Roots.

Sometimes a quadratic equation has no solutions in the set of real numbers. Consider the following equation: $4x^2 + 2x + 9 = 0$. This trinomial cannot be factored, so use the quadratic formula, where $a = 4$, $b = 2$, and $c = 9$. The formula gives us $x = \dfrac{-2 \pm \sqrt{2^2 - (4 \times 4 \times 9)}}{2 \times 4}$, or $x = \dfrac{-2 \pm \sqrt{4 - 144}}{8}$, which simplifies to $x = \dfrac{-2 \pm \sqrt{-140}}{8}$.

In the set of real numbers, the square root of a negative number does not exist. Thus, there is no real solution to this quadratic equation.

REMEMBER THIS!

The **quadratic formula** is a formula used to solve a quadratic equation in the form $ax^2 + bx + c = 0$. The solutions to the equation are found by substituting the values of the coefficients a, b, and c into the formula

$$x = \frac{-b \pm \sqrt{b^2 - 4ac}}{2a}.$$

You can use the quadratic formula on any quadratic equation, even those with a factorable trinomial. Note, however, that it is very rare for a trinomial on the GMAT to be unfactorable. Factor trinomials whenever possible to bypass the need for this complicated formula.

PRACTICE 5

Use your knowledge of quadratic equations to solve for the following variables. Answers and explanations are located at the end of the chapter.

26. Solve for x: $x^2 + 10x + 25 = 0$

27. Solve for x: $x^2 - 5x = 14$

28. Solve for x: $2x^2 - 7x - 8 = 0$

29. If the area of the rectangle below is equal to nine square units, what is the value of x?

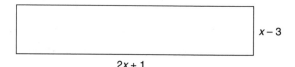

$x - 3$

$2x + 1$

INEQUALITIES

On the GMAT, you'll often see inequalities, such as $x < 3$ and $3 - \dfrac{3x}{5} > \dfrac{48}{5}$. Though inequalities look different from equations, you can perform all the same operations on an inequality that you can on an equation, with only one new rule to remember: multiplying or dividing both sides by a negative value causes the inequality sign to reverse direction. Other than that, you can follow the five-step process described at the beginning of this chapter to solve inequalities just as you would equations.

For an example, we'll use the second inequality from the previous paragraph, $3 - \dfrac{3x}{5} > \dfrac{48}{5}$. First, eliminate the fractions by multiplying by 5: $15 - 3x > 48$. Next, get the $-3x$ term by itself by subtracting 15 from both sides: $-3x > 33$. To isolate x, you need to divide both sides by -3, and here's where the new rule comes in. Since -3 is a negative number, you have to flip, or reverse the direction of, the inequality sign to finish with $x < -11$.

SUMMARY

In conclusion, if you learn only eight things about equations, they should be the following:

1. To solve an equation, you must isolate the variable.

2. To isolate the variable, first use multiplication to eliminate any fractions. Then get all the terms with the variable on the same side, combine like terms, and factor out the variable if necessary. Finally, divide to isolate the variable.

3. You can easily check solutions to an equation by plugging them into your original equation.

4. The two algebraic methods for solving a system of equations are substitution and combination.

5. In order to solve a system of equations, you need to have at least as many distinct equations as you have variables.

6. To solve a quadratic equation, first try to factor the quadratic. If it can be factored, set each of these factors equal to 0 to find the possible real number answers.

7. To solve a quadratic equation that cannot be factored, use the quadratic formula.

8. Operations on inequalities follow the same rules as those on equations, except that multiplying or dividing both sides of an inequality by a negative value causes the inequality sign to reverse direction.

Practice Answers and Explanations

1. Isolate

Once you have the variable alone on one side of the equation (isolated), you have solved the equation for the given variable.

2. Add 7

Addition is the inverse operation of subtraction, so you add 7 to both sides of the equation to isolate x: $x - 7 + 7 = 10 + 7$, or $x = 17$, the solution to the equation.

3. Subtract 9

First you need to subtract 9 to get the x term by itself; then you can divide by 3 to isolate x.

4. $x = -18$

Subtract 10 from both sides of the equation.

5. $w = -15$

Add 6 to both sides to get $-2w = 30$. Then divide both sides by -2.

6. $x = 80$

The equation is $\frac{x}{4} - 3 = 17$. Add 3 to both sides of the equation to get $\frac{x}{4} = 20$. Then multiply both sides by 4 to isolate the variable. Note that in this case, it was convenient to eliminate the fraction (Step 1) *after* getting the variable term by itself (Step 2).

7. -24

Apply the distributive property to get $-2x - 16 = 32$. Add 16 to both sides to get $-2x = 48$. Finally, divide both sides by -2 to isolate the variable.

8. -0.5

Apply the distributive property to get $-5x - 15 = -12.5$. Add 15 to both sides to get $-5x = 2.5$. Divide both sides by -5 to isolate the variable.

9. -11

Combine the like terms $4x$ and $-7x$ to get $-3x - 6 = 27$. Add 6 to both sides to get $-3x = 33$. Finally, divide both sides by -3 to get $x = -11$.

10. 4.375

Apply the distributive property and then combine like terms: $10x - 2x + 24 = 59$, or $8x + 24 = 59$. Subtract 24 from both sides to get $8x = 35$. Finally, divide both sides by 8 to isolate x.

11. 8

The equation is $2(x + 4) = 24$. Apply the distributive property: $2x + 8 = 24$. Subtract 8 from both sides to get $2x = 16$. Divide both sides by 2 to get $x = 8$.

12. 18.4

Recall from chapter 8 that the sum of the degree measures of the angles in a triangle is 180. Use this fact to write the equation $3x + 3x + 4(x - 1) = 180$. Apply the distributive property: $3x + 3x + 4x - 4 = 180$. Combine like terms to get $10x - 4 = 180$. Add 4 to both sides and then divide both sides by 10 to get $x = 18.4$.

13.   13

The sum of the interior angles of a triangle is $180°$. Set the sum of the three angle measures equal to 180: $2(x - 1) + 6x + 6x = 180$. Distribute on the left side of the equation to get $2x - 2 + 6x + 6x = 180$. Combine like terms to get $14x - 2 = 180$. Add 2 to both sides and then divide by 14 to get $x = 13$.

14. $c = \dfrac{42}{6 - 4b}$

Start by simplifying the left side of the equation: $6c - 24 = 4cb + 18$. Next, get all the c terms on one side: $6c - 4cb = 24 + 18$; $6c - 4cb = 42$. Since you can't combine like terms, factor out c: $c(6 - 4b) = 42$. At last, divide by $(6 - 4b)$ to isolate c: $c = \dfrac{42}{6 - 4b}$.

15.   –18

First combine like terms to get $-2y + 12 = 48$. Then subtract 12 from both sides: $-2y = 36$. Finally, divide both sides by -2 to get $y = -18$.

16. $\dfrac{8}{5x - 3}$

Start by getting all the y terms on one side: $5yx - 3y = 8$. Factor out the y: $y(5x - 3) = 8$. Finally, divide by $(5x - 3)$ to isolate y: $y = \dfrac{8}{5x - 3}$.

17. $\dfrac{45}{4}$, or 11.25

Multiply each term by the LCM (least common multiple) of 2 and 3, which is 6, to eliminate both fractions: $6\left(\dfrac{2}{3}x + \dfrac{1}{2}\right) = 6(8)$, which simplifies to $4x + 3 = 48$. Subtract 3 from both sides: $4x + 3 - 3 = 48 - 3$, or $4x = 45$. Finally, divide both sides by 4 to isolate x: $x = \dfrac{45}{4}$, or 11.25.

18.   238

Multiply each term by the LCM of 6 and 12, which is 12: $12\left(\dfrac{5x}{12} + \dfrac{5}{6}\right) = 12(100)$, which simplifies to $5x + 10 = 1,200$. Subtract 10 from both sides to get $5x = 1,190$.

Finally, divide both sides by 5: $x = 238$.

19. $\dfrac{6}{5}$**, or 1.2**

Multiply each term by the LCM of 2 and 3, which is 6: $6\left(\dfrac{1}{2}x + \dfrac{1}{3}x\right) = 6(1)$, which simplifies to $3x + 2x = 6$. Combine like terms: $5x = 6$. Finally, divide both sides by 5: $x = \dfrac{6}{5}$, or 1.2.

20.   (2, 4)

You can multiply each term of the first equation by 2 and use the combination method:

$$12x + 2y = 32$$
$$-4x - 2y = -16$$

Combine the two equations: $[12x + (-4x)] + [2y + (-2y)] = [32 + (-16)]$, which simplifies to $8x = 16$. Divide each side of this simplified equation by 8 to get $x = 2$. Now substitute the value of 2 for x in the original first equation: $6x + y = 16$ becomes $(6 \times 2) + y = 16$, or $12 + y = 16$. Subtract 12 from both sides to get $y = 4$. The ordered pair is (2, 4).

21.   (5, −2)

You can solve using the substitution method: solve the first equation for x, then use this value to find y. The first equation becomes $x = -3y - 1$ when you isolate the variable x. Substitute this value for x in the second equation: $3(-3y - 1) + 2y = 11$. Apply the distributive property: $-9y - 3 + 2y = 11$. Now combine like terms to get $-7y - 3 = 11$. Add 3 to both sides: $-7y = 14$. Finally, divide both sides by −7 to get $y = -2$. Use the value of −2 in the first equation to find the value of x: $x + 3y = -1$ becomes $x + (3 \times -2) = -1$, or $x - 6 = -1$. Add 6 to both sides, and $x = 5$. The ordered pair is (5, −2).

22.   12 jerseys and 9 pants

Let j represent the number of jerseys and p represent the number of pants. The total number of items bought is 21, so the first equation is $j + p = 21$. The total cost is \$214.50, so the second equation is $8.5j + 12.5p = 214.50$. Multiply the first equation by −8.5 to eliminate j:

$$-8.5j - 8.5p = -178.50$$
$$8.5j + 12.5p = 214.50$$

Combine the two equations: $(-8.5j + 8.5j) + (-8.5p + 12.5p) = -178.50 + 214.50$. Simplify to get $4p = 36$. Divide both sides by 4 to get $p = 9$. A total of 21 items were bought, so the number of jerseys is $21 - 9 = 12$.

23. **False**

Multiplying the second equation by 15 to eliminate fractions yields $15y = 30 - 6x$. Adding $6x$ to both sides yields $6x + 15y = 30$, and this equation can be divided by 3 to get $2x + 5y = 10$, which is the same as the first equation. These equations are not distinct, so it's impossible to solve for x and y.

24. **True**

Dividing the second equation by 4 yields $3x - y = 8$. This looks similar to the first equation, but since the y is subtracted instead of added, the equations are distinct, so this system of equations can be solved for values of x and y.

25. **False**

Dividing the second equation by -1 produces $7x + 8y = 13$, which is the first equation. The two equations are not distinct, so it's impossible to solve for x and y.

26. $\{-5\}$

The left-hand side of this equation is a perfect square trinomial. Factor it to get $(x + 5)(x + 5) = 0$. If either of the two factors is 0, the equation is true. In both cases, this occurs when $x = -5$.

27. $\{7, -2\}$

Subtract 14 from both sides to get the equation into the form of $ax^2 + bx + c = 0$: $x^2 - 5x - 14 = 0$. Now factor the trinomial on the left to get $(x - 7)(x + 2) = 0$. If either of these factors is 0, the equation is true. Therefore, $x = 7$ and $x = -2$ are the two solutions to the quadratic equation.

28. $\left\{ \dfrac{7 + \sqrt{113}}{4}, \dfrac{7 - \sqrt{113}}{4} \right\}$

The trinomial on the left-hand side of the equation cannot be factored. Use the quadratic formula to solve for x, with $a = 2$, $b = -7$, and $c = -8$: $\dfrac{-(-7) \pm \sqrt{(-7)^2 - (4 \times 2 \times -8)}}{(2)(2)}$

$= \dfrac{7 \pm \sqrt{49 + 64}}{4} = \dfrac{7 \pm \sqrt{113}}{4}$.

29. $\{4\}$

The formula for the area of a rectangle is base times height, and the problem states that this area is equal to 9 square units. Set up the equation: $(2x + 1)(x - 3) = 9$. Multiply, using the distributive property (in this case, FOIL): $2x^2 - 6x + x - 3 = 9$.

Combine like terms: $2x^2 - 5x - 3 = 9$. Then subtract 9 from both sides of the equation to solve: $2x^2 - 5x - 3 - 9 = 9 - 9$ simplifies to $2x^2 - 5x - 12 = 0$. The left-hand side can be factored: $(2x + 3)(x - 4) = 0$. For the equation to be true, either $2x + 3 = 0$, or $x - 4 = 0$. Subtract 3 from both sides of the first equation to get $2x = -3$. Divide both sides by 2: $x = -\dfrac{3}{2}$. The second equation is true when $x = 4$. The quadratic equation has two solutions: $\left\{ -\dfrac{3}{2}, 4 \right\}$. However, when $x = -\dfrac{3}{2}$, the base value of the rectangle is $2\left(-\dfrac{3}{2} \right) + 1$, which equals $-3 + 1$. Add to get -2 for the length of the base. This is a negative number. Because length cannot be a negative value, the solution of $x = -\dfrac{3}{2}$ is rejected as impossible, and the only possible solution for x is 4.

CHAPTER 12 TEST

Try the following questions to see what you've learned about solving equations. Following the questions are complete answer explanations to help you assess your understanding. Unless otherwise noted, round each answer to the nearest tenth.

1. Solve for x: $x + 21 = 15$

    (A) 315

    (B) 36

    (C) −36

    (D) 6

    (E) −6

2. Solve for x: $−12x = 138$

    (A) 11.5

    (B) −11.5

    (C) 150

    (D) 126

    (E) −150

3. Solve for y: $\frac{1}{4}y + 8 = 12$

    (A) 2

    (B) 4

    (C) 5

    (D) 8

    (E) 16

4. Solve for x: $3(x − 2) = 36$

    (A) 14

    (B) 10

    (C) 12.7

    (D) 13.7

    (E) 10.3

5. Solve for b: $-4(b - 6) = -60$

   (A) -9

   (B) 21

   (C) -21

   (D) 9

   (E) 13.5

6. If you multiply 5 times the sum of a number and 13, the result is 100. What is the number?

   (A) 20

   (B) 33

   (C) 7

   (D) 17.4

   (E) 22.6

7. Solve for z: $3z + 23 + 6z = 104$

   (A) 14.1

   (B) 25

   (C) 72

   (D) 9

   (E) 3.4

8. Solve for x: $4x - 8 = x + 1$

   (A) 1.8

   (B) 3

   (C) -1.4

   (D) 1.4

   (E) 2.25

9. Solve for x: $25 - 4(x + 3) = 4x + 33$

   (A) -5

   (B) -7.625

   (C) -0.75

   (D) 2.5

   (E) -2.5

10. In the figure below, what is the value of the variable *x*?

    (A) 117

    (B) 4.2

    (C) 23.4

    (D) −117

    (E) −4.2

11. In the figure below, lines *l* and *m* are parallel. What is the value of the variable *x*?

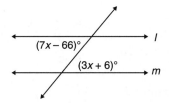

    (A) 6

    (B) 7.2

    (C) 15

    (D) 18

    (E) −6

12. Solve for *x*: $\dfrac{4x}{7} - \dfrac{2}{5} = 6$

    (A) $2.\overline{2}$

    (B) 0.4

    (C) 11.2

    (D) 1

    (E) 9.8

13. Solve for x: $\dfrac{1}{6}x + \dfrac{1}{8}x = 1$

   (A) 3.4

   (B) 12

   (C) 7

   (D) 4.5

   (E) 4.2

14. Solve the system of equations:

   $3x + y = 4$

   $2x - 8y = -58$

   (A) $(1, -7)$

   (B) $(-7, 1)$

   (C) $(7, -1)$

   (D) $(7, 1)$

   (E) $(-1, 7)$

15. Solve the system of equations:

   $y = 6x + 10$

   $2x + 3y = 110$

   (A) $(5, 40)$

   (B) $(7, 52)$

   (C) $(4, 34)$

   (D) $(34, 4)$

   (E) $(40, 5)$

16. For the Valentine's Day dance, 120 favors were purchased in either red or pink. The pink favors cost $2.00 each, and the red favors cost $1.75 each. If the total cost of the favors was $222.50, how many pink favors were purchased?

   (A) 50

   (B) 70

   (C) 60

   (D) 111

   (E) 9

17. For brunch, 25 adults and children went to a restaurant. The cost of brunch was $11.95 for adults and $3.95 for children. If the total bill was $266.75, how many adults attended the brunch?

    (A) 4

    (B) 46

    (C) 21

    (D) 11

    (E) 22

18. Solve for x: $x^2 - 14x = -49$

    (A) $\{-7\}$

    (B) $\{7\}$

    (C) $\{-7, 7\}$

    (D) $\{40, 9\}$

    (E) $\{-40, 9\}$

19. Solve for x: $x^2 - 36 = 0$

    (A) $\{-18\}$

    (B) $\{6\}$

    (C) $\{-6\}$

    (D) $\{18\}$

    (E) $\{6, -6\}$

20. Solve for x: $2x^2 - 3x - 5 = 15$

    (A) $\left\{-\dfrac{5}{2}, 4\right\}$

    (B) $\left\{-\dfrac{5}{2}, -4\right\}$

    (C) $\left\{\dfrac{5}{2}, 4\right\}$

    (D) $\left\{\dfrac{5}{2}, -4\right\}$

    (E) $\left\{\dfrac{3 + \sqrt{89}}{4}, \dfrac{3 - \sqrt{89}}{4}\right\}$

21. Solve for x: $3x^2 + 2x - 15 = 0$

    (A) $\{5, -3\}$

    (B) $\left\{ \dfrac{-1+\sqrt{46}}{3}, \dfrac{-1-\sqrt{46}}{3} \right\}$

    (C) $\{-5, 3\}$

    (D) $\{-15, 1\}$

    (E) No real number solution

22. If the area of the triangle below is 8 square units, what is the value of the variable x?

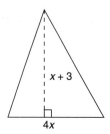

$x + 3$

$4x$

    (A) 4

    (B) 1

    (C) $\{1, -4\}$

    (D) $\{2, -1\}$

    (E) $\{1, 4\}$

23. If $-7x + \dfrac{20}{3} < \dfrac{x}{3} - 8$, then which of the following must be true?

    (A) $x > 4$

    (B) $x < 4$

    (C) $x > 0$

    (D) $x < 2$

    (E) $x < -2$

Answers and Explanations

1. E

Because subtraction is the inverse operation to addition, subtract 21 from both sides of the equation: $x + 21 - 21 = 15 - 21$. This simplifies to $x = -6$.

2. B

The inverse operation of multiplication is division; therefore, divide both sides of the equation by -12: $\dfrac{-12x}{-12} = \dfrac{138}{-12}$, or $x = -11.5$.

3. E

The inverse of addition is subtraction, so subtract 8 from both sides: $\dfrac{1}{4}y + 8 - 8 = 12 - 8$. This simplifies to $\dfrac{1}{4}y = 4$. Now undo multiplication by dividing both sides by $\dfrac{1}{4}$, which is the same as multiplying both sides by 4: $4 \times \dfrac{1}{4}y = 4 \times 4$. This simplifies to $y = 16$.

4. A

First apply the distributive property to get $3x - 6 = 36$. Add 6 to both sides of the equation: $3x - 6 + 6 = 36 + 6$, or $3x = 42$. Divide both sides of the equation by 3 to get $x = 14$.

5. B

First apply the distributive property: $(-4 \times b) - (-4 \times 6) = -60$, so $-4b - (-24) = -60$, which simplifies to $-4b + 24 = -60$. Subtract 24 from both sides of the equation to get $-4b + 24 - 24 = -60 - 24$, or $-4b = -84$. Now divide both sides by -4 to get $b = 21$.

6. C

Translate the words into an algebraic equation: $5(x + 13) = 100$. Use the distributive property to get $5x + 65 = 100$. Subtract 65 from both sides to get $5x = 35$. Finally, divide both sides by 5 to get $x = 7$.

7. D

Combine like terms to get $3z + 6z + 23 = 104$, or $9z + 23 = 104$. Subtract 23 from both sides of the equation to get $9z + 23 - 23 = 104 - 23$, or $9z = 81$. Divide both sides by 9 to isolate the variable and find that $z = 9$.

8. B

Add $-x$ to both sides to get the variable on one side of the equation: $4x + (-x) - 8 = x + (-x) + 1$. Combine like terms to get $3x - 8 = 1$. Add 8 to both sides of the equation: $3x - 8 + 8 = 1 + 8$, or $3x = 9$. Divide both sides by 3 to get $x = 3$.

9. E

The first step is to apply the distributive property: $25 - 4x - 12 = 4x + 33$. Combine like terms on the left-hand side: $25 - 12 - 4x = 4x + 33$ becomes $13 - 4x = 4x + 33$. Add $4x$ to both sides to get the variable on one side of the equation: $13 - 4x + 4x = 4x + 4x + 33$, or $13 = 8x + 33$. Subtract 33 from both sides to get $-20 = 8x$. Now divide both sides by 8: $x = -\dfrac{20}{8}$, or $x = -2.5$.

10. B

These angles are a linear pair, or supplementary angles, in which the sum of the degree measures is $180°$. Set up the equation: $8x + 117 + 7x = 180$. Combine like terms to get $15x + 117 = 180$. Subtract 117 from both sides of the equation: $15x = 63$. Divide both sides of the equation by 15 to isolate x: $x = 4.2$.

11. D

The angles marked are alternate interior angles, so their measures are equal. Set up the equation: $7x - 66 = 3x + 6$. Add $-3x$ to both sides of the equation to get the variable on one side: $7x + (-3x) - 66 = 3x + (-3x) + 6$. Combine like terms and add 66 to both sides: $4x = 72$. Divide both sides by 4: $x = 18$.

12. C

Multiply all terms in this equation by 35, the LCM (least common multiple) of 7 and 5. This will clear the fractional terms of the equation. The equation then becomes $35\left(\dfrac{4x}{7} - \dfrac{2}{5}\right) = 35(6)$, which simplifies to $20x - 14 = 210$. Add 14 to both sides to get $20x = 224$. Divide both sides by 20: $x = 11.2$.

13. A

Multiply each term by 24, the LCM of 6 and 8. The equation then becomes $24\left(\dfrac{1}{6}x + \dfrac{1}{8}x\right) = 24(1)$, which simplifies to $4x + 3x = 24$. Combine like terms: $7x = 24$. Divide both sides by 7: x is approximately 3.4.

14. E

Because the coefficient of y is 1 for the first equation and -8 for the second equation, multiply the first equation by 8 to eliminate the y variable by combining the two equations:

$$24x + 8y = 32$$
$$2x - 8y = -58$$

The equation $(24x + 2x) + [8y + (-8y)] = 32 + (-58)$, when simplified, becomes $26x = -26$. Divide both sides by 26: $x = -1$. Substitute the value of -1 for x in the original first equation to find the value of y: $3x + y = 4$ becomes $3(-1) + y = 4$, or $-3 + y = 4$. Add 3 to both sides of the equation: $y = 7$. The solution is the ordered pair $(-1, 7)$.

15. C

The first equation is already solved for the variable y, so use the substitution method and substitute the expression $6x + 10$ for the value of y in the second equation: $2x + 3y = 110$ becomes $2x + 3(6x + 10) = 110$. Apply the distributive property: $2x + 18x + 30 = 110$. Next combine like terms: $20x + 30 = 110$. Subtract 30 from both sides of the equation to get $20x = 80$. Divide both sides by 20: $x = 4$. Substitute the value of 4 for x in the first equation to find y: $y = 6x + 10$ becomes $y = 6(4) + 10$, or $y = 34$. The solution is the ordered pair $(4, 34)$.

16. A

Let r represent the number of red favors and p represent the number of pink favors. There were a total of 120 favors purchased, so the first equation is $r + p = 120$. Using the cost of each type of favor and the total purchase price, the second equation is $2.00p + 1.75r = 222.50$. The problem asks for the number of pink favors purchased, so solve the first equation for r in terms of p, which is $r = 120 - p$. Substitute this expression for r in the second equation: $2.00p + 1.75(120 - p) = 222.50$. Apply the distributive property to get $2p + 210 - 1.75p = 222.50$. Combine like terms: $0.25p + 210 = 222.50$. Subtract 210 from both sides to get $0.25p = 12.5$. Divide both sides by 0.25: $p = 50$.

17. C

Let a represent the number of adults and c represent the number of children. There were a total of 25 people, so the first equation is $a + c = 25$. Using the cost of brunch for each type of customer and the total bill, the second equation is $11.95a + 3.95c = 266.75$. The problem asks for the number of adults, so solve the first equation for c in terms of a: $c = 25 - a$. Now substitute this expression for c in the second equation:

$11.95a + 3.95(25 - a) = 266.75$. Apply the distributive property to get $11.95a + 98.75 - 3.95a = 266.75$. Combine like terms: $8a + 98.75 = 266.75$. Subtract 98.75 from both sides to get $8a = 168$. Divide both sides by 8: $a = 21$.

18. B

First add 49 to both sides to get the equation in the correct form: $x^2 - 14x + 49 = 0$. The left-hand side is a perfect square trinomial when factored: $(x - 7)(x - 7) = 0$. When either of these factors is 0, the equation is true, so the solution is $x = 7$.

19. E

The binomial on the left-hand side is, when factored, the difference of two squares: $(x + 6)(x - 6) = 0$. The equation will be true when either of the factors is equal to 0; this is when either $x = 6$ or $x = -6$.

20. A

First subtract 15 from both sides of the equation to get the equation in the correct form: $2x^2 - 3x - 5 - 15 = 15 - 15$, or $2x^2 - 3x - 20 = 0$. Factor the left-hand side of the equation to get $(2x + 5)(x - 4) = 0$. The equation will be true when either $2x + 5 = 0$ or $x - 4 = 0$. Subtract 5 from both sides of the first equation to get $2x = -5$. Divide both sides by 2, and the first value for x is $-\frac{5}{2}$. The second equation, $x - 4 = 0$, is true when $x = 4$, which is the second value for x.

21. B

This trinomial cannot be factored, so you must use the quadratic formula, where $a = 3$, $b = 2$, and $c = -15$:

$$x = \frac{-(2) \pm \sqrt{2^2 - (4 \times 3 \times -15)}}{2(3)} = \frac{-2 \pm \sqrt{4 + 180}}{6} = \frac{-2 \pm \sqrt{184}}{6}$$

Simplify the radical: $\frac{-2 \pm 2\sqrt{46}}{6}$. Now cancel out the common factor of 2 in each term of the numerator and the denominator to get the two values of x: $\frac{1 \pm \sqrt{46}}{3}$.

22. B

The formula for the area of a triangle is $\frac{1}{2}b \times h$. In this triangle, the base (b) is $4x$, and the height (h) is $x + 3$. The area of the triangle is thus $\frac{1}{2}(4x)(x+3)$, which equals 8 square units. Multiply $\frac{1}{2} \times 4x$ to get $2x$; therefore, $2x(x + 3) = 8$. Distribute the $2x$ to get $2x^2 + 6x = 8$. Now subtract 8 from both sides: $2x^2 + 6x - 8 = 0$. Factor the left-hand side: $(2x - 2)(x + 4) = 0$.

The equation is true if either of the factors equals 0. This will be when either $x = 1$ or $x = -4$. Even though the equation does have two solutions, the value of -4 must be rejected, because it is not possible to have a negative length. The solution is $x = 1$.

23.   C

Simplify the inequality by treating it like an equation and applying the five-step process for isolating a variable. Multiply both sides by 3 to eliminate the fractions: $-21x + 20 < x - 24$. Next, get all the x terms on one side: $-21x - x < -24 - 20$. Combine like terms: $-22x < -44$. Lastly, divide both sides by -22 to solve for x. Remember to reverse the direction of the inequality sign since -22 is negative: $x > 2$.

This does not match any of the choices. However, if x is greater than 2, then it's certainly also greater than 0, so choice (C) must be true and is the correct answer. Be wary of choice (D), which uses the wrong inequality sign, and choice (A), which is deceiving: if x is greater than 2, it could be 3 or 4, neither of which is greater than 4. Thus, choice (A) could be true but doesn't have to be true.

Cumulative Test

Cumulative Test

Congratulations! You have made your way through the basic building blocks of math and have built a solid understanding of basic math concepts ranging from number properties to decimals to coordinate geometry, and more! The following cumulative review tests the skills you have learned throughout *GMAT Math Foundations*. Try the following questions to assess how far you've come. Answers with detailed explanations follow to help further your study and understanding.

1. On a series of plays, a football team loses 9 yards on the first play, loses 5 more yards on the second play, gains 12 yards on the third play, and loses 2 yards on the fourth play. If the first play started at the 22nd yard line, what yard line did they end up on after the fourth play?

   (A) 18th
   (B) 4th
   (C) 36th
   (D) 6th
   (E) 26th

2. Factor the expression: $x^2 + 8x + 16$

   (A) $(x + 4)(x - 4)$
   (B) $(x + 4)^2$
   (C) $(x + 1)(x + 16)$
   (D) $(x + 8)^2$
   (E) $(x + 2)(x + 8)$

3. Find the product: $\dfrac{5x-15}{9y^2} \times \dfrac{18y}{x-3}$

   (A) $\dfrac{10}{y}$

   (B) $10y$

   (C) $\dfrac{7}{y}$

   (D) $\dfrac{10y}{x-3}$

   (E) $\dfrac{7y}{x-3}$

4. Evaluate: $(-90 \div 45) \times -3$

   (A) -6
   (B) -135
   (C) 15
   (D) 6
   (E) 135

5. A boat sights the top of a lighthouse, known to be 45 feet tall. The angle of elevation is 30°. How far is the boat from the base of the lighthouse?

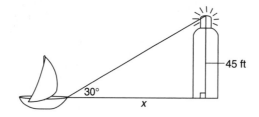

   (A) $9\sqrt{5}$ ft
   (B) 90 ft
   (C) 75 ft
   (D) $45\sqrt{3}$ ft
   (E) $45\sqrt{2}$ ft

6. How many square feet of carpeting is needed to cover a floor that is 32 feet by 28 feet?

   (A) 120 ft^2

   (B) 896 ft^2

   (C) 1,792 ft^2

   (D) 60 ft^2

   (E) 1,808 ft^2

7. Which concept is demonstrated in $7 \times (12 - 3) = (7 \times 12) - (7 \times 3)$?

   (A) Order of operations

   (B) Distributive property

   (C) Associative property

   (D) Commutative property

   (E) None of the above

8. What is the slope of the line that contains the points $(9, 2)$ and $(6, -1)$?

   (A) 3

   (B) -3

   (C) -1

   (D) $\dfrac{1}{3}$

   (E) 1

9. What is the solution to the system of equations below?

$x = 4$

$y = x + 5$

   (A) $(5, 0)$

   (B) $(5, 9)$

   (C) $(9, 4)$

   (D) $(4, 0)$

   (E) $(4, 9)$

10. The formula to convert from degrees Fahrenheit to degrees Celsius is $C = \frac{5}{9}(F - 32)$, where F is the degrees in Fahrenheit. What are the degrees Celsius of a temperature of 104 degrees Fahrenheit?

    (A) 40
    (B) 54
    (C) 360
    (D) 3,240
    (E) 8

11. Which of the following numbers is divisible by 9?

    (A) 996
    (B) 17,145
    (C) 980
    (D) All of the above
    (E) None of the above

12. $3\frac{5}{8} - 4\frac{1}{4} =$

    (A) $7\frac{7}{8}$

    (B) $\frac{5}{8}$

    (C) $\frac{1}{2}$

    (D) $-\frac{5}{8}$

    (E) $1\frac{3}{8}$

13. Kate had $19.03 left on her gift card. She used the card to purchase an item for $9.99. How much money is now left on the gift card?

    (A) $90.40
    (B) $9.05
    (C) $0.90
    (D) $0.09
    (E) $9.04

14. Which of the following sets of side lengths could be the measures of the sides of a triangle?

    (A) {6, 7, 14}
    (B) {5, 5, 10}
    (C) {6, 8, 10}
    (D) All the above sets are possible.
    (E) None of the above sets are possible.

15. If you take one-half of a number and add 19, the result is 44. What is the number?

    (A) 50
    (B) 25
    (C) 12.5
    (D) 31.5
    (E) 22

16. Which of the following is *TRUE*?

    (A) All rectangles are parallelograms.
    (B) All trapezoids are quadrilaterals.
    (C) All squares are rhombuses.
    (D) All of the above are true.
    (E) None of the above are true.

17. Simplify: $\dfrac{(2^4 \times 2^5)}{2^3}$

    (A) 2^6

    (B) 2^9

    (C) 2^{12}

    (D) 2^{17}

    (E) 2^{23}

18. $2\sqrt{150} =$

    (A) $2\sqrt{6}$

    (B) $5\sqrt{6}$

    (C) $15\sqrt{10}$

    (D) $10\sqrt{10}$

    (E) $10\sqrt{6}$

19. Solve for x: $x^2 - 4x - 96 = 0$

    (A) $\{12, 8\}$

    (B) $\{-12, -8\}$

    (C) $\{12, -8\}$

    (D) $\{-12, 8\}$

    (E) No real number solution

20. In a local high school band, the ratio of trombone players to trumpet players is 3 to 4. Which of the following can *NOT* be the total number of musicians that play either the trombone or trumpet?

    (A) 14

    (B) 84

    (C) 126

    (D) 196

    (E) 204

21. For a $4,500.00 certificate of deposit, the bank will pay 8.5% simple interest if it is invested for 18 months. How much interest will the certificate accrue?

    (A) $6,885.00

    (B) $38,250.00

    (C) $573.75

    (D) $6,750.00

    (E) $688.50

22. When rolling one die, what is the probability of landing on a prime number?

    (A) $\dfrac{1}{4}$

    (B) $\dfrac{1}{2}$

    (C) $\dfrac{2}{3}$

    (D) $\dfrac{1}{3}$

    (E) $\dfrac{1}{6}$

23. How many different three-digit area codes can be made if repetition is allowed and the first digit cannot be 0 or 1?

    (A) 800

    (B) 100

    (C) 80

    (D) 28

    (E) 1,000

24. What is the sale price of a snow blower originally priced at $370.00 and now on sale for 40% off?

(A) $330.00

(B) $222.00

(C) $148.00

(D) $14,800.00

(E) $22.20

25. Water is draining out of a pool at a rate of 50 gallons per minute. If there are 12,650 gallons of water in the pool, how many hours will it take to empty the entire pool?

(A) 25 hours 18 minutes

(B) 6 hours

(C) 4 hours 13 minutes

(D) 352 hours

(E) 253 hours

Answers and Explanations

1. A

This problem can be written as an expression. Since the first play started at the 22nd yard line, the expression becomes 22 + −9 (loss of 9 yards) + −5 (loss of 5 yards) + 12 (gain of 12 yards) + −2 (loss of 2 yards). Use the commutative property from chapter 1 to change the order of the numbers to 22 + 12 + −9 + −5 + −2. By combining the positive values and the negative values, the expression yields a result of 34 + −16 = 18. After the fourth play, they were on the 18th yard line.

2. B

To find the factors of the trinomial, write the factors in the form $(x + a)(x + b)$ where the sum of a and b is 8 and the product of a and b is 16. Since the factors of 16 that have a sum of 8 are 4 and 4, the factors are $(x + 4)(x + 4)$. This is also equivalent to $(x + 4)^2$ because it is a perfect square trinomial.

3. A

First factor, and then cancel any common factors between the numerators and denominators. $\dfrac{5x-15}{9y^2}\times\dfrac{18y}{x-3}=\dfrac{5\,\cancel{(x-3)}}{\cancel{9}\,y^{\cancel{2}}}\times\dfrac{\cancel{18}^{2}\,\cancel{y}}{\cancel{x-3}}$. Multiply the remaining factors to get $\dfrac{5\times2}{y}=\dfrac{10}{y}$.

4. D

Using the correct order of operations that was explained in chapter 1, first divide inside the parentheses to get $-90\div45=-2$. Keep in mind that the result was negative because there was one negative within the parentheses. Now multiply -2 by -3 to get 6. In this step, an even number of negatives gives a positive result.

5. D

This is a 30-60-90 right triangle, so its sides are in the ratio $x:x\sqrt{3}:2x$. Since the side opposite the 30° angle is 45, the side opposite the 60° angle is $45\sqrt{3}$.

6. B

The area of a rectangle is $A=b\times h$. $A=32\times28=896$ ft^2.

7. B

This represents the distributive property, choice (B), which states that multiplication distributes over subtraction. Instead of subtracting first, you can multiply 7×12 and then 7×3 and, as a last step, find the difference of these products to get the same answer. This is not an example of the order of operations, choice (A), which is a set order for performing arithmetic operations. This is not an example of the associative property, choice (C), which states that changing the grouping of either addends or factors does not affect the resultant sum or product. Likewise, choice (D) is not correct because the commutative property states that changing the order of addends or factors does not affect the resultant sum or product.

8. E

Use the slope formula:

$$m=\frac{\text{change in }y}{\text{change in }x}=\frac{y_1-y_2}{x_1-x_2}=\frac{2-(-1)}{9-6}=\frac{3}{3}=1$$

9. E

As shown below, on a coordinate grid the two equations in the system would intersect at the point (4, 9). Therefore, this is the solution to the system of equations.

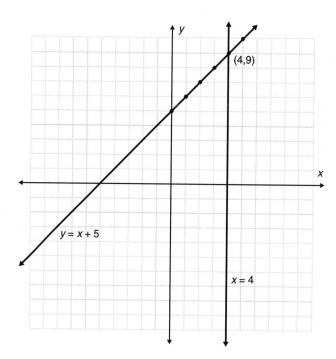

10. A

You need to follow the correct order of operations for this formula. Substitute in 104 for F, and then subtract because this expression is within parentheses. $104 - 32 = 72$. Now multiply this result by $\frac{5}{9}$: $\frac{5}{9} \times 72 = \frac{5 \times 72}{9} = \frac{360}{9} = 40$ degrees Celsius.

11. B

Choice (A) is not divisible by 9 because the sum of the digits, $9 + 9 + 6 = 24$, is not divisible by 9. Choice (B) fits the criteria: $1 + 7 + 1 + 4 + 5 = 18$, which is divisible by 9. Choice (C) does not work; $9 + 8 + 0 = 17$, and 17 is not divisible by 9.

12. D

First change the mixed numbers to improper fractions: $\frac{(3)(8)+5}{8} = \frac{29}{8}$; $4\frac{1}{4} = \frac{(4)(4)+1}{4} = \frac{17}{4}$. Then, change the second fraction to have a denominator of 8: $\frac{17}{4} = \frac{34}{8}$. Then subtract your numerators: $\frac{29}{8} - \frac{34}{8} = \frac{-5}{8}$.

13. E

This is a decimal subtraction problem. Both numbers have two digits to the right of the decimal point, so just line up the decimal points and subtract. $19.03 - 9.99 = \$9.04$.

14. C

The sum of the measure of any two sides of a triangle must be greater than the other side. The only set that passes this condition is choice (C), $\{6, 8, 10\}$. For choice (A), $6 + 7 = 13$, which is less than the third side, 14. For choice (B), $5 + 5 = 10$, which is not greater than 10.

15. A

These words translate into the two-step equation $\frac{1}{2}x + 19 = 44$. Subtract 19 from both sides of the equation to undo addition: $\frac{1}{2}x + 19 - 19 = 44 - 19$. This simplifies to $\frac{1}{2}x = 25$. Now, undo multiplication by dividing both sides by $\frac{1}{2}$, which is equivalent to multiplying by 2: $2 \times \frac{1}{2}x = 25 \times 2$, or $x = 50$.

16. D

All of the three statements are true.

17. A

First perform multiplication in the numerator by adding the exponents: $2^4 \times 2^5 = 2^9$. Then divide by subtracting the exponents: $\frac{2^9}{2^3} = 2^{9-3} = 2^6$.

18. E

First simplify the square root of 150. The largest perfect square factor of 150 is 25, so $\sqrt{150} = \sqrt{25} \times \sqrt{6} = 5\sqrt{6}$. Then multiply this by the coefficient of $2 : 2 \times 5\sqrt{6} = 10\sqrt{6}$.

19. C

To factor the trinomial, look for two numbers that multiply to -96 and add to -4. Trial and error yields -12 and 8: $-12 \times 8 = -96$, and $-12 + 8 = -4$. The factored form of the quadratic equation is therefore $(x - 12)(x + 8) = 0$. This means that $x = 12$ or $x = -8$. Don't be fooled by choice (D): when $x = -12$ or 8, the expression $x^2 - 4x - 96$ is not equal to 0.

20. E

Since the part-to-part ratio of trombone players to trumpet players is 3 to 4, then the parts can be expressed as $3x$ and $4x$. Thus, the total number of trombone and trumpet players can be expressed as $3x + 4x = 7x$. The total, therefore, would need to be a multiple of 7. The only answer choice that is not a multiple of 7 is choice (E).

21. C

Use the simple interest formula: $I = prt$, where I is the interest earned, p is the principal invested ($4,500.00), r is the percentage rate (8.5%, or 0.085), and t is the time (18 months, or 1.5 years). $I = 4,500.00 \times 0.085 \times 1.5$, or $I = \$573.75$.

22. B

The prime numbers on a die are 2, 3, and 5. The probability of rolling a prime number is therefore $\dfrac{3}{6} = \dfrac{1}{2}$.

23. A

Since the first digit cannot be a 0 or a 1, there are eight choices for the first digit. Since there are no restrictions on the second or third digit, and repetition is allowed, there are ten choices for each of these digits. The total number of area codes is therefore $8 \times 10 \times 10 = 800$.

24. B

Because the snow blower is 40% off of the original price, the sale price will be 100% − 40% = 60% of the original price. Multiply: $0.60 \times 370.00 = \$222.00$.

25. C

Total amount = rate × time. Since the water is draining at a rate of 50 gallons per minute, 12,650 gallons = 50 × time. Divide the total gallons by this rate. $\dfrac{12,650\,\text{gallons}}{50\,\text{gallons per minute}} = 253$ minutes. Divide the number of minutes by 60 (to find the hour amount) and you get 4, remainder 13. This is equivalent to 4 hours 13 minutes.